CAMBRIDGE LIBRARY COLLECTION

Books of enduring scholarly value

British and Irish History, Nineteenth Century

This series comprises contemporary or near-contemporary accounts of the political, economic and social history of the British Isles during the nineteenth century. It includes material on international diplomacy and trade, labour relations and the women's movement, developments in education and social welfare, religious emancipation, the justice system, and special events including the Great Exhibition of 1851.

The Christian and Civic Economy of Large Towns

This three-volume study by the Scottish churchman and social reformer Thomas Chalmers (1780–1847) is a revealing work of Christian morality as applied to urban economic theory. Having moved to Glasgow in 1815, Chalmers was given a free hand in 1819 for an experiment in urban ministry at the new parish of St John's in the poorest district of the city. His reforms improved education and reduced the need for institutional poor relief by dividing the area into manageable 'proportions' that were closely looked after by parish elders and deacons, reviving a traditional community spirit and promoting self-help. Although sometimes severe, Chalmers' system and this influential work reflect Enlightenment optimism regarding human nature, suggesting the need for the Church of Scotland to respond actively to problems of urban industrialisation. Volume 1, published in 1821, outlines his theories of locality and the ways in which the Church could support the community.

Cambridge University Press has long been a pioneer in the reissuing of out-of-print titles from its own backlist, producing digital reprints of books that are still sought after by scholars and students but could not be reprinted economically using traditional technology. The Cambridge Library Collection extends this activity to a wider range of books which are still of importance to researchers and professionals, either for the source material they contain, or as landmarks in the history of their academic discipline.

Drawing from the world-renowned collections in the Cambridge University Library and other partner libraries, and guided by the advice of experts in each subject area, Cambridge University Press is using state-of-the-art scanning machines in its own Printing House to capture the content of each book selected for inclusion. The files are processed to give a consistently clear, crisp image, and the books finished to the high quality standard for which the Press is recognised around the world. The latest print-on-demand technology ensures that the books will remain available indefinitely, and that orders for single or multiple copies can quickly be supplied.

The Cambridge Library Collection brings back to life books of enduring scholarly value (including out-of-copyright works originally issued by other publishers) across a wide range of disciplines in the humanities and social sciences and in science and technology.

The Christian
and Civic Economy
of Large Towns

VOLUME 1

THOMAS CHALMERS

CAMBRIDGE UNIVERSITY PRESS

Cambridge, New York, Melbourne, Madrid, Cape Town,
Singapore, São Paolo, Delhi, Mexico City

Published in the United States of America by Cambridge University Press, New York

www.cambridge.org
Information on this title: www.cambridge.org/9781108062350

© in this compilation Cambridge University Press 2013

This edition first published 1821
This digitally printed version 2013

ISBN 978-1-108-06235-0 Paperback

THE

CHRISTIAN

AND

CIVIC ECONOMY

OF

LARGE TOWNS.

BY

THOMAS CHALMERS, D.D.

MINISTER OF ST. JOHN'S CHURCH, GLASGOW.

VOL. I.

Glasgow.

Printed by James Starke, Nelson Street,

FOR CHALMERS & COLLINS, GLASGOW;

A. CONSTABLE & Co.; W. BLACKWOOD; W. WHYTE & Co.; OLIVER & BOYD;
WAUGH & INNES; W. OLIPHANT; FAIRBAIRN & ANDERSON; MANNERS & MILLER;
AND JAMES ROBERTSON, EDINBURGH;
BALDWIN, CRADOCK & JOY; LONGMAN, HURST, REES, ORME & BROWN;
G. & W. B. WHITTAKER; HURST, ROBINSON & Co.;
T. HAMILTON; OGLE, DUNCAN & Co.; W. BAYNES & SON,
E J. HOLDSWORTH; AND J. NISBET, LONDON.

1821.

CONTENTS.

PREFACE.

THERE is a great deal of philanthropy afloat in this our day. At no period, perhaps, in the history of the human mind, did a desire of doing good so earnest, meet with a spirit of inquiry so eager, after the best and likeliest methods of carrying the desire into accomplishment. Amid all that looks dark and menacing, in the present exhibitions of society, this, at least, must be acknowledged, —that never was there a greater quantity of thought embarked on those speculations which, whether with Christian, or merely economical writers, have the one common object of promoting the worth and comfort of our species.

It must be confessed, at the same time, that much of this benevolence, and more particularly, when it aims at some fulfilment, by a combination of many individuals, is rendered abortive for want of a right direction. Were the misleading causes to which

B

philanthropy is exposed, when it operates among a crowded assemblage of human beings, fully understood, then would it cease to be a paradox,—why there should either be a steady progress of wretchedness in our land, in the midst of its charitable institutions; or a steady progress of profligacy, in the midst of its churches, and Sabbath schools, and manifold reclaiming societies.

The Author of the following work has been much in the way of comparing the habitudes of a city, with those of a country population; and he cannot more fitly express its subject than by assigning to it the title of "The Christian and Civic Economy of our Large Towns."

Though he counts himself in possession of materials ample enough for an immediate volume, yet it suits better with his other engagements, to come forth in quarterly numbers, with the successive chapters of it.

CHRISTIAN & CIVIC ECONOMY

OF

LARGE TOWNS.

CHAP. I.

THE ADVANTAGE AND POSSIBILITY OF ASSIMILATING A TOWN TO A COUNTRY PARISH.

THERE are two classes of writers, whose prevailing topics stand intimately connected with the philosophy of human affairs, but who, in almost all their habitudes of thinking, have hitherto maintained an unfortunate distance from each other. There are political economists, who do not admit Christianity, as an element, into their speculations; and there are Christian philanthropists, who do not admit political science, as an element, into theirs. The former very generally regard the professional subject of the latter, if not with contempt, at least with unconcern; and the latter as generally regard the professional subject of the former, with a somewhat sensitive kind of prejudice, bordering upon disapprobation and dislike. It is thus, that two classes of public labourers, who, with a mutual respect and understanding, might have, out of their united contributions, rendered a most important offering to society—have, in fact, each in the prosecution of their own separate walk, so shut out the light, and so rejected the aid, which the other could have afforded, as either, in many instances, to have merely amused the intellectual public, with inert and unproductive theory, on the one hand, or as to have misled the practically benevolent public, into measures of well-meaning, but mischievous, and ill-directed activity, on the other.

And indeed, it is only in the later walks of political science, that the aid of Christianity has obviously become of practical importance to her; nor did this aid appear to be at all requisite for the purpose of giving effect to her earlier speculations. Till within these last fifteen years, the great topic of inquiry among our abstract politicians, was the theory of commerce; and the moral habit of the labouring classes, as founded on their religion, did not enter, as an element, or as a component part, into that theory. By the simple fiat of an enlightened parliament, the freedom of trade could be established; and every artificial restraint or encouragement, alike be done away; and all intermeddling with a concern, which is best provided for on the part of government, by its being simply let alone, could henceforth be left to the operation of nature's own principles, and nature's own processes. And thus, without borrowing any other aid from the religion of the

New Testament, than that general benefit which she has conferred upon society, by the greater currency she has given to the virtues of truth, and justice, and liberality, among men, may all that is sound in the political economy of Smith, and his immediate followers, have been carried into accomplishment, by a series of enactments, or rather of repeals, on the part of a country's legislature, without any concurrence of principle and habit whatever, either sought after or obtained, on the part of a country's population.

But the case is widely different, with respect to the later contributions, which have been rendered to this science. We allude more especially to the Essay of Mr. Malthus, whose theory of population, had it been present to the mind of Mr. Smith, would, we think, have modified certain of those doctrines and conclusions, which he presented to the world, in his Essay on the Theory of Commerce. It is true, that government, by her obtrusive interferences, has put the country into a worse condition, in respect of her population, than it would have been in, had this branch of its economy been left altogether to itself—just as she has put the country into a worse condition, in respect of its trading prosperity, than it would have been in, had this branch of its economy been also left to itself. There are certain artificial encouragements to population, which government ought never to have sanctioned, and which it were the wisdom of government, with all prudent and practicable speed, to abolish. There are certain bounties that the law has devised upon marriage, in every way as hurtful and impolitic, as her bounties upon trade, and which it were greatly better for the interest of all classes, and more especially of the labouring classes, that she should forthwith recal. There is a way, in which, by stepping beyond her province, and attempting to provide for that which would have more effectually been provided for without her, by the strong principle of self-preservation, on the one hand, and the free, but powerful sympathies of individual nature, on the other—there is a way, in which she has lulled the poor into improvidence, and frozen the rich into apathy towards their wants and their sufferings; and this way, it were surely better that she had never entered upon, and better now, that she should retrace, with all convenient expedition. Now, all this may be done, and with a certain degree of benefit, even in the midst of an unchristian population. Their comfort would be advanced so far, merely by the principles of nature being restored to their unfettered operation; and this is desirable, even though we should fall short of that additional comfort, which would accrue from the principles of Christianity being brought more prevalently amongst them, than before. And thus, it is a possible thing, that government, acting exclusively in the temper, and with the views of the wisdom of this world, may exert herself, with beneficial

influence, on that great branch of political economy, which relates to the population of a state,
just as she may on that other great branch of it,
which relates to the commerce of a state. She may
at least erase her own blunders from the statute-
book, and conclusively do away the whole of that
mischief, which the erroneous policy of our ancestors has entailed on the present generation.

But there is one wide and palpable distinction
between the matter of commerce, and the matter
of population. Government may safely withdraw
from the former concern altogether, and abandon
it to the love of gain, and the spirit of enterprise,
and the sharp-sighted sagacity, that guides almost
all the pursuits of interest, and the natural securities for justice, between man and man in society.
Let her simply commit the cause of commerce to
the joint operation of these various influences, and
she will commit it to the very elements which are
most fitted to prosper it forward to the pitch of
its uttermost possible elevation. And it were also
well, that government withdrew from the concern
of ordinary pauperism altogether, which stands so
nearly associated with the question of population.
She would, in this way, do much to call forth a
resurrection of those providential habits, which
serve both to restrain the number, and to equalise
the comforts of our people; and she would also
do much to bring out, those otherwise checked
and superseded sympathies, that, in the flow of
their kindly and spontaneous exercise, are more

fitted to bind the community in gentleness together, than all the legalised charities of our land.
But though she may thus do much, she cannot
do all; and there will still be left a mighty reversion of good, that can only be achieved by the
people themselves. For, though the unfettered
principles of nature, may suffice for carrying all
that interest which is connected with the state of a
country's commerce, onwards to the condition that
is best and safest for the public weal; the mere
principles of nature will not suffice for carrying
the interest that is connected with the state of a
country's population, onwards to the condition
that is best and safest for the public weal. It is
very true, that a compulsory provision for the
poor, aggravates the poverty of the land, by augmenting the pressure of its population upon its
subsistence, and that by the repeal of such a system, the whole amount of this aggravation would
be reduced. But the reduction were only partial.
For, so long as profligacy remains, the pressure in
question, will, though lessened in amount, remain
along with it. So long as the sensual predomi-
nates over the reflective part of the human constitution, will there be improvident marriages,
and premature families, and an overdone competition for subsistence, and a general inadequacy
in the wages of labour, to the fair rate of human
enjoyment, and, in a word, all the disorder and
discomfort of an excessive population. So long
as there is generally a low and grovelling taste

among the people, instead of an aspiring tendency towards something more in the way of comfort, and cleanliness, and elegance, than is to be met with in the sordid habitations of a rude and demi-barbarous country, will they rush, with precipitation, into matrimony, and care not how unable they are to meet its expenses, and forfeit the whole ease ‹and accommodation of the future, to the present ascendency of a blind and uncalculating impulse. And thus, while government may reduce this pressure, up to the amount of what it has brought on by its own mismanagement, it is a pressure which it can never wholly, and never nearly extinguish. The tendency to excessive population, can only find its thorough and decisive counteraction, among the amended habits, and the moralised characters, and the exalted principles, of the people themselves. To bring the economy of a nation's wealth into its best possible condition, it may suffice to go up to the legislature, and beg that she may withdraw her intermeddling hand from a concern, which her touch always mars, but never medicates. To bring the economy of its population into the best possible condition, it is right to go up to the legislature, and beg that she may recal the mischief of her own interferences. But it is further necessary, to go forth among the people, and there to superinduce the principles of an efficient morality, on the mere principles of nature—and there to work a transformation of taste and of character—and

c

there to deliver lessons, which, of themselves, will induce a habit of thoughtfulness, that must insensibly pervade the whole system of a man's desires and his doings; making him more a being of reach, and intellect, and anticipation, than he was formerly—raising the whole tone of his mind, and infusing into every practical movement, along with the elements of passion and interest, the elements of duty, and of wisdom, and of self-estimation.

It is thus, that the disciples of political science, however wisely they may speculate upon this question, are, if without the element of character among the general population, in a state of impotency as to the practical effect of their speculation. So long as the people remain either depraved or unenlightened, the country never will attain a healthful condition in respect of one of the great branches of her policy. This is an obstacle which stands uncontrollably opposed to the power of every other expedient for the purpose of mitigating the evils of a redundant population; and, till this be removed, legislators may devise, and economists may demonstrate as they will, they want one of the data, indispensable to the right solution of a problem, which, however clear in theory, will, upon trial, mock the vain endeavours of those who overlook the moral principles of man, or despise the mysteries of that faith, which can alone inspire them.

It is thus that our political writers, if at all honestly desirous of obtaining a fulfilment for their own speculation, should look towards the men who are fitted to expatiate among the people, in the capacity of their most acceptable and efficient moralists. It is evident that they themselves are not the best adapted for such a practical movement through a community of human beings. It is not by any topic or any demonstration of theirs, that we can at all look for a general welcome and admittance amongst families. Let one of their number, for example, go forth with the argument of Malthus, or any other of the lessons of political economy, and that, for the purpose of enlightening the practice and observation of his neighbourhood. The very first reception that he met with, would, in all likelihood, check the farther progress of this moral and benevolent adventure, and stamp upon it all the folly and all the fruitlessness of Quixotism. People would laugh, or wonder, or be offended, and a sense of the utterly ridiculous, would soon attach itself to this expedition, and lead him to abandon it. Now, herein lies the great initial superiority which the merely Christian has over the merely civil philanthropist. He is armed with a topic of ready and pertinent introduction, with which he may go round a population, and come into close and extensive contact with all the families. Let his errand be connected with religion, and, even though a very obscure, and wholly unsanctioned individual, may he enter within the precincts of nearly every household, and not meet with one act of rudeness or resistance during the whole of his progress. Should he only, for example, invite their young to his Sabbath-School, he, with this for his professed object, would find himself in possession of a passport, upon which, and more especially among the common ranks of society, he might step into almost every dwelling-place— and engage the inmates in conversations of piety— and leave, at least, the sensations of cordiality and gratitude behind him—and pave the way for successive applications of the same influence—and secure this acknowledgment in favour of his subject, that it is worthy of being proposed on the one side, and worthy of being entertained and patiently listened to, on the other. It is not of his final success that we are now speaking. It is of his advantageous outset. It is of that wide and effectual door of access to the population, which the Christian philanthropist has, and which the civil philanthropist has not—and from which it follows, that if the lessons of the former are at all fitted to induce a habit favourable to the objects of the latter, the economist who underrates the gospel of Jesus Christ, and the zeal of its devoted labourers, is deposing from their rightful estimation, the best auxiliaries of his cause.

And, it would save a world of misconception, were it distinctly kept in mind, that, for the purpose of giving effect to the lessons of the economist, it is not necessary for him who labours in the gospel vineyard, either to teach, or even so much as to understand, these lessons. Let him simply confine himself to his own strict and peculiar business—let him labour for immortality alone—let his single aim be to convert and to christianise, and, as the result of prayer and exertion, to succeed in depositing with some, the faith of the New Testament, so as that they shall hold forth to the esteem and the imitation of many, the virtues of the New Testament—and he does more for the civil and economical well-being of his neighbourhood, than he ever could do by the influence of all secular demonstration. Let his desire and his devotedness be exclusively towards the life that is to come, and without borrowing one argument from the interest of the life that now is, will he do more to bless and to adorn its condition, than can be done by all the other efforts of patriotism and philosophy put together. It were worse than ridiculous, and it most assuredly is not requisite for him to become the champion of any economic theory, with the principles of which he should constantly be infusing either his pulpit or his parochial ministrations. His office may be upheld in the entire aspect of its sacredness—and the main desire and prayer of his heart towards God, in behalf of his brethren, may be that they should be saved—and the engrossment of his mind with the one thing needful, may be as complete as was that of the Apostle, who determined to know nothing among his hearers, save Jesus Christ, and him crucified—and yet, such is the fulness of the blessing of the gospel with which he is fraught, that while he renders the best possible service to the converts whom, under the spirit of God, he has gained to its cause; he also, in the person of these converts, renders the best possible contribution to the temporal good of society. It is enough, that they have been rescued from the dominion of sensuality;—it is enough, that they have become the disciples of that book, which, while it teaches them to be fervent in spirit, teaches them also to be not slothful in business;—it is enough, that the Christian faith has been formed with such power in their hearts, as to bring out the Christian morals into visible exemplification upon their history;—it is enough, that the principle within them, if it do not propagate its own likeness in others, can at least, like the salt to which they have been compared, season a whole vicinity with many of its kindred and secondary attributes. There is not a more familiar exhibition in humble life, than that alliance, in virtue of which a Christian family is almost always sure to be a well-conditioned family. And yet its members are utterly unversant either in the maxims or in the speculations of political science. They occupy the right place in a rightly constituted and well-going mechanism; but the mechanism itself is what they never hear of, and could not comprehend. Their Christian adviser never reads them a lesson from the writings of any economist, and yet the moral habit to which the former has been the instrument of conducting them, is that which brings them into a state of practical conformity with the soundest and most valuable lessons which the latter can devise. And now, that habit, and character, and education, among the poor, have become the mighty elements of all that is recent in political theory, as well may the inventor of a philosophical apparatus, disown the aid of those artizans, who, in utter ignorance of its use, only know how to prepare and put together its materials, as may the most sound and ingenious speculator in the walks of civil economy, disown the aid of those Christian labourers, who, in utter ignorance of the new doctrine of population, only know how to officiate in that path of exertion, by which the members of our actual population may be made pure, and prudent, and pious.

And if we revert to the habit of the last generation in Scotland, which is still fresh in the remembrance of many who are now alive, we shall find an ample verification of all these remarks. At that time, Malthus had not written, and his speculation had little more than an embryo existence in the pages of Wallace; and, certain it is, that, in the minds of our solid, and regular, and well-doing peasantry, it had no existence at all. It was acted upon, but without being at all counted upon. It was one of the cherished and domestic decencies of a former age, transmitted from every matron to her daughters, not to marry without a costly and creditable provision; and the delay of years, was often incurred, in the mighty work of piling together, the whole *materiel* of a most bulky and laborious preparation—and the elements of future comfort and future respectability, behoved to be accumulated to a very large extent, ere it was lawful, or, at least, reputable, to enter upon the condition of matrimony—and thus the moral preventive check of our great economist, was in full and wholesome operation, long before it was offered by him to public notice, in the shape of a distinct and salutary principle. And, if we wish to revive its influence among the people, this will not be done, we apprehend, by cheapening the currency of his doctrine, and bringing it down to the level of popular understanding. It must be by other tracts than those of political economy, that we shall recover the descending habit of our countrymen. It must be by addresses of a more powerful character, than those which point to the futurities of an earthly existence. It must be, not by men labouring, however strenuously, after some great political achievement, but by men labouring for the good of imperishable spirits— by men who have their conversation in heaven, and who, with their eye full upon its glories, feel the comparative insignificance of the pilgrimage which leads to it. And not, till we recal the Christianity, shall we ever recal the considerate sobriety, the steady equalised comfort, the virtuous independence of a generation, the habit and the memory of which are so fast departing away from us.

Let me finish my observations on this part of
the subject, with adverting to the way in which
the re-action of a people's turbulence is ever sure
to follow the neglect of a people's Christianity—
how, of all modes of intolerance, that intolerance
of irreligion, which denounces the faith of the
New Testament as fanaticism, brings, in its train,
the most woful forfeiture of all civil and all political advantages; insomuch, that the deadliest
enemy of our state, is not what has been called
a methodistical spirit among the people; but its
deadliest enemy, by far, is a persecuting church,
which would thwart all that is serious and evangelical in the desires of the people—and which, in
so doing, tramples on those sacred accommodations
that God has established between the longings
of an awakened heart, and the truth that is unto
salvation.

So much for the prevailing tendency of the civil
to underrate or disregard the labours of the Christian philanthropist. But there is no less prevailing
a tendency, on the part of the latter, to neglect
many of the principles, and to underrate many of
the propositions of the former.

It is certainly to be regretted, that many of our
most pious, and even our most profound theolo-
gians, should be so unfurnished as they are with
the conceptions of political economy. But it is
their active resistance to some of its clearest and
most unquestionable principles—it is their blindly
sentimental dislike of a doctrine, which stands

on the firm basis of arithmetic—it is their misre-
presentation of it, as hostile to the exercise of our
best feelings, when, in fact, all its hostility is
directed against such perverse and unfortunate
arrangements, as have served to chill and to counteract the sympathies of our nature—it is the dog-
matism of their strenuous asseverations, against
that which experience and demonstration are ever
obtruding upon the judgment as irrefragable truth—
it is this which is mainly to be regretted, for it has
enlisted the whole of their high and deserved influence on the side of institutions pernicious to
society—and what, perhaps, is still worse, it has led
a very enlightened class in our land, to imagine a
certain poverty of understanding as inseparable
from religious zeal—thus bringing down our Christian labourers, from that estimation, which, on
their own topic, so rightfully belongs to them, and
deducting from the weight of that professional
testimony, which it were the best interest of all
classes most patiently to listen to, and most re-
spectfully to entertain.

But the mischief which has thus been inflicted
on the good of humanity, is not to be compared
with the still deadlier mischief of a certain error,
which has received the utmost countenance and
support from a large class of religionists. What
we allude to, is their distaste towards all kinds of
external machinery, for the furtherance of any
Christian enterprise—founded on their misapplica-
tion of an undoubted doctrine, that all the ebbs

and all the revivals of Christianity, are primarily
to be traced to the alternations of a direct influence from heaven. They look, and they rightly
look, to the Spirit of God, as the agent of every
prosperous revolution in the Christianity of our
land. When there is a general torpor of irreligion
amongst us, it is because there is a famine of
spiritual nourishment, and God has withdrawn
the manifestations of the Holy Ghost, from a
careless, and thoughtless, and worldly generation.
When there is the awakening of a thoughtful and
repentant seriousness, it is because the Spirit of
it has been poured out of that upper Sanctuary,
into which prayer has ascended from beneath, and
from which a regenerating influence has come
down, as a descending return, for the intercessions
of the devoted few, in behalf of a world lying
in wickedness. All this is sacred and substantial
truth, which no speculation can impair; and it
were folly to think, that, by the mere erection of
a material frame-work, the cause of Christianity
can be advanced, by a single hair-breadth, should
there be a withholding of that especial and sanc-
tifying grace, without which, the builders labour
in vain, and the watchmen wake but in vain.
And hence, with many, is there a total indolence
and unconcern as to all outward arrangements;
and every thing like a visible apparatus, appears
insignificant in their eyes; and with something
like the complacency of one who fancies himself
in possession of the recondite principle of a given

operation, do they view with contempt, all that man can do externally, and with his hands, for the purpose of achieving it: and thus do they hold in a kind of ineffable disdain, the proposal of building more churches, for the increase of Christianity in our land; and this is only one out of the many instances, in which, under a sense of the utter impotency of all mechanism, they would restrain human activity from putting itself forth on any palpable subject, and would sit in a sort of mystic and expectant quietism, till there come down upon us from the skies, the visitation of that inspiring energy, which is to provide for all, and to do all.

It may serve to reconcile these people, and perhaps to engage them in the work of outward arrangements, if we point their regards to that season, in the history of the world, which was most signalised by the visitations of a moral and spiritual energy from heaven. We instance the apostolic age, when living water flowed more abundantly than it has ever done since, among those who wear the denomination of Christians; and yet, if we may extend the simile, did the leaders of the church give much of their earnestness to the work of providing it with ducts of conveyance. There never was perhaps so goodly and so various an external apparatus, for the transmission of Christianity from one human being to another, as at that period, when the Spirit descended most plentifully, and that, too, for the

purpose of depositing Christianity in the hearts
of men. Paul, who prayed without ceasing for the
supply of this essential influence, also pondered
without ceasing such a constitution of offices,
and such a routine of services, as would ensure
the right distribution of it. The falling of rain
from the clouds, no more supersedes the preparation of receptacles for gathering, and of channels
for conveying it, than the descent of living water,
as the aliment of all that is acceptable in human
virtue and spiritual in human discernment, supersedes the question of the best and fittest construc-
tion of an external system, for the circulation of
it through a neighbourhood. The Apostle, who
felt most his dependence on the Spirit for the
conversion of the souls of men, laboured most in
the rearing of an outward and a visible agency,
for the furtherance of the cause. And whether
we read of the great variety of offices in the
Christian church, as of prophets, and interpreters,
and evangelists, for the edifying of the body of
Christ, or observe the labour of the great Apostle
to set things in order, and the provision he made
for ordaining elders in every city, we may perceive, that the age of greatest spiritual influence,
was also an age of busy external regulation. Nor
does it follow, that he who places all his confidence on the former, should neglect and undervalue the latter, or that he who expends thought
and judgment upon the machinery of a Christian-

ising process, thereby disowns to the Holy Spirit that supremacy which belongs to him.

It was at a period when the religious spirit run high, that schools were instituted in Scotland, and such a system of education was devised and established, as has at least struck out a fountain of scholarship in every parish, which has been the place of uniform repair for the young of many successive generations. In this we see the good of what may be called a material organization. It survives all the ebbs and alternations of the spirit which gave it birth; and who can fail to perceive, that in virtue of its existence, when this spirit re-appears in the country, it finds channels for a readier and more abundant access into all the families, than it would do in a country where there was no parochial endowment, and no regular or universal habit of scholarship among the population? But what is more, the religious spirit may decline in a country, when, of course, it will move scantily through those conveyances which have been established in it, between the teacher and the taught. And yet it must not be denied, that there continues to move such an influence, as is still favourable to the temporal well-being of society. Even in seasons of the greatest abandonment, as to the light and faith of the gospel, there is an intelligence, and an enlargement, and a reflective sobriety, gotten at these schools, all of which have stamped a great civic and economic superiority of character on the peasantry of Scotland. Such a machinery, with its numerous rills of distribution, is well adapted to the object of propagating the dominant spirit of the times through the nation at large. When that happens to be the warm, and affectionate, and evangelical spirit of the New Testament, there will be a far wider and more effectual door of access for it through the families of that land which has the apparatus, than of that land which has it not. So that it is well for the christian economy of every country to have such an establishment. And even where the evangelical spirit has declined, there is still in the quiet and ordinary tenor of every nation's history, a spirit among the public functionaries, on the side of order and good conduct; so that, with the softening and humanising effect of scholarship, on the habit of the mind, it is further well, for the civic economy of every country, to have such an establishment.

We hold the very same principles to be applicable to the question of religious establishments. It is true, that our present goodly apparatus of churches and parishes was reared and perfected in days of thickest darkness. But when the light of reformation arose, it broke its way with greater force and facility, because of the very passages which Popery had opened; and let our ecclesiastical malcontents ascribe what corruption they may to the establishments of England and Scotland, we hold them to be the destined instruments both for propagating and for augmenting the Christianity of our land, and should never cease to regret the overthrow of this mighty apparatus, as a catastrophe of deadliest import to the religious character of our nation.

We are the more in earnest upon this subject, that we believe the difference, in point of moral and religious habit, between a town and country population, to be more due to the difference, in point of adequacy, between the established provision of instruction, for the one and the other, than to any other cause which can be assigned for it. The doctrine of a celestial influence does not supersede, but rather calls, for a terrestrial mechanism, to guide and to extend the distribution of it; and it is under the want of the latter, that a mass of heathenism has deepened, and accumulated, and attained to such a magnitude and density in our large towns. The healing water is a treasure which must be looked for and prayed for from heaven; but still, it is put into earthen vessels, and is conveyed through the whole body of corruption by earthen path-ways. Nor do we think it more rational to look for the rise of Christianity in Pagan lands, without a missionary equipment, and missionary labour, than to look for its revival among the enormous and now unpervaded departments of the city multitude, without such a locomotive influence, as shall bring the Word of God into material contact with its still, and sluggish, and stationary families.

We hold the possibility, and we cannot doubt the advantage of assimilating a town to a country parish. We think that the same moral regimen, which, under the parochial and ecclesiastical system of Scotland, has been set up, and with so much effect, in her country parishes, may, by a few simple and attainable processes, be introduced into the most crowded of her cities, and with as signal and conspicuous an effect on the whole habit and character of their population—that the simple relationship which obtains between a minister and his people in the former situation, may be kept up with all the purity and entireness of its influences in the latter situation; and be equally available to the formation of a well-conditioned peasantry; in a word, that there is no such dissimilarity between town and country, as to prevent the great national superiority of Scotland, in respect of her well-principled and well-educated people, being just as observable in Glasgow or Edinburgh, for example, as it is in the most retired of her districts, and these under the most diligent process of moral and religious cultivation. So that, while the profligacy which obtains in every crowded and concentrated mass of human beings, is looked upon by many a philanthropist as one of those helpless and irreclaimable distempers of the body politic, for which there is no remedy—do we maintain, that there are certain practicable arrangements which, under the blessing of God, will stay this growing calamity, and would, by the perseverance

E

of a few years, land us in a purer and better generation.

One most essential step towards so desirable an assimilation in a large city parish, is a numerous and well-appointed agency. The assimilation does not lie here in the external frame-work; for, in a small country parish, the minister alone, or with a very few coadjutors of a small session, may bring the personal influence of his kind and Christian attentions to bear upon all the families. Among the ten thousand of a city parish, this is impossible; and, therefore, what he cannot do but partially and superficially in his own person, must, if done substantially, be done in the person of others. And he, by dividing his parish into small manageable districts—and assigning one or more of his friends, in some capacity or other, to each of them—and vesting them with such a right either of superintendence or of inquiry, as will always be found to be gratefully met by the population— and so, raising, as it were, a ready intermedium of communication between himself and the inhabitants of his parish, may at length attain an assimilation in point of result to a country parish, though not in the means by which he arrived at it. He can in his own person maintain at least a pretty close and habitual intercourse with the more remarkable cases; and as for the moral charm of cordial and Christian acquaintanceship, he can spread it abroad by deputation over that part of the city which has been assigned to him. In this way, an influence, long unfelt in towns, may be speedily restored to them; and they, we affirm, know nothing of this department of our nature, who are blind to the truth of the position—that out of the simple elements of attention, and advice, and civility, and good-will, conveyed through the tenements of the poor, by men a little more elevated in rank than themselves, a far more purifying and even more gracious operation can be made to descend upon them, than ever will be achieved by any other of the ministrations of charity.

And here, let it be remarked, that just as the material apparatus of schools subserves the civic as well as the Christian economy of a nation, by its operating as a medium for other good influences than those which are purely sacred—so, this eminently holds true of every such arrangement as multiplies the topics and the occurrences of intercourse between the higher and the lower orders of society. There is no large city which would not soon experience the benefit of such an arrangement. But when that city is purely commercial, it is just the arrangement which, of all others, is most fitted to repair a peculiar disadvantage under which it labours. In a provincial capital, the great mass of the population are retained in kindly and immediate dependence on the wealthy residenters of the place. It is the resort of annuitants, and landed proprietors, and members of the law, and other learned professions, who give impulse to a great amount of domestic industry, by their ex-

penditure; and, on inquiring into the sources of
maintenance and employment for the labouring
classes there, it will be found that they are chiefly
engaged in the immediate service of ministering
to the wants and luxuries of the higher classes in
the city. This brings the two extreme orders of
society into that sort of relationship, which is
highly favourable to the general blandness and
tranquillity of the whole population. In a manu-
facturing town, on the other hand, the poor and
the wealthy stand more disjoined from each other.
It is true, they often meet, but they meet more
on an arena of contest, than on a field where the
patronage and custom of the one party are met
by the gratitude and good will of the other. When
a rich customer calls a workman into his presence,
for the purpose of giving him some employment
connected with his own personal accommodation,
the general feeling of the latter must be altogether
different from what it would be, were he called
into the presence of a trading capitalist, for the
purpose of cheapening his work, and being dis-
missed for another, should there not be an agreement in their terms. We do not aim at the most
distant reflection against the manufacturers of our
land; but it must be quite obvious, from the
nature of the case, that their intercourse with the
labouring classes is greatly more an intercourse
of collision, and greatly less an intercourse of
kindliness, than is that of the higher orders in such
towns as Bath, or Oxford, or Edinburgh. In this

way, there is a mighty unfilled space interposed
between the high and the low of every large manu-
facturing city, in consequence of which, they are
mutually blind to the real cordialities and attrac-
tions which belong to each of them; and a resentful
feeling is apt to be fostered, either of disdain or
defiance, which it will require all the expedients
of an enlightened charity effectually to do away.
Nor can we guess at a likelier, or a more immediate arrangement for this purpose, than to multiply the agents of Christianity amongst us, whose
delight it may be to go forth among the people,
on no other errand than that of pure good-will,
and with no other ministrations than those of respect and tenderness.

There is one lesson that we need not teach, for
experience has already taught it, and that is, the
kindly influence which the mere presence of a human being has upon his fellows. Let the attention
bestowed upon another, be the genuine emanation
of good-will, and there is only one thing more to
make it irresistible. The readiest way of finding
access to a man's heart, is to go into his house, and
there to perform the deed of kindness, or to acquit
ourselves of the wonted and the looked for acknowledgment. By putting ourselves under the
roof a poor neighbour, we in a manner put
ourselves under his protection—we render him
for the time our superior—we throw our reception on his generosity, and we may be assured
that it is a confidence which will almost never

fail us. If Christianity be the errand on which the movement is made, it will open the door of every family; and even the profane and the profligate will come to recognise the worth of that principle, which prompts the unwearied assiduity of such services. By every circuit which is made amongst them, there is attained a higher vantage ground of moral and spiritual influence; and, in spite of all that has been said of the ferocity of a city population, in such rounds of visitation there is none of it to be met with, even among the lowest receptacles of human worthlessness. This is the home walk in which is earned, if not a proud, at least a peaceful popularity—the popularity of the heart—the greetings of men, who, touched even by the cheapest and easiest services of kindness, have nothing to give but their wishes of kindness back again; but, in giving these, have crowned such pious attentions with the only popularity that is worth the aspiring after—the popularity that is won in the bosom of families, and at the side of death-beds.

We must refer to the following chapter, on the effect of locality in towns, for a more full elucidation of this influence, and of its beneficial operation. And, indeed, we can do little more at present, than clear and open our way to the task of demonstrating the various facilities by which a city may be likened, in constitution and effect, to a country parish. We shall therefore confine ourselves to what, in the main, may be regarded

as preliminary. And as we have already adverted
to the trivial estimation in which the work of
purely Christian labourers is apt to be held by
our political theorists, let us now expose a very
sore and hurtful invasion that has been actually
made upon them by our political practitioners, by
which their religious usefulness has been grievously
impaired, and even their civil and political usefulness has been impaired along with it. It is indeed
a topic altogether pertinent to the title of our
present chapter, as standing intimately associated
with the cause of one of the greatest dissimilarities
that obtains between a town and a country parish.
It is an example of the slender homage which is
rendered to Christianity by our political economists, embodied into shape and practice by our
political functionaries, and in virtue of which, the
best objects of all civil and legislative policy are
in danger of being entirely frustrated.

What we allude to, is, the mischief of those secularities, which have been laid on the clerical office;
and for the purpose of exposing it, do we offer a
short narrative of the way in which the sanctity of
a profession, that ought ever to have been held
inviolable, has been laid open to all the rude and
random invasions which are now ready to over-
whelm it,—though we shall find it impossible to
advert to every one item in that strange medley
of services, by which the minister of a large city
parish now feels himself plied at every hour, and
beset at every path, and every turning point, in
the history of his movements.

Among the people of our busy land, who are
ever on the wing of activity, and, whether in circumstances of peace or of war, are at all times
feeling the impulse of some national movement or
other, it is not to be wondered at, that a series of
transactions should be constantly flowing between
the metropolis of the empire, and its distant
provinces. There are the remittances which pass
through our public offices, from soldiers and sailors,
to their relatives at home;—there are letters of
inquiry sent back again from these relatives;—
there is all the correspondence, and all the business of drafts, and other negociations, which ensue
upon the decease of a soldier, or a sailor;—there
is the whole tribe of hospital allowances, the pay-
ment of pensions, and a variety of other items,
which, all taken together, would make out a very
strange and tedious enumeration.

The individuals with whom these transactions
are carried on, need to be verified. They live in
some parish or other; and who can be fitter for
the required purpose, than the parish minister?
He is, or he ought to be, acquainted with every
one of his parishioners; and this acquaintance,
which he never can obtain in towns, but by years
of ministerial exertion amongst them, is turned
to an object destructive of the very principle on
which he was selected for such a service. It
saddles him with a task which breaks in upon his
ministerial exertions—which widens his distance
from his people; and, in the end, makes him as

unfit for certifying a single clause of information
about them, as the most private individual in his
neighbourhood.

Yet so it is. The minister is the organ of many
a communication between his people and the
offices in London,—and many a weary signature
is exacted from him,—and a world of management
is devolved upon his shoulders,—and, instead of
sitting like his fathers in office, surrounded by the
theology of present and of other days, he must now
turn his study into a counting-room, and have his
well-arranged cabinet before him, fitted up with
its sections and its other conveniences, for notices,
and duplicates, and all the scraps and memoranda
of a manifold correspondence.

But the history does not stop here. The
example of Government has descended, and is
now quickly running through the whole field of
private and individual agency. The regulation of
the business of prize-moneys, is one out of several
examples that occur to us. The emigration of
new settlers to Canada, was another. The business
of the Kinloch bequest, is a third. It does not
appear, that there is any act of Government
authorising the agents in this matter to fix on the
clergy, as the organs either for the transaction of
their business, or the conveyance of their information to the people of the land. But they find it
convenient to follow the example of Government,
and have accordingly done so; and, in this way,
a mighty host of schedules, and circulars, and

printed forms, with long blank spaces, which the minister is required to fill up, according to the best of his knowledge, come into mustering competition with the whole of his other claims, and his other engagements. It is true, that the minister may, in this case decline; but, then, the people are apprised of the arrangement, and, trained as they have been, too well, to look up to the minister as an organ of civil accommodation, will they lay siege to his dwelling-place, and pour upon him with their inquiries; and the cruel alternative is laid upon him either to obstruct the convenience of his parishioners, and bid them from his presence, or to take the whole weight of a management that has been so indiscreetly and so wantonly assigned to him.

If, for the expediting of business, we are made free with, even by private individuals, it is not to be wondered at, if charitable bodies should, at all times, look for our subserviency to their schemes and their operations of benevolence. When a patriotic fund, or a Waterloo subscription, blazons in all the splendour of a nation's munificence, and a nation's gratitude, before the public eye,—who shall have the hardihood to refuse a single item of the bidden co-operation that is expected from him? Surely, such a demand as this is quite irresistible; and, accordingly, from this quarter too, a heavy load of consultations and certificates, with the additional singularity of having to do with the drawing of money, and the keeping of it in safe custody, and the dealing of it out in small discretionary parcels according to the needs and circumstances of the parties;—all, all is placed upon the shoulders of the already jaded and overborne minister.

We know not where this is to end, or what new and unheard-of duties are still in reserve for us. But this much we know, that they are in the way of an indefinite augmentation. We have heard obscurely of some very recent additions to our burdens; but of what it particularly is, we have not got the distinct or the authentic information. We are not civilians enough to know, if even an Act of Parliament carry such an omnipotence along with it, as to empower this strange series of wanton and arbitrary infringements on the individual homes and liberties of clergymen. But we are patriots enough to feel, that the rulers of our country are, for an accommodation which might be easily rendered to them by another method, bartering away the best interests of its people,— that, through the side of its public instructors, they are reaching a blow to the morality and principle of the commonwealth,—that, by every such impolitic enactment as we have now attempted to expose, they are slackening the circulation of Christianity, and of all its healthful and elevating influences amongst our towns and families,— that they are sweeping away from the face of every large city, the best securities for order, and contentment, and loyalty;—nor should we wonder,

if, in some future period of turbulence and disorder, they shall rue the infatuation which led
them to tamper so with the religion of our land, by
the inroads they are now making, and the cruel
profanation they are now inflicting, on the sacredness of its officiating ministers.

It is needless to expatiate on the mischievous
effect of all this upon the great mass of our
population. In virtue of the grievous desecration
that has thus been inflicted on the office, we hold
out, in their eyes, a totally different aspect from the
ministers of a former age. We are getting every
year more assimilated, in look and in complexion,
to surveyors, and city-clerks, and justices, and
distributors of stamps; and all those men of place,
who have to do with the people, in the matters of
civil or municipal agency. Every feature in the
sacredness of our character is wearing down, amid
all the stir, and hurry, and hard-driving, of this
manifold officiality. And thus it is, that our
parishioners have nearly lost sight of us altogether,
as their spiritual directors, and seldom or never
come near to us, upon any spiritual errand at all—
but, taking us, as they are led by the vicious
system that is now in progressive operation to find
us—they are, ever and anon, overwhelming us
with consultations about their temporalities; and
the whole tact of a spiritual relationship between
the pastor and his flock is thus dissipated and done
away. There is little of the unction of Christianity, at all, in the intercourse he holds with

them—and every thing that relates to the soul, and to the interests of eternity, and to the religious care of themselves, and of their families, is elbowed away by the work of filling up their schedules, and advising them about their moneys, and shuffling, along with them, amongst the forms and the papers of a most intricate correspondence.

The principle which we lay down is,—that the work of a Christian teacher is enough, by itself, to engross and take possession of the entire powers of any single man. The business of meditation is a fatiguing business, and leaves a general exhaustion behind it. There is such a thing as a weariness of the mind; and surely, if the right ministration for weariness be repose—then, there must be an overworking of the mind, when after having taken exercise up to the limits of its strength, it is plied with a multiplicity of other and overbearing demands on its attention, and its memory, and its judgment, and the various faculties which belong to it. The likest thing to it, in the experience of ordinary citizens, which we can imagine, is the case of a merchant exhausting himself by the forenoon labours of his desk, or his counting-house, and retiring to the sweets of a comfortable home, and there solacing himself with the conversations of friendship, or recruiting the languor of his worn-out spirits among the endearments of a family. There is a wall of defence, which, we understand, many of them have thrown around their persons, and, in virtue of

which, no one application about business is at all
entertained, or listened to, excepting on business
hours. Let them just guess, then, how much
they would be teased, and jaded, and positively
enfeebled, were this wall of defence broken down;
and there regularly passed through the breach, in
force and in frequency, every evening, upon them,
a host of invaders, armed with their miscellany of
mixed and multiform applications. Let them take
this back to the case of a man, whose business is
meditation. They, perhaps, may never have engaged to any great extent in this business. Then,
we do not wait for the conviction of their personal experience on the subject; but we demand
it as a right, that the man who has the experience
should be believed. His positive testimony should
be made to outweigh all that inexperience may
conceive, or may utter, on such a case. If he
happen to stand confronted with a public, who are
utter strangers to the labour of intense thoughtfulness, the voice of such a public, if lifted in
condemnation against him, should not be sustained
as a voice of authority. They are not a competent
jury upon this question. And, having premised
this, we assert what we are not afraid to carry, by
appeal, to the higher reason of the country—that
the labour of intense study, if persisted in, for a
few hours, is just as exhausting as the busiest and
most lengthened forenoon of an ordinary citizen.
He who has borne this labour, through the day,
has purchased by it, as good a right to exemption

from all that can disturb or annoy him—and if, nevertheless, these annoyances shall be obstinately presented to him, he is put into a state of mental and bodily suffering. There is a pressure upon his whole constitution, greater than the strength of it can enable him to carry. And, under these circumstances, he must cast about for relief, in some change of his daily and habitual arrangements.

We are all aware of the restless appetite of a sentient being, for a comfortable state of existence. In the case which we have now specified, this principle must tell. If a student was in the habit of labouring at his own peculiar exercise, up to the measure of his constitutional ability, then the additional labour that is thus laid upon him, lays also upon him the necessity of an abridgement upon his studies. He must just make a curtailment upon his business hours. There is a familiar advice, that is often given to a man under hardship, and which will come upon him with all the power of a most insinuating temptation: "Take matters easily." Are you busied with foreign applications? Take them easily. Are you cumbered with official patronage? Take it easily. Are you plied for your personal attendance on the work of secularities? Take it easily. Are you put into requisition, through the week, for a variety of manifold engagements? Take them all easily. Are you, in addition to other things, burdened with the duty of Sabbath preparation? It is true, that there is something in this employment, which may well weigh a man down with a feeling of its importance. He is to address a number of unperishable creatures, about the affairs of immortality. But he has no other resource, than just to do with them what he does with the crowd and the frequency of his other affairs. He must throw together such thoughts as he can, and get up a half-hour exhibition, in some way or other; but, in self-defence, and as he values the great objects of comfort and endurance, he must, by all means, take the matter easily.

We need not say more about the direct blow which the prevailing system of our towns must, at length, in this way, give to the cause of practical Christianity, in our congregations and parishes. We proceed to another effect, still more palpable, if not more prejudicial, than the former. It will keep back and degrade the theological literature of Scotland.

There is nothing in the contrast which we are now to offer, between the theology of one age and that of another, which is not highly honourable to the present race of clergymen. The truth is, that they have kept their ground so well, against the whole of this blasting and degenerating operation, as to render it necessary, for the purpose of giving full effect to our argument, that we should look forward, in perspective, to the next age, and compute the inevitable difference which must obtain between its literature and that of the last generation.

On looking back to the distance of half a century, we behold the picture of a church adorned
by the literature of her clergy. It is of no consequence to the argument, that the whole of this
literature was not professional. Part of it was
so; and every part of it proved, at least, the fact,
that there was time, and tranquillity, and full
protection from all that was uncongenial for the
labours of the understanding. We cannot but
look back with regret, bordering upon envy, to
that period in the history of our church—when
her ministers companied with the sages of philosophy, and bore away an equal share of the
public veneration—when the levities of Hume, as
he sported his unguarded hour, among the circles
of the enlightened, were met by the Pastors of
humble Presbyterianism, who, equal in reach and
in accomplishment to himself, could repel the
force of all his sophistries, and rebuke him into
silence—when this most subtle and profound of
infidels aimed his decisive thrust at the Christian
testimony, and a minister of our church, and he,
too, the minister of a town, dared all the hazards
of the intellectual warfare, and bore the palm of
superiority away from him—In a word, we look
back, as we do upon a scene of departed glory, to
that period, when the clergy of our cities could
ply the toils of an unbroken solitude, and send
forth the fruits of them, in one rich tide of moral
and literary improvement over our land. It is
true, that all the labours of that period were not

rendered up, in one consecrated offering, to the
cause of theology. It is true, that among the
names of Wallace, and Henry, and Robertson,
and Blair, and Macknight, and Campbell, some
can be singled out, who chose the classic walk, or
gave up their talent to the speculations of general
philosophy. Yet the history of each individual
amongst them, proves that, in these days, there
was time for the exercise of talent—that these
were the days, when he, among the priesthood,
who had an exclusive taste for theology, could
give the whole force of his mind to its contemplations—that these were the days, when a generous
enthusiasm for the glories of his profession, met
with nothing to stifle or vulgarise it—that these
were the days, when the man of prayer, and the
man of gospel ministrations, could give himself
wholly to these things, and bring forth the evidence of his profiting, either in authorship to all,
or in weekly addresses to the people of his own
congregation. It is true, that the names which
we have now gathered, are all from the field of
a lofty and conspicuous literature. Yet we chiefly
count upon them, as the tokens of such a leisure,
and of such a seclusion, and of such an habitual
opportunity, for the exercises of retirement, as
would give tenfold effect to the worthiest and
most devoted ministers of a former generation—as
enabled the Hamilton and Gillies of our own city,
to shed a holier influence around them, and have
throned, in the remembrance of living men, the

Erskine, and Walker, and Black, of our metropolis, who maintained, throughout the whole of their history, the aspect of sacredness, and gave every hour of their existence to its contemplations and its labours.

What is it that must cause all resemblance of this to disappear from a future generation? Not that their lot will be cast in an age of little men. Not that Nature will send forth a blight over the face of our establishment, and wither up all the graces and talents, which, at one time, signalised it. Not that some adverse revolution of the elements will bring along with it some strange desolating influence on the genius and literature of the priesthood. The explanation is nearer at hand, and we need not seek for it among the wilds or the obscurities of mysticism. Nature will just be as liberal as before; and bring forth the strongest and the healthiest specimens of mind, in as great abundance as ever; and will cast abroad no killing influence at all, to stunt any one of its aspiring energies; and will just, if she have free play, be as vigorous with the moral as with the physical productions of a former generation. This change, of which the fact will be unquestionable, however much the cause may elude the public observation, will not be the work of Nature, but of man. There will be no decay of talent whatever, in respect to the existence of it. The only decay will be in the exercise of talent. It will be— that her solitudes have all been violated—that her claims have all been unheeded and despised—that her delicacies have all been overborne—above every thing, that her exertions and her capabilities have been grossly misunderstood—it not being known how much restraint stifles her—and the employments of ordinary business vulgarise her—and distraction impedes the march of her greater enterprises—and the fatigue she incurs by her own exercises, if accumulated by the fatigue of other exercises, which do not belong to her, may, at length, enervate and exhaust her altogether. Thus it is, that an unlearned public may both admit the existence of the mischief, and lament the evils of it, and yet be utterly blind to the fact, that it is a mischief of their own doing. They lay their own rude estimate on a profession, of the cares and the labours of which they have no experience—and, instead of cheering, do they scowl upon the men who vindicate the privileges of our order. They are perpetually measuring the habits and the conveniences of literary business, of which they know nothing, by the habits and the conveniences of ordinary business, of which they know something. And thus it is, that instead of the blind leading the blind, the blind, in the first instance, turn upon their leaders—they give the whole weight of their influence and opinion to that cruel process, by which the most enlightened priesthood in the world, if they submit to it, may, by the lapse of one generation more, sink down into a state of contentment with the tamest, and the humblest, and the paltriest attainments. Nor will it at all alleviate, but fearfully embitter, the whole malignity of this system, should its operation be such, that, in a succeeding age, both our priests and our people will sit down in quietness, and in great mutual satisfaction with each other—the one, fired by no ambition for professional excellence; the other, actuated by no demand for it—the one, peaceably leaning down to the business of such services as they may be called to bear; the other, not seeking, and not caring for higher services.

Every thing that is said for the evils of such a system, should elevate, in public estimation, all our living clergymen. It came upon them in the way of gradual accumulation; and, at each distinct step, it wore the aspect of a benevolent and kind accommodation to the humbler orders of society. They are not to blame that it has been admitted; and we call upon the public to admire, that they have stood so well its adverse influence on all their professional labours. But there is one principle in human nature, which, if the system be not done away, will, in time, give a most tremendous certainty to all our predictions. It does not bear so hard on the natural indolence of man, to spend his life in bustling and miscellaneous activity, as to spend his life in meditation and prayer. The former is positively the easier course of existence. The two habits suit very ill together; and, in some individuals, there is an utter incompatibility betwixt them. But should the alternative be presented, of adopting the one habit or the other, singly, the position is unquestionable, that it were better for the ease, and the health, and the general tone of comfort and cheerfulness, that a man should lend out his person to all the variety of demands for attendance, and of demands for ordinary business, which are brought to bear upon him, than that he should give up his mind to the labours of a strenuous and sustained thoughtfulness. Now, just calculate the force of the temptation to abandon study, and to abandon scholarship, when personal comfort and the public voice, both unite to lure him away from them—when the popular smile would insinuate him into such a path of employment, as, if he once enter, he must bid adieu to all the stern exercises of a contemplative solitude; and the popular frown glares upon that retirement, in which he might consecrate his best powers to the best interests of a sadly misled and miscalculating generation—when the hosannahs of the multitude cheer him on to what may be comparatively termed, a life of amusement; and the condemnation both of unlettered wealth and unlettered poverty, is made to rest upon his name, should he refuse to let down the painful discipline of his mind, by frittering it all away amongst those lighter varieties of management, and of exertion, which, by the practice of our cities, are habitually laid upon him. Such a temptation must come, in time, to be irresistible; and, just in proportion as it is yielded to, must there be a portion of talent withdrawn from the literature of theology. There must be the desertion of all that is fine, and exquisite, and lofty, in its contemplations. There must be a relapse from the science and the industry of a former generation. There must be a decline of theological attainments, and theological authorship. There must be a yearly process of decay and of deterioration, in this branch of our national literature. There must be a descending movement towards the tame, and the feeble, and the commonplace. And thus, for the wretched eclat of getting clergy to do, with their hands, what thousands can do as well as they, may our cities come, at length, to barter away the labour of their minds, and give such a blow to theology, that, amongst men of scholarship and general cultivation, it will pass for the most languishing of the sciences.

And here we cannot but advert to the observation of Hume, who, be his authority in religion what it may, must be admitted to have very high authority in all matters of mere literary experience. He tells us, in the history of his own life, that a great city is the only fit residence for a man of letters; and his assertion is founded on a true discernment of our nature. In the country, there may be leisure for the pursuits of the understanding; but there is a want of impulse. The mind is apt to languish in the midst of a wilderness, where, surrounded perhaps, by uncongenial spirits, it stagnates and gathers the rust of decay, by its

mere distance from sympathy and example, and
the animating converse of men who possess a kindred taste, and are actuated by a kindred ambition.
Transport the possessor of such a mind to a town,
and he there meets with much to arouse him out
of all this dormancy. He will find his way to men,
whose views and pursuits are in harmony with his
own—and he will be refreshed for action, by
the encouragement of their society—and he will
feel himself more linked with the great literary
public, by his personal approximation to some of
its most distinguished members—and communications from the eminent, in all parts of the
country, will now pour upon him in greater a-
bundance—and above all, in the improved facilities of authorship, and from his actual position
within the limits of a theatre; where his talents are
no sooner put forth into exercise, than the fruits
of them may be brought out into exhibition—in
all this, we say, there is a power and a vivacity of
excitement, which may set most actively agoing,
the whole machinery of his genius, and turn to its
right account, those faculties which, else, had with-
ered in slothfulness, and, under the bleak influences
of an uncheered and unstimulated solitude, might
finally have expired.

This applies, in all its parts, to the literature of
theology, and gives us to see, how much the cities
of our land might do for the advancement of its
interests. They might cast a wakeful eye over
the face of the country—and single out all the

splendour and superiority of talent which they see
in our establishment—and cause it to emerge out
of its surrounding obscurity—and deliver it from
the chill and langour of an uncongenial situation
—and transplant it into a kindlier region, where,
shielded from all that is adverse to the play or
exercise of mind, and encouraged to exertion by
an approving and intelligent piety, it may give
its undivided labour to things sacred, and have its
solitude for meditation on these things, varied only
by such spiritual exercises out of doors, as might
have for their single object the increase of Christian
worth and knowledge amongst the population.

This is what cities might do for Theology. But
what is it that they in fact do for it? The two
essential elements for literary exertion, are excitement and leisure. The first is ministered in abundance out of all those diversities of taste and understanding which run along the scale of a mighty
population. The second element, if we give way
much longer to the system which prevails among
them—if we lay no check upon their exertions,
and make no stand against the variety of their
inconsiderate demands upon us—if we resign our
own right of judgment upon our own habits and
our own conveniencies, and follow the impulse of
a public, who, without experience on the matter,
can feel no sympathy and have no just calculation
about the peculiarities of clerical employment—
then should we be robbed of this second element
altogether. We should lie under the malignity of

an Egyptian bondage,—bricks are required of us, and we have no straw. The public would like to see all the solidities of argument, and all the graces of persuasion, associated with the cause of sacred literature. But then they would desolate the sanctuaries of literature. They would drag away mind from the employments of literature. They would leave not one moment of time or of tranquillity for the pursuits of literature. They would consume, by a thousand preposterous servilities, all those energies of the inner man, which might, every one of them, be consecrated with effect, to the advancement of literature. In one word, they would dethrone the guardians of this sacred cause from the natural eminency of their office altogether; —and, weighing them down with the burden of other services, they would vulgarise them out of all their taste and all their generous aspirings after literature.

Here, then, is the whole extent of this sore and two-edged calamity. In the country, there is time for the prosecution of a lofty and laborious walk; but there is not the excitement. In the town, there is the excitement; but under the progress of such a system as we have attempted to expose, there will not be the time. There is a constant withdrawment of the more conspicuous members of our establishment from the solitude of their first parishes. But it is withdrawment into a vortex which stifles and destroys them. Those towns, which, with a few most simple and practicable reformations, might be the instruments of sustaining the cause of theology, and of sending abroad over the face of our country, a most vigorous and healthful impulse towards the prosecution of theological learning, may, under that yearly process of extinction, which is now going forward, depress the whole literature of our profession, and by every translation from the country, may, in fact, absorb so much of promise and ability from the cause of the gospel. The atmosphere of towns, may at length become so pestilential, as to wither up the energies of our church, and shed a baleful influence over all that lustre of ministerial accomplishment, which otherwise might adorn it. And we have only to look to the last fifty years, and think of the new direction to our habits which has taken place in that period, in order to compute how soon our national establishment may, by the simple cause of its ministers being turned to the drudgery of other services, be shorn of her best and most substantial glories, and how soon that theology of which she is the appointed guardian, may come to sink both in vigour and illustration, beneath the spirit, and literature, and general philosophy, of the times.

Should no arrest be laid on this mischievous operation, then, by another age, will we behold two great absorbing eddies for the theology of our land. An Argus is stationed at each of them, whose office now, is to watch for all the rising excellence that shoots into visibility on the face of our establishment—and whose office then, will be to lure it to inevitable destruction. In the short-lived whirl of some fair and even brilliant exhibitions, may it be able, in each individual case, to sustain itself for a few circling years above the surface of mediocrity, when it will at length touch the brink of its final engulfment, and disappear for ever.

Should any reader think that we have drawn the above picture with too faithful, or even with too strong a hand, we ask him further to think, that it is such a picture, as, by its very exhibition, may scare away the realities which it anticipates. The case, we are persuaded, requires only to be understood, and then will it be provided for, since the restoration of the clergy to their own proper and peculiar influence over the hosts of a city population, must appear both to the Christian and the general philanthropist, one of the most important all our national desiderata.

CHAP. II.

ON THE INFLUENCE OF LOCALITY IN TOWNS.

WE do not know how the matter is ordered in London; but, in the second-rate towns of our empire, it will often be found, that, when a philanthropic society is formed in them for any assigned object, it spreads its operations over the whole field of the congregated population. This holds generally true both of the societies for relief, and of the societies for instruction. Take a clothing society, or an old man's friend society, or a destitute sick society, as examples of the former— or take a Sabbath school society, as an example of the latter—and, in by far the greater number of instances, will it be seen, that, instead of concentrating their exertions upon one district or department of the city, they expatiate at large, and over the face of its entire territory, recognising no other boundary, than that which lies indefinitely but fully beyond the final outskirts of the compact and contiguous dwelling-places.

We do not offer at present to discuss the specific merits of any of these societies; and though, in the remarks which immediately follow, we attach ourselves chiefly to the last of them—yet it is not with the view of appreciating or vindicating Sabbath schools; but, through them, to illustrate a principle of philanthropic management, for which we can find no better designation, than the influence of locality in large towns.

In most of the Sabbath school societies with which we are acquainted, this principle is disregarded. The teachers are indiscriminately stationed in all parts of the city, and the pupils are as indiscriminately drawn from all parts of the city. Now, what we affirm, is, that the effectiveness of each individual teacher is greatly augmented, if a definite locality be given to him; and that a number of teachers spread over any given neighbourhood on this principle, is armed, in consequence of it, with a much higher moral power, over the habits and opinions of the rising generation.

Let a small portion of the town, with its geographical limits, be assigned to such a teacher. Let his place of instruction be within this locality, or as near as possible to its confines. Let him restrain his attentions to the children of its families, sending forth no invitations to those who are without, and encouraging, as far as it is proper, the attendance of all who are within. Under such an arrangement, he will attain a comfort and an efficiency in his work, which, with the common arrangement, is utterly unattainable. And, we farther conceive, that, if this local assignation of teachers were to become general, it would lead to far more precious and lasting consequences of good to society.

However thoroughly we may be convinced of the benefit that would result from the influence of locality, we feel that it is not an easy task didactically to set forth this influence, by any process of argument or explanation. The conviction is far more readily arrived at by the tact of real and living experience, than by the lessons of any expounder. There is a charm in locality, most powerfully felt by every man who tries it; but which, at the same time, it is most difficult so to seize upon as to embody it in language, or to bring it forth in satisfying demonstration to the public eye. We do not know an individual who has personally attached himself to a manageable portion of the civic territory, and has entered with taste and spirit upon its cultivation—and who does not perceive, with something like the force and the clearness of intuition, that, if this way of it were spread over an assembled million of human beings, it would quickly throw a new moral complexion over the teeming expanse that is on every side of him. But what he feels, it is not easy to make others see. For, however substantial the influence of locality is, there is a certain shadowy fineness about it, in virtue of which it eludes the efforts of an observer to lay hold of it, and to analyse it. It is no bad evidence, however, of the experimental soundness of this operation, that the incredulity about it, is all on the side of those who stand without the field of local management; and the confidence about it, on the side of those who stand within; and that, while the former regard it as a mystic and undefinable fancy, the latter find in it as much of sureness and solidity, as if their eyes saw it, and their hands handled it.

Let us attempt, however, in the face of all these difficulties, to offer some developement of the precise character and tendency of the arrangement which we have now recommended.

The first effect of it which falls to be considered, is that which it has upon the teacher. He, with a select and appropriate vineyard thus lying before him, will feel himself far more powerfully urged, than when under the common arrangement, to go forth among its families. However subtle an exercise it may require from another, faithfully to analyse the effect upon his mind, he himself has only to try it, and he will soon become sensible of the strong additional interest that he acquires, in virtue of having a small and specific locality assigned to him. When the subject on which he is to operate, thus offers itself to his contemplation, in the shape of one unbroken field, or of one entire and continuous body, it acts as a more distinct and imperative call upon him, to go out upon the enterprise. He will feel a kind of property in the families; and the very circumstance of a material limit around their habitations, serves to strengthen this impression, by furnishing to his mind a sort of association with the hedges and the landmarks of property. At all events, the very visibility of the limit, by constantly leading him to perceive the length and the breadth of his task, holds out an inducement to his energies, which, however difficult to explain, will be powerfully felt and proceeded on. There is a very great difference, in respect of its practical influence, between a task that is indefinite, and a task that is clearly seen to be overtakeable. The one has the effect to paralyze; the other, to quicken exertion. It serves most essentially to spirit on his undertaking, when, by every new movement, one feels himself to be drawing sensibly nearer to the accomplishment of it—when, by every one house that he enters, he can count the lessening number before him, through which he has yet to pass with his proposals for the attendance of their children—and when, by the distinct and definite portion which is still untravelled, he is constantly reminded of what he has to do, ere that district, which he feels to be his own, is thoroughly pervaded. He can go over his families too, with far less expense of locomotion, than under the common system of Sabbath schools; and, for the same reason, can he more fully and frequently reiterate his attentions; and it will charm him onwards, to find that he is sensibly translating himself into a stricter and kinder relationship with the people of his district; and, if he have a taste for cordial intercourse with the fellows of his own nature, he will be gladdened and encouraged by his growing familiarity with them all; and thus will he turn the vicinity which he has chosen, into a home-walk of many charities; and recognised as its moral benefactor, will his kindness, and his judgment, and his Christianity,

be put forth, with a well-earned and well-estab-
lished influence, in behalf of a grateful population.

Thus one great benefit of such an arrangement,
is, its effect in calling out the exertion of the
teachers; the next, is, its effect in calling out the
attendance of the taught. The invitation comes
upon them with far greater power, when it is to
attend the weekly lessons which are given out in
the close vicinity of their own habitations, than
were it to attend at some distant place, where
children are assembled from all quarters of the
city. And the vicinity of the place of instruction
to the taught, is not the only point of juxtaposition
which goes to secure and to perpetuate their attendance. There is also much in the juxtaposition
of the taught to one another. This brings what
may be called the gregarious principle into fuller
play. What children will not do singly, they will
do with delight and readiness in a flock. This
comes powerfully to the aid of the other advantages which belong to the local system—where the
teacher will not only experience a kind reception
at his first outset among the families, but will find,
that in the course of a very few rounds, he en-
gages, for his scholars, not a small proportion of
the young, but a great majority of those in the
district. And if he just follow up each act of
absence, on the part of the children, by a call of
inquiry upon their parents, he will succeed in con-
trolling them to regular and continued attendance—
a habit, which, with a slight exertion of care upon

his part, may be so kept up and strengthened, as to obtain, in the little vicinage over which he presides, all the certainty of a mechanical operation.

The third peculiar benefit of this local arrangement, is, its effect on the population of the district. That very influence which binds the teacher to the families, does, though by a looser and feebler tie, bind the families to each other. One great desideratum in large towns, is acquaintanceship among the contiguous families. And to promote this, every arrangement in itself right, should be promoted, which brings out the indwellers of one vicinity to one common place of repair, and brings upon them one common ministration. We believe, that the total want of parish schools, and the total neglect of the right of parishioners, to a preference for seats in parish churches, have, in addition to a mischief of a deadlier and more direct character, withheld from our population, the great, though collateral advantage that we are now insisting on. It is an advantage, which is, to a certain degree, made up by the local arrangement of Sabbath-schools—where, by next-door neighbours being supplied with one common point of reference; and their children being led to meet in each other's houses, at one common work of preparation; and all being furnished with one common topic of simple, but heart-felt gratitude—that moral distance is somewhat alleviated, which obtains in our great cities, without any counteraction whatever, even among those living under the same roof, and which powerfully contributes, among other causes, to stamp a louring and unsocial aspect, on a city population.

The common system of Sabbath-schooling, has none of these advantages. The families that furnish children to the same teacher, may lie at a wide physical distance from each other; and it is therefore seldom that he holds any week-day intercourse at all, with the few and scattered houses out of which his scholars repair to him—or that he maintains any common understanding with the parents about their young—or that he joins his guardianship with theirs, in calling the absentees to account, for their acts of non-attendance—or that he forms acquaintance with them upon that most gratifying and welcome of all intimations, that their children are doing well. The close and oft-repeated influences, in virtue of which, a local teacher may incorporate his school, with the habit of all the families that are allotted to him, are wanting to the general teacher. The latter may still, however, head a most numerous and respectable school; but this is more in virtue of a pre-existent desire for Christian instruction, than of any desire which he himself has excited among the families. Attendance upon a general teacher, in spite of distance and other disadvantages, generally argues, and is indeed the fruit of a certain value and pre-disposition for the lessons of Christianity. Attendance on a local teacher, is oftener the fruit, not of an original, but of a communicated taste for his instructions. It is a produce of his own gathering. It is the result, not of a spontaneous, but of a derived movement, to which he himself gave the primary impulse, by going aggresively forth upon a given territory; and which he perpetuates and keeps up by his frequent calls and his unremitting vigilance, and his oft-repeated applications, brought to bear upon one and the same neighbourhood.

Under a local system, the teachers move towards the people. Under a general system, such of the people as are disposed to Christianity, move towards them. To estimate the comparative effect of these two, take the actual state of every mixed and crowded population, where there must be many among whom this disposition is utterly extinguished. The question is, how shall the influence of a Sabbath school be brought most readily and most abundantly into contact with their families? Which of the two parties, the teacher or those to be taught, should make the first advances to such an approximation? To meet this question, let it ever be remembered, that there is a wide and a mighty difference between the wants of our physical, and those of our moral and spiritual nature. In proportion to our want of food, is our desire for food; but it is not so with our want of knowledge, or virtue, or religion. The more destitute we are of these last, the more dead we are as to any inclination for them. A general system of Sabbath schooling may attract

K

towards it all the predisposition that there is for Christian instruction, and yet leave the majority as untouched and as unawakened as it found them. In moving through the lanes and the recesses of a long-neglected population, will it be found of the fearful multitude, that not only is their acquaintance with the gospel extinguished, but their wish to obtain an acquaintance with it is also extinguished. They not only have no righteousness; but they have no hungering nor thirsting after it. A general teacher may draw some kindred particles out of this assemblage. He may bring around him such families as are of a homogeneous quality with himself. Those purer ingredients of the mass, which retain so much of the etherial character as to have an etherial tendency, may move towards a place of central and congenial attraction, though at a considerable distance from them; and, even though, in so doing, they have to come separately out from that overwhelming admixture with which they are encompassed. But the bulky sediment remains untouched and stationary; and, by its power of assimilation, too, is all the while adding to its own magnitude. And thus it is both a possible thing that schools may multiply, under a general system, and that out of the resources of a mighty population, an overflowing attendance may be afforded to each of them, while an humble fraction of the whole is all that is overtaken; and below the goodly superficies of a great apparent stir and activity, may an unseen structure of baser materials

deepen and accumulate underneath, so as to furnish a solution of the fact, that with an increase of Christian exertion amongst us, there should, at one and the same time, be an increase of heathenism.

It is the pervading operation of the local system, which gives it such a superior value and effect in our estimation. It is its thorough diffusion through that portion of the mass in which it operates. It is that movement, by which it traverses the whole population, and by which, instead of only holding forth its signals to those of them who are awake, it knocks at the doors of those who are most profoundly asleep, and, with a force far more effective than if it were physical, drags them out to a willing attendance upon its ministrations. In this way, or indeed in any way, may it still be impossible to reach the parents of our present generation. But the important practical fact is, that, averse as they may be to Christianity on their own account, and negligent as they often are, in their own persons, of the Christianity of their children, still, there is a pride and a satisfaction felt in their attendance upon the Sabbath schools, and their proficiency at the Sabbath schools. Let the system be as impotent as it may in its efficiency upon the old, still, it comes into extensive contact with the ductile and susceptible young; and, from the way in which it is fitted to muster them nearly all into its presence, is it fitted, in proper hands, to wield a high and a presiding influence over the destinies of a future age.

The schools, under a general system, are so many centres of attraction for all the existing desire that there is towards Christianity; and what is thus drawn, is, doubtless, often bettered and advanced by the fellowship into which it has entered. The schools, under a local system, are so many centres of emanation, from which a vivifying influence is actively propagated through a dead and putrid mass. It does not surprise us to be told, that, under the former operation, there should be an increase of youthful delinquency, along with an increase of public instruction for the young. Should the latter operation become universal in cities, we would be surprised if there were still an increase of youthful delinquency; and it were a phenomenon we would be unable to explain.

The former, or general system, draws around it the young of our more decent and reputable families. It can give an impulse to all the matter that floats upon the surface of society. It is the pride of the latter, or local system, while it refuses not these, that it also fetches out from their obscurities, the very poorest and most profligate of children. It may have a painful encounter at the outset, with the filth, and the raggedness, and the other rude and revolting materials, which it has so laboriously excavated from those mines of depravity, that lie beneath the surface of common observation. But it may well be consoled with the thought, that, while much good has been done by its predecessor, which, we trust, that it is on the eve of supplanting, it holds in its own hands the materials of a far more glorious transformation.

This is an age of many ostensible doings, in behalf of Christianity. And it looks a paradox to the general eye, that, with this feature of it standing out so conspicuously, there should also be an undoubted increase of crimes, and commitments, and executions, all marking an augmented depravity among our population. A very slight degree of arithmetic, we are persuaded, can explain the paradox. Let it simply be considered, in the case of any Christian institution, whether its chief office be to attract or to pervade. Should it only be the former, we have no doubt, that a great visible exhibition may be drawn around it—and that stationary pulpits and general Sabbath schools, and open places of repair for instruction indiscriminately to all who will, must give rise to a great absolute amount of attendance. And whether we look at the streets, when all in a fervour with church-going—or witness the full assemblage of children, who come from all quarters, with their weekly preparations, to a pious and intelligent teacher—or compute the overflowing auditory, that Sabbath after Sabbath, some free, evening sermon is sure to bring out from among the closely peopled mass—or, finally, read of the thousands which find a place in the enumerations of some great philanthropic society—we are apt, from all this, to think that a good and a religious influence is in full and busy circulation on every side of us. And yet, there is not a second-rate town in our empire, which does not afford materials enough, both for all this stir and appearance, on the one hand, and for a rapid increase, in the quantum of moral deterioration, on the other. The doings to which we have adverted, may bear, with a kind of magnetic influence, on all that is kindred in character to their own design and their own principle. They may communicate a movement to the minority who will, but leave still and motionless the majority who will not. Whole streets and whole departments may be nearly untouched by them. There is the firm and the obstinate growth of a sedentary corruption, which will require to be more actively assailed. It is certainly cheering to count the positive numbers on the side of Christianity. But, beyond the ken of ordinary notice, there is an outnumbering both on the side of week-day profligacy, and of Sabbath profanation. There is room enough for apparent Christianity, and real corruption, to be gaining ground together, each in their respective territories; and the delusion is, that, while many are rejoicing in the symptoms of our country's reformation, the country itself may be ripening for some awful crisis, by which to mark, in characters of vengeance, the consummation of its guilt.

In these circumstances, do we know of no expedient, by which this woful degeneracy can be arrested and recalled, but an actual search and entry upon the territory of wickedness. A mere signal of invitation is not enough. In reference to the great majority, and in reference to the most needful, this were as powerless as was the bidding to the marriage-feast of the parable. We must have recourse, at last, to the final expedient that was adopted on that occasion; or, in other words, go out to the streets and the highways, and, by every fair measure of moral, and personal, and friendly application, compel the multitude to come in. We must do with the near, what we are doing with the distant world. We do not expect to Christianise the latter, by messages of entreaty, from the regions of paganism. But we send our messages to them. Neither do we give a roving commission to the bearers, but assign to each of them their respective stations in that field, which is the world. And we most assuredly need not expect to Christianise any city of nominal Christendom, by waiting the demand of its various districts, for religious instruction, and acting upon the demands, as they arrive. There must just be as aggressive a movement in the one case as in the other. There is not the same physical distance, but there is nearly the same moral distance, to be described with both; and they who traverse this distance, though without one mile of locomotion to the place of their labour, do, in effect, maintain the character, and fulfil the duty of missionaries.

Any one, or, at most, two philanthropists, may set forth upon such an experiment. They will

soon, in the course of their inquiries, be enabled
to verify the actual state of our city families, and,
at the same time, their openness to the influence
of a pervading operation. Let them, for this
purpose, make their actual entrance upon a district, which they have previously chalked out as
the ground of their benevolent enterprise; and it
were better, that it should be in some poor and
neglected part of the city. Let the one introduce
the other to every family; and on the simple
errand, that he meant to set up a Sabbath school,
to be just at hand, and for the vicinity around
him. With no other manner than that which
Christian kindness would dictate, and just such
questions as are consistent with the respect which
every human being should entertain for another,
we promise him, not merely a civil, but a cordial
reception in almost every house, and a discreet
answer to all his inquiries. The first thing which,
in all likelihood, will meet his observation, is the
mighty remainder of good that is left for him to
do, amid the number and exertion of the general
Sabbath schools that are on every side of him. It
may be otherwise in some few accidental districts.
But, speaking generally, he will assemble a sufficient school out of a population of three hundred.
Parents of all characters will accept his proposition
with gratitude. And if, on his first meeting with
their children in some apartment of the district,
he should be disappointed by the non-attendance
of some whom he was counting on, a few calls of

inquiry on the subject, will generally, at length, secure the point of their attendance; and, by following up every case of absence with a week-day inquiry at the parents, he will secure the regularity of it; and thus may he bring his moral and personal influence into contact with their young, for a few hours of every recurring Sabbath; and also keep up an influence through the whole week, by the circulation of books from a small library attached to his institution. It will prove a mighty accession to the good that he is doing, if he hold frequent intercourse with the families. Their kindness and his enjoyment will grow with the growth of their mutual acquaintanceship. And should he, in the spirit of a zealous philanthropy, resolve to cultivate the district as his own—should he fill up every opening to usefulness which occurs in it—should he mix consideration with sympathy—and, in all his services and all his distributions, bear a respect to their character as well as to their comfort—we cannot confidently say, that he will turn many from Satan unto God, but he will extinguish many an element, both of moral and political disorder.

A few months of perseverance will thoroughly engage him to the cause that he has undertaken. He will feel a comfort in this style of philanthropy, which he does not feel in the bustle and distraction of manifold societies. He will enjoy both the unity and the effectiveness of his doings. And, instead of pacing, as he does now, among dull

L

committees, and perplexing himself among the questions of a large and laborious superintendence, will he expatiate, without encumbrance, upon his own chosen field, and rejoice in putting forth his immediate hand, on the work of reclaiming it from that neglected waste of ignorance and improvidence by which it is surrounded.

To be effective in such a walk of benevolence as this, it is not necessary to be rich. Should, for example, the defective education of a whole district be repaired by one individual, without the expense of a single shilling; and that, by the mere force of moral suasion, he, prevailing on every parent who required urgency upon the subject, to send all the children of a right age, to a week-day school upon their own charges—or, should another individual, standing in the relation that we are now explaining, to a particular district, put a debt, which bears most oppressively over one of the families, into a sure and rapid process of liquidation, and that, not by advancing one fraction, but by simply recommending the expedient of a small weekly deposite—and such instances as these, be varied and multiplied to the extent that is conceivable, would not this be enough to prove, that it is not by the influence which lies in wealth, but by the power which resides in the moral elements of intelligence and affection, that the good is to be accomplished? The weapons of this warfare are, advice—and friendship—and humanity, at all times ready, without being at any time impertinent—and the well-earned confidence, which is ever sure to follow, in the train of tried and demonstrated worth—these, when wielded for a time by the same individual, on the same contiguous families, will work an effect of improvement, which never can be attained by all the devices and labours of ordinary committeeship.

There are so many philanthropists in this our day, that if each of them, who is qualified, were to betake himself, in his own line of usefulness, to one given locality, it would soon work a great and visible effect upon society. One great security for such an arrangement being propagated, is the actual comfort which is experienced by each, after he has entered on his own separate portion of it. But there is, at the same time, a temporary hindrance to it, in the prevailing spirit of the times. The truth is, that a task so isolated as that which we are now prescribing, does not suit with the present rage for generalising. There is an appetite for designs of magnificence. There is an impatience of every thing short of a universal scheme, landing in a universal result. Nothing will serve but a mighty organization, with the promise of mighty consequences; and, let any single person be infected with this spirit, and he may decline from the work of a single court or lane in a city, as an object far too limited for his contemplation. He may like to share, with others, in the enterprise of subordinating a whole city to the power of some great and combined operation. And we may often have to deliver a man from this ambitious tendency, ere we can prevail upon him to sit humbly and perseveringly down to his task—ere we can lead him to forget the whole, and practically give himself to one of its particulars—ere we can satisfy him, that, should he moralise one district of three hundred people, he will not have lived in vain—ere we can get him to pervade his locality, and quit his speculation.

This spirit has restrained the march of philanthropy as effectually, as, in other days, it did that of philosophy. In the taste for splendid generalities, it was long ere the detail and the drudgery of experimental science were entered upon. There is a sound and inductive method of philanthropy, as well as a sound and inductive method of philosophising. A few patient disciples of the experimental school, have constructed a far nobler and more enduring fabric of truth, than all the old schoolmen put together could have reared. And could we prevail on those who are unwearied in well-doing, each to take his own separate slip, or portion of the vast territory that lies before us, and to go forth upon it with the one preparation of common sense and common sympathy; and, resigning his more extended imaginations, actually to work with the materials that are put into his hand—would we, in this inductive way of it, arrive at a far more solid, as well as striking consummation, than ever can be realised by any society of wide and lofty undertakings.

The individual who thus sits soberly down to a work, that is commensurate with the real mediocrity of the human powers, will soon meet with much to reconcile him to the enterprise. He will not fail to contrast the impotency of every general management, in reference to the whole, with the efficacy of his own special management, in reference to a part. His feeling of the superior comfort of his own walk, and his conviction of its superior productiveness, will soon make up to him for the loss of those more comprehensive surveys that are offered to his notice by Societies, which, however gigantic in their aim, are so inefficient in their performance. He loses a splendid deception, and he gets, in exchange for it, a solid reality, and a reality too, which will at length grow and brighten into splendor, by the simple apposition of other districts to his own—by the mere summation of particulars—by each philanthropist betaking himself to the same path of exertion, and following out an example that is sure to become more alluring by every new act of experience.

There is an impatience on the part of many a raw and sanguine philanthropist, for doing something great; and, akin to this, there is an impatience for doing that great thing speedily. They spurn the condition of drivelling amongst littles; and unless there be a redeeming magnificence in the whole operation, of which they bear a part, are there some who could not be satisfied with a humble and detached allotment in the great

vineyard of human usefulness. A Sabbath school
society for one city parish, has a greatly more
limited aim, than a Sabbath school society for the
whole city, or than a similar society for the whole
of Scotland. And yet, in opposition to the maxim,
that union is power, would we strongly advise the
managers of every parochial society, to refuse every
other alliance than that of good will, with any
wider association—to maintain, within its own
limits, the vitality and the spirit of a wholly independent existence—to resist every offered extension of its mechanism, and rather leave the contiguous parish to follow its example, than lay upon
it a chain of fellowship, which will only damp the
alacrity and impede the movements of both. Not
that we at all admire the narrowness of an unsocial
spirit, which cares for nothing beyond the confines
of its own territory. It is simply, that we hold
it to be bad moral tactics, thus to extend the field
of management—thus to bring a whole city or a
whole province under one unwieldy jurisdiction—
thus to weaken, by dispersion, the interest which
we think is far more vivid and effective when
concentrated upon one given locality—thus to exchange the kindliness of a small appropriated home
for the cold lustre of a wider and more public
management—thus to throw ourselves abroad, over
an expanse of superficiality, instead of thoroughly
pervading and filling up each of its subordinate
sections. We have, in fact, somewhat of the same
antipathy to a general society for matters spiritual,

that we have to a general session for matters temporal; and are most thoroughly persuaded, that the less we are linked and hampered with one another, the more effective will be all our operations.

In the work of filling up a parish with Sabbath schools, we would recommend the local system in its purest form; that is, that a small separate district should be assigned to each teacher, and that it should no more be his practice to draw the young from all parts of the parish indiscriminately, than to draw them from all parts of the city indiscriminately. There are many parishes in the empire, of a population, that would require fifty teachers for their thorough cultivation; and the danger is, that in the hurry of an ambitious desire to get up a complete apparatus, there may be a rapidity and a regardlessness of qualification in the admissions of new agency. It were greatly better, that the promoters of such an undertaking, should begin with one extremity of the ground upon which they have entered—cautiously provide for each department as they move onwards to the other extremity—and leave a portion, for a time, in an outfield state, rather than precipitate the appointments, or assign to any, a larger allocation than he can comfortably or effectually pervade.

It was a matter of speculation, some months ago, to subordinate the whole of Glasgow to this local system, and that, by a simultaneous movement on the part of many individuals. It is greatly better that this was abandoned. The projectors of such a scheme never could have found their way through the conflict and perplexity of many opinions, to its accomplishment. To muster a force, in any way adequate to the commencement of such an enterprise, there behoved to be a very wide and crowded arena of consultation upon the subject; and this, to a moral certainty, would have turned out an arena of controversy, where, after a very great deal of unproductive speechifying, the parties would have neutralized each other's propositions, and the project been given up in despair. Even though it had been possible to institute a society for this object, the work of filling up the city with local schools, would have gone on most languidly—the agency would have sunk under the consciousness of a burden too heavy for them—it would have been utterly impossible to send, over this wide extent, the impetus of such a common spirit as is often observed to animate a more small and select band of philanthropists—in proportion to the sublimity of the aim, would have been the shortness and slenderness of the execution: and one delusion more would have been added to the number of others, by which the public have been blinded to the fact, that, amid all the zeal and variety of our apparent doings in behalf of Christianity, we live at a time when irreligion is multiplying her proselytes every day, and vice, and ignorance, and ferocity, are making their most frightful advances over a rapidly degenerating population.

But we have to record a far more fortunate attempt that was made some time ago, to institute a
society of the same kind, on a more limited scale.
We allude to the Saltmarket Sabbath School Society. The field of its operations takes in both
sides of the street, with the deep, and narrow, and
numerous lanes which branch off from them.
It bears a population of 3624; and to cultivate
this extent, there were only four individuals, at
the outset of the undertaking, who, instead of
spreading themselves over the whole, appropriated
each a small locality, and waited for more agents,
ere they proceeded to lay out the remainder.
And, such is the impulse that lies in a field of
exertion, with its boundaries lying visibly before
you—such is the excitement given to human
power, when linked with a task that may be
surmounted, instead of being left to expatiate
at random, over an obscure and fathomless unknown—such is the superior charm of a statistical
over an extended territory, and such the more
intense sympathy of a devoted few, in the prosecution of their common and defined object, than
that of the scattered many, who have spread
beyond the limits either of mutual inspection or
of general control, that, in a few months, did this
little association both complete its numbers, and
thoroughly allocate and pervade the whole ground
of its projected operations. It has now opened
fourteen schools, and provided them with teachers. The number of scholars is 420, amounting to

M

more than a ninth of the whole population. This
is a very full proportion indeed; for, on pretty
extensive surveys, is it found, that the whole
number of children, from the age of six to fifteen,
comes to about one-fifth of the population. Certain it is, that all the general societies in previous
operation, had brought out but a very slender
fraction, indeed, of the number brought out by
this local and pervading society—that many a
crowded haunt of this district, was as completely
untouched by the antecedent methods, as are the
families in the wilds of Tartary—that hundreds of
young, never in church, and without one religious
observation to mark and to separate their Sabbath from the other days of the week, have thus
been brought within an atmosphere, which they
now breathe for the first time in their existence—
that, with a small collection of books attached to
each humble seminary, there is a reading of the
purest and most impressive character, in full circulation amongst both the parents and the children
who belong to it; and, what is not the least
important effect of all, that, by the frequent
recurrence of week-day visitations, there is both
a Christian and a civilizing influence sent forth
upon a whole neighbourhood, and a thousand
nameless cordialities are constantly issuing out of
the patriarchal relationship, which has thus been
formed between a man of worth, and so many
outcast and neglected families.

We know that there are many who look coldly and suspiciously to the whole system of Sabbath schools. We postpone, to some future number of this work, our direct vindication of them,—our sole object at present being to illustrate, by a reference to them, a principle which will afterwards be seen to bear, with effect, on a number of other questions, that respect both the Christian and the civic economy of our towns. But thus much we may at least say, that many of the objections proceed on an ignorance of the actual state of a crowded society;—it not being sufficiently known, how utterly alienated the great majority of our young are from all Christian opportunities; and that there is an unobserved heathenism amongst us, which stands as much in need of being aggressively entered upon from without, as the heathenism of antiquity stood in need of apostles. Such is the lack of churches, and such is the dreary and unprovided extent of our city parishes, that the majority of our people may be said to live in a state of excommunication from all the privileges of a Christian land. The disgrace of their present habits is not theirs alone, but must be shared with them by others. And, if they have sunk in moral or religious worth, under a treatment, the necessary effect of which was thus to degrade them, let us not utter one sentence of disrespect, till we first try the effect of a treatment, the natural effect of which is to raise and to transform them. We could not, without this preliminary remark, have adverted to the outset of one of these Saltmarket schools, or looked back on the first raw exhibition of the children, or revealed thus publicly what they once were, if we had not been enabled further to relate what, under the energetic superintendence of one of the teachers, they have actually become. Certain it is, that we never witnessed so rapid a cultivation; and when, on visiting the school a few months after its establishment, we beheld the dress and decency of their exterior, and marked the general propriety of their manners, and observed the feeling that was evident in the replies of some, and the talent and promptitude that shone forth in the replies of many—when, along with all this, we were made to rejoice in the greetings of the assembled parentage, and shared their triumph and satisfaction in the proficiency of their own offspring, whom, poor as they were, they, out of their own unaided resources, had so respectably arrayed—when we further reflected, that the living scene before us, was not made up of the scantlings of a whole city, but was formed by the compact population of one small but thoroughly explored vicinage,—with our eyes open to what had thus been done by the moral force of care and kindness on the part of one individual, we could not miss the inference, that, with a right distribution, it was in the power of a number of individuals, to throw another aspect over the habit and character of another generation.

There is much of experimental wisdom to be gathered, we think, from the circumstances attendant on the origin and progress of this little association. We learn, by its history, first, what unsanctioned and wholly unofficial individuals can do. They had no superior to introduce or to accompany them in their rounds; and yet did they find their way to a gracious reception, and a firm practical concurrence with their scheme, on the part of the general population. They have also proved how much more stimulating a manageable section of the city is, than a mighty whole, over which there hangs the feeling of a weight and a difficulty insuperable. From the very outset of their undertaking, they were within clear sight of its termination, and felt themselves urged onwards at every new step, by a new inspiration of hope and energy, till, in a very few weeks, their establishment was completed. Their lists, furthermore, teach us how this is the effectual system for most thoroughly pervading any given space. The Sabbath scholars amount to more than a ninth of the whole population. There is one district, consisting of 264 people, which furnishes no less than 50 pupils; and, before they are admitted, they must previously be able to read the New Testament. For the object of such institutions is greatly different from their general object in England. It is not to teach them the reading of the Scriptures; but to exercise their memory, and judgment, and conscience, on the lessons of Scripture. The

Sabbath schools of our country do not supersede, but stimulate the processes of week-day education. This has been their effect, in many instances, under the society in question. Were it otherwise, it might lead to the substitution of a worse for a better scholarship. But, as it is actually conducted, scholarship is not the fruit of attendance on these little seminaries, but the essential preparation for entering them. And thus have we the pleasure of recording, that, under the care and vigilance of a few associated individuals, an impulse, not merely on the side of Christianity, but on the side of ordinary learning, has been sent abroad among the families of a department, that, in both respects, was fast languishing into utter degeneracy. The machinery which they have so speedily raised, need only to be diligently wrought; and even the performance of a few months, warrants the largest expectation of good from their steady and unfaltering perseverance.

The number of scholars from this part of the town, in attendance upon the general schools, at the erection of this Society, was 128, being greatly less than a third of the number who attend the present schools. But the most cheering part of the whole operation, was, the great and immediate effect of the local interest, in calling out a well qualified agency for the work of this association. It consists of fourteen teachers, ten of whom were never employed in this capacity before; and who were allured to the enterprise by the peculiar motives and facilities which were attached to it. In other words, to multiply and extend the good which has been done on this portion of the territory, we do not need to starve any one department of public usefulness that is now in operation. In answer to the prayers and the pains of Christians, will labourers come forth, as the work of the harvest is entered upon; and an influence, which never could have emanated from any one fountain of general superintendence, will spread itself among the contiguous districts, by a mere process of distinct and successive imitations.

It is the feeling of the writer of these remarks, that, for the purposes both of good superintendence and good workmanship, the extent of the Saltmarket district, is perhaps the most desirable that can be fixed upon, as being about the right extent of field, for a separate and independent management. It is scarcely possible to proceed far beyond such limits, without a growing sense of unwieldiness, and a proportional deadening of that interest and activity, which are far better kept up among the members of a small association. Certain it is, that the present size of our parishes in Glasgow, is greatly beyond the fittest magnitude, either for this or for any other operation, which points to the moral and religious welfare of our people. But there is a comfortable hope, that there will be a reduction and a splitting down of these enormous masses—that the process which clergymen, of late years, have had to undergo, will be altogether inverted; and, instead of over-grown charges, where the care of souls and the care of secularities were mingled together, into one disgusting compound, and laid upon their persons—that they will be disengaged, in toto, from the latter care; and, to prosecute the former with effect, will, by the multiplication of churches, have their respective managements then rendered strictly ecclesiastical, and gradually so lessened, as at length to be brought each within the grasp of one individual.

Strong, however, as our partialities are for the Saltmarket Society, we are not sure but that we feel a still greater interest in the solitary, yet eminently successful, attempt of a gentleman in our city, whose name, from motives of delicacy, we forbear to mention. It is now about a year and a half ago, since he assumed a district to himself, which he resolved to cultivate, on the system of local philanthropy. We believe that, in respect of the rank and condition of those who live in it, it is greatly beneath the average of Glasgow. It comprises a population of 996; whom he, in the first instance, most thoroughly surveyed, and all of whom, we are confident, he has now most thoroughly attached, and that, by a series of the most friendly and enlightened services. He has found room, within its limits, for four Sabbath schools, which he provided with teachers of his own selecting, and who, like him-self, labour, of course, gratuitously in the cause;

as, indeed, we believe, do all the other Sabbath teachers in the city. The scholars amount to 110; which is, also, in very full proportion to the number of inhabitants. He has also instituted a Savings Bank, which takes in deposites only from those who live, and from those who work, within the bounds of this little territory. With this last extension of his plan, the bank may embrace a population of 1200; and, from its commencement, in December 19th, 1818, to December 18th, 1819, the whole sum deposited is 235*l*. 12*s*. 3*d*. During the twelvemonth, sixty families of this small district, have opened their accounts with the bank, and received an impulse from it, on the side of economy and foresight. This, in such a year, proves what might be made of the neglected capabilities of our labouring classes. Any general savings bank for the town at large, would not have called out one tenth of this sum, from the obscure department which this gentleman occupies, and which, with the doings and the devices of a most judicious benevolence, he is so fast rescuing from all the miseries which attach to a crowded population. We hold this to be one of the most signal triumphs of locality. The sum deposited in this local bank, is about proportional to the sum of 30,000*l*. for the town and suburbs of Glasgow; and forms another proof, among the many others which multiply around us, of the superiority, in point of effect, which a small and, at the same time, distinct and unfettered management holds, over a wide and ambitious superintendence.

We read, in the book of Genesis, how few the righteous men were, that would have sufficed to save a city from destruction. It is cheering to calculate on the powers of human agency, and how much even an individual may do, when those powers are wisely and steadily directed, and, above all, what is the number of individuals required, who, if each, labouring in his own duteous and devoted walk, would altogether assure the magnificent result of a country recovered from vice and violence, and placed conclusively beyond the reach of all moral and all political disorders.

This result, will, at length be arrived at, not by the working of one mighty organization, for the achievement of great things, but by the accumulation of small things—not by men, whose taste it is to contemplate what is splendid in philanthropy, but by men whose practical talent it is, to do what is substantial in philanthropy— not by men, who eye, with imaginative transport, the broad and boundless expanse of humanity, but by men, who can work in drudgery and in detail, at the separate portions of it. But, before we can sit down and be satisfied with doing thoroughly and well, that which lies within the compass of our strength—there must be a conquest over the pride of our nature—there must be a calling in of the fancy, from those specious generalities, which have lured so many from the path of sober and productive exertion—we must resign the glory of devising a magnificent whole, and count it enough to have rendered, in our narrow sphere, and in our little day, the contribution of a part to the good of human society. The whole it is only for Him to contemplate fully, whose agents we are, and who assigns a portion of usefulness to each severally, as he will. It is our part to follow the openings of his Providence, and to do, with our might, that work which he hath evidently put into our hands. Any great moral or economical change in the state of a country, is not the achievement of one single arm, but the achievement of many; and though one man walking in the loftiness of his heart, might like to engross all the fame of it, it will remain an impotent speculation, unless thousands come forward to share among them all the fatigue of it. It is not to the labour of those who are universalists in science, that she stands indebted for her present solidity, or her present elevation, but to the separate labours of many—each occupying his own little field, and heaping, on the basis of former acquisitions, his own distinct and peculiar offering. And it is just so in philanthropy. The spirit of it has gone marvellously abroad amongst us of late years; but still clouded and misled by the bewildering glare which the fancy of ambitious man is apt to throw around his own undertakings. He would be the sole creator of a magnificent erection, rather than a humble contributor to it, among a thousand more, each as necessary and important as himself. And yet, would he only resign his speculations, and give himself to the execution of a task, to which his own personal faculties were adequate, he would meet with much to compensate the loss of those splendid delusions, which have hitherto engrossed him. There would be less of the glare of publicity, but there would be more of the kindliness of a quiet and sheltered home. He could not, by his own solitary strength, advance the little stone into a great mountain, but the worth and the efficacy of his labours, will be sure to recommend them to the imitation of many— and the good work will spread, by example, from one individual, and from one district to another— and, though he may be lost to observation, in the growing magnitude of the operations which sur-round him, yet will he rejoice even in his very insignificance, as the befitting condition for one to occupy, among the many millions of the species to which he belongs—and it will be enough for him, that he has added one part, however small, to that great achievement, which can only be completed by the exertions of an innumerable multitude—and the fruit of which is to fill the whole earth.

CHAP. III.

It is perhaps the best among all our more general
arguments for a religious establishment in a country, that the spontaneous demand of human beings
for religion, is far short of the actual interest which
they have in it. This is not so, with their demand
for food or raiment, or any article which ministers
to the necessities of our physical nature. The
more destitute we are of these articles, the greater
is our desire after them. In every case, where
the want of any thing serves to whet our appetite,
instead of weakening it, the supply of that thing
may be left, with all safety to the native and
powerful demand for it, among the people themselves. The sensation of hunger is a sufficient
guarantee for there being as many bakers in a
country, as it is good and necessary for the country to have, without any national establishment of
bakers. This order of men will come forth, in
number enough, at the mere bidding of the people;
and it never can be for want of them, that society
will languish under the want of aliment for the
human body. It is wise in government to leave
the care of the public good, wherever it can be
left safely, to the workings of individual nature;
and, saving for the administration of justice be-

o

tween man and man, it were better that she never
put out her hand either with a view to regulate or
to foster any of the operations of common mer-
chandise.

But the case is widely different, when the appetite for any good, is short of the degree in
which that good is useful or necessary; and, above
all, when just in proportion to our want of it, is
the decay of our appetite towards it. Now this is,
generally speaking, the case with religious instruction. The less we have of it, the less we desire
to have of it. It is not with the aliment of the
soul, as it is with the aliment of the body. The
latter will be sought after; the former must be
offered to a people, whose spiritual appetite is in a
state of dormancy, and with whom it is just as necessary to create a hunger, as it is to minister a
positive supply. In these circumstances, it were
vain to wait for any original movement on the
part of the receivers. It must be made on the
part of the dispensers. Nor does it follow, that
because government may wisely abandon to the
operation of the principle of demand and supply, all those interests, where the desires of our
nature, and the necessities of our nature, are adequate the one to the other, she ought, therefore,
to abandon all care of our interest, when the
desire, on the part of our species, is but rare, and
feeble, and inoperative, while the necessity is of
such a deep and awful character, that there is not
one of the concerns of earthliness which ought,
for a moment, to be compared with it.

This we hold to be the chief ground upon which
to plead for the advantage of a religious establishment. With it, a church is built, and a teacher is
provided, in every little district of the land. Without it, we should have no other security for the
rearing of such an apparatus, than the native
desire and demand of the people for Christianity,
from one generation to another. In this state of
things, we fear, that Christian cultivation would
only be found in rare and occasional spots over
the face of extended territories; and instead of
that uniform distribution of the word and ordinances, which it is the tendency of an establishment to secure, do we conceive that in every
empire of Christendom, would there be dreary,
unprovided blanks, where no regular supply of instruction was to be had, and where there was no
desire after it, on the part of an untaught and
neglected population.

We are quite aware, that a pulpit may be cor-
ruptly filled, and that there may be made to
emanate from it, the evil influence of a false or
mitigated Christianity on its surrounding neighbourhood. This is an argument, not against the
good of an establishment, but for the good of
toleration. There is no frame-work reared by
human wisdom, which is proof against the frequent incursions of human depravity. But if
there do exist a great moral incapacity on the
part of our species, in virtue of which, if the
lessons of Christianity be not constantly obtruded

upon them, they are sure to decline in taste and
in desire for the lessons of Christianity; and if an
establishment be a good device for overcoming
this evil tendency of our nature, it were hard to
visit, with the mischief of its overthrow, the future
race either of a parish or of a country, for the
guilt of one incumbency, or for the unprincipled
patronage of one generation. We trust, therefore, in the face of every corruption which has
been alleged against them, that our parochial
establishments will stand, so as that churches shall
be kept in repair, and ministers, in constant succession, shall be provided for them. At the same
time, we hope that no restriction whatever will be
laid on the zeal and exertion of dissenters; and
that any legal disability, under which they still
labour, will, at length, be done away. The truth
is, that we know not a better remedy against the
temporary and incidental evils of an establishment,
than a free, entire, and unexcepted toleration;
nor how an endowed church can be more effectually preserved, either from stagnation or decay,
than by being ever stimulated and kept on the
alert, through the talent, and energy, and even
occasional malignity and injustice of private adventurers. Still, however, such is our impression
of the overwhelming superiority of good done by
an establishment, that, in addition to the direct
christian influence which it causes to descend
upon the country, from its own ministers, we
regard it as the instrument of having turned the

country into a fitter and more prepared field, for the reception of a Christian influence from any other quarter. Insomuch, that had the period of the reformation from Popery, in Britain, been also the period for the overthrow and cessation of all religious establishments whatever, we apprehend that there would not only have been no attendance of people upon churches, but a smaller attendance of people upon meeting-houses than there is at this moment. They are our establishments, in fact, which have nourished and upheld the taste of the population for Christianity; and when that taste is accidentally offended, they are our establishments which recruit the dissenting places of worship with such numbers as they never would have gotten out of that native mass which had been previously unwrought, and previously unentered on.

In order that men may become Christians, there must either be an obtruding of Christianity on the notice of the people, or the people must be waited for, till they move themselves in quest of Christianity. We apprehend that the former, or what may be called the aggressive way of it, is the most effectual. Nature does not go forth in search of Christianity, but Christianity goes forth to knock at the door of nature, and, if possible, awaken her out of her sluggishness. This was the way of it at its first promulgation. It is the way of it in every missionary enterprise. And seeing, that the disinclination of the human heart to entertain the overtures of the gospel, forms a mightier obstacle to its reception among men, than all the oceans and continents which missionaries have to traverse, there ought to be a series of aggressive measures in behalf of Christianity, carried on from one age to another, in every clime and country of Christendom. To wait till the people shall stir so effectually, as that places of worship shall be built by them, and the maintenance of teachers shall be provided by them, and that, abundantly enough for all the moral and spiritual necessities of our nation, is very like a reversal of the principle on which Christianity was first introduced amongst us, and on which, we apprehend, Christianity must still be upheld amongst us. We, therefore, hold it to be wise, in every Christian government, to meet the people with a ready-made apparatus of Christian education. It is like a constant and successive going forth amongst them with those lessons which they never would have sought after, through all the sacrifices that they else would have had to make, and all the obstacles that they else must have overcome. It is in order to perpetuate the religion of the people, keeping up the same aggressiveness of operation, which first originated the religion of the people. We are aware that itinerancy is an aggressive operation, and that dissenters do itinerate. But we are mistaken if, in this way, there is more of the gospel brought into contact with the inhabitants of our country, throughout the space of a year, than is heard on every single Sabbath within the pale of its two establishments. This is not fastening the contempt of insignificance upon dissenters; for, in truth, the good done by their locomotive proceedings, forms, we believe, a very humble fraction, indeed, of the good that emanates from their pulpits, and is performed through the week, and around the vicinity of their pulpits, by the ministers who fill them. It is a mere question of moral and spiritual tactics, which we are at present engaged with. The ability and the Christian worth of dissenters, and the precious contributions which they have rendered to sacred literature, should ever screen them from being lightly or irreverently spoken of. And yet, among all their claims to the gratitude of the public, we think that they have a higher still, in their wholesome re-action on the establishments of the land, in their fresh, and vigorous, and ever-recurring impulses on a machinery, the usefulness of which they may disown in words, while, in fact, they are among the most effective instruments of its usefulness.

So much for the question of a religious establishment over a country at large. But we think that it has a special advantage in towns, which has been, in a great measure, overlooked, or, at least, been wofully defeated in the practical management of towns.

In our last chapter, we made a comparison between local and general Sabbath schools. Now, a church is, or easily might be, in effect, a local

Sabbath school. Its district is, or ought to be, the parish with which it stands nominally associated, and its sitters ought to be the inhabitants of that parish. The established ministers of a large town, should be enabled, each to concentrate the full influence of his character and office, on his own distinct and separate portion of the whole territory. Any thing that can disturb the reiteration of his attentions to the same local quarter of the city, should be resisted as a detraction from his real usefulness. And what we affirm, is, that the united influence of the exertions of all the clergy, when generalised and extended over the town, will never nearly amount to the sum of their separate influences, when each is permitted to give the whole both of his Sabbath and week-day labour to the people of his own geographical vineyard.

To demonstrate this at length, we would just have to repeat the argument of the last chapter, with the substitution of other terms. We could not offer a complete analysis of that influence which lies in parochial locality, without a frequent recurrence to the very considerations upon which we have already decided in favour of Sabbath-school locality. We shall, therefore, at present, study to observe all the brevity that is consistent with the importance of the subject.

The influence of locality may be resolved into two influences; first, that which operates on the agent to whom the locality is assigned; and, secondly, that which operates on the people who reside within the field of his undertaking.

In the first place, then, it is not so likely that a minister will go forth on his share of the population, when spread at random over the whole city, as when they lie within the limits of a space that is overtakable. He feels an incitement to move in the latter way of it, which he does not feel when his attentions are dispersed over a wide and bewildering generality. He, under the one arrangement, may have rare, and rapid, and transient intercourse with the individuals of a diffused multitude; but this can never ripen into solid acquaintanceship with more than a very few. Under the other arrangement, he may, at a greatly less expense, attain to terms of confidence with some, and of familiarity with many. And it would add prodigiously to this operation, were his hearers, on the Sabbath, also his parochial acquaintances through the week. By this simple expedient alone, he would attain such an establishment of himself in his parish, in a single month, as he will not otherwise reach, but by the labour and assiduity of years. The very consciousness that, in a certain quarter of the city, lay the great body of his congregation, would be enough to assure him of a welcome there, and a friendship there, that would ever be inclining his footsteps to his parish, as the fittest scene of promise and of preparation for all his enterprises. And he would soon find, that the business of the Sabbath and the business of the week, had a most wholesome, reciprocal influence the one upon the other. The former business

P

would immediately open a wide and effectual door of intercourse with the people, and the latter business would not only retain their people in attendance upon their minister, but would rapidly extend their demand of attendance upon him, whenever there was room for it. So that, like as the local Sabbath school teacher recruited his seminary out of the families of the district that was assigned to him; so may the local minister, with far less fatigue and locomotion, than are now incurred by the distractions of too manifold and scattered a concern, not only recruit his church out of the parish to which it has been appropriated, but keep up an effective demand for seats, which shall press on the existing accommodation, and must at length be provided with more.

But the second influence of locality in this matter, is perhaps of greater efficacy still. The first is, that by which the minister obtains a more intense feeling of his relationship to his people. The second is, that by which the people obtains a more intense feeling of their relationship to their minister. It is incalculable how much this last is promoted, by the mere juxta-position of the people to one another. There is a great deal more than perhaps can be brought out by a mere verbal demonstration, in a number of contiguous families, all related by one tie to the same place of worship, and the same minister. It would go to revive a feeling, which is now nearly obliterated in towns, whereby the house which a man occupies, should be connected, in his mind, with the parish in which it is situated, and an ecclesiastical relationship be recognized with the clergyman of the parish. In these circumstances, where there was no interference of principle, and no personal disapprobation of the clergyman, attendance upon the parish church, would at length pass into one of the habitual and established proprieties of every little vicinage. Old families would keep it up, and new families would fall into it; and the demand for seats, instead of slackening under such an arrangement, would become more intense every year, so as to form a distinct call for more churches, whenever they were called for by the exigencies of a growing population.

There is nothing fanciful in the charm which we thus ascribe to locality. It is the charm of tact and of experience. It is better, when the people who live beside each other, are under one common impression of good from their minister, than when these same people live asunder from each other. It is not known how much that impression is heightened by sympathy. Did each of the thousand who attend a dramatic performance, satisfy himself with reading the composition at home, the total impression among them were not half so powerful, as when, within the infection of one another's feelings, they sit together, at its representation in a theatre. This is, in part, due to the power of sensible exhibition in the acting. But it is also due, in great part, to the operation of sympathy. And when contiguous families hear the same minister on the Sabbath, or come within the scope of the same household attentions on other days, there is between them, through the week, a prolonged, and often a cherished sympathy, which, were the families widely apart in distant places of the town, would have no operation. Such a common topic, too, of reference and attention, would have a cementing influence on every little neighbourhood. It would draw next-door families into closer and nearer relationship with each other, and shed a mild, moral lustre, over many vicinities, now crowded with human beings, but desolate in respect of all those feelings which go to sweeten and to solace human bosoms. It would, in fact, go a certain way, to transplant into our larger towns, the kindliness of select and limited intercourse; so that, even though the minister could be the visitant of as many families, and the friend of as many individuals, on the general, as on the local system, yet the very circumstance of their being scattered, instead of being contiguous, makes a heavy deduction from the amount of his influence upon them. And, on these various accounts, do we think, that a city clergy would be greatly more effective under an arrangement, where, instead of the hearers of all churches being intermingled in every direction over the town, they were as much as may be, recalled from this state of dispersion, so as that they may be found together in their respective parishes, and there offer to each of the ministers one separate and compact body of acquaintance-ship.

But, after all, the argument of greatest strength for a strictly parochial system in towns, is identical with the argument for a religious establishment all over the country. People will not be drawn in such abundance to Christianity, by a mere process of attraction, as Christianity can be made to radiate upon them, by a process of emanation. We have not yet heard of any dissenting minister in towns, who assumed to himself a locality for the purpose of its moral and religious cultivation. We think, that it would greatly add to the power of his ministrations, if he did so. But, as the case stands, his pulpit operates on the neighbourhood, chiefly as a centre of attraction; and the people move, in the first instance, towards him, instead of him, in the first instance, going forth among the people. We can see, how he may form his congregation out of the pre-disposition for Christianity, that there already is in the place; and, in this way, how dissenters have, in fact, rendered this important service to the nation, that they have retarded the decline of its religious spirit and character. But we do not see, in their system, what the forces are, by which the nation can be recalled from the declension into which it has actually sunk. We do not see, how the torpid, and lethargic, and ever-augmenting mass, can be effectually wrought upon. Many will continue to attend their meeting-houses, and thus be retained by them on the side of Christianity. But we do not see, how it is likely that many will be recovered and brought over from the side of practical Heathenism. And, thus it is, that, along with the multiplication of their pulpits, and the undoubted zeal and ability of those who fill them, there has been, in our chief towns, an increasing alienation from the word and ordinances, on the part of the inhabitants, and that, greatly beyond the rate of the increasing population.

The pulpit of an established minister, may, like a local sabbath-school, be turned into a centre of emanation. Instead of having a merely attractive influence, which can operate only where a taste for Christianity already exists, there may, in the person of him who fills it, and in virtue of the peculiar advantages which we have just explained, go forth a pervading influence, which may be made to spread itself through every portion of the space that he occupies, and be reiterated upon it at short intervals, and with successive applications. He, and the auxiliaries with whom he stands associated, may keep up an incessant locomotion among the families, and they will scarcely meet with one solitary exception in the way of a cordial and universal welcome. This is the way in which a local teacher recruits his school out of families that felt no moving inclination whatever towards a general teacher; and this, in effect, is the way in which a parochial clergyman, had he room and space for it, may reclaim to congregational habits, a whole multitude that have sat motionless for years, and grown most alarmingly in number, under all that churches and meeting-houses have yet done for them.

The ideas of rest, and stillness, and stagnancy, have long been associated with an establishment. But the truth is, that they are its facilities for a busy movement of circulation over a given space, which confer upon it, in our apprehension, a mighty superiority over a mere system of dissenterism. It is true, that the movement is, in a great measure, internal; and, for this reason, it does not bear ostensibly upon it the character of a missionary enterprise. But surely, a missionary object is as much fulfilled by the movement that comprehends all who are within, as by the movement that extends to all who are without. The precept of " Go and preach the gospel to every creature," includes an application to the outcasts at home, as well as to the outcasts abroad; and, on the very principle which inclines us to the frame-work of a missionary society, do we feel inclined to the frame-work cf a national establishment.

It will readily be asked, why, if an establishment be an engine of such mighty operation, it has done so little. Is it at all palpable, that, with the same talent and professional ardour, an established clergyman does more to stay the declension of a religious habit in towns, than the dissenting minister who labours on the same field along with him?

And would the difference, in point of result, have been great, from the state of matters as it now exists around us, though, instead of so many endowed churches with territorial portions of the city annexed to them, there had just been the same number of additional meeting-houses, all drawing such hearers as they could out of a common population?

It is quite true that the establishment has been greatly more powerless in cities, than, with care and vigilance on the part of our rulers, it might have been. It is not merely of the inadequate number of churches that we complain, though these, in some of the chief cities of our empire, could not harbour more than a tenth part of the inhabitants. Neither is it of the manner in which the clergy have been loaded with such extra-professional work, as, in fact, has reduced their usefulness as ministers, greatly beneath the level of that of their dissenting brethren. But, in addition to all this, the most precious advantages of an establishment, have been virtually thrown away, and its ministers disarmed of more than half their influence, by a mere point of civic practice and regulation. By what may be called a most unfortunate blunder in moral tactics, an apparatus that might have borne with peculiar effect on the hosts of a rapidly degenerating population, has been sorely thwarted and impeded in the most essential part of the mechanism which belongs to it. Not by the fault of any, but through the mere oversight of all, a wide disruption has been made between city ministers, and the people of their respective localities; and we should esteem it a truly ·important epoch in the Christian economy of towns, were effectual measures henceforth taken, to repair gradually, and without violence, the mischief alluded to.

What we complain of is, the mode which has obtained hitherto of letting the vacant church-seats. They are open to applications from all parts of the town and neighbourhood, and that, till very lately, without any preference given to the inhabitants of the parish.

It is this, which, trifling as it may appear, has struck with impotency our church establishment in towns, and brought it down from the high vantage ground it might else have occupied. In this way each church is made to operate, by a mere process of attraction, over an immense field, instead of operating, by a process of emanation, on a distinct and manageable portion of it. With the exception of his civil immunities, and his civil duties, which last form a heavy deduction from his usefulness, there remains nothing to signalise an established over a dissenting minister, though the capabilities of his office ought to give him the very advantage which a local has over a general Sabbath school. That which, in argument, forms the main strength of our establishment, has, in practice, been so utterly disregarded, as, in fact, to have brought every city of our land under a mere system of dissenterism. It is not of the powerful influence of dissenters that we complain. It is of the feeble influence of their system. It is not that they are become so like unto us, as to have gained ground upon the establishment. It is, that we have become so like unto them, as both of us to have lost ground on the general population. Locality, in truth, is the secret principle wherein our great strength lieth; and our enemies could not have devised more effectual means of prevailing against us, in order to bind us and to afflict us, than just to dissever this principle from our establishment. Our city rulers, without the mischievous intent, have inflicted upon us the mischievous operation of Delilah; and since we are asked, why it is that, with all the strength and superiority which we assign to an establishment, we put forth so powerless an arm on the general community—we reply, that it is, because, under this operation, our strength has gone from us, and we have become weak, and are like unto other men.

It is well enough, that every article of ordinary sale is to be had in stationary shops, for the general and indiscriminate use of the public at large; for all who need such articles, also feel their need, and have a moving force in themselves to go in quest of them. But this is no reason why the same thing should have been done with Christianity. It is what all men need, but what few feel the need of; and, therefore it is, that, under our present arrangement in towns, there are many thousands who will never move towards it; but where still it is in our power to reclaim and to engage, did we obtrude it upon them. We cannot think of a more effectual device, by which to send a reaching and a pervading influence to this sedentary part of our population, than by binding one church, with one minister, to one locality. Under the opposite, and, unfortunately, the actual system, the result, that is now visibly before us, was quite unavoidable. All the activity of dissenters, aided by the established church, whose activity and influence have been, in fact, reduced to that of dissenters, could not have prevented it. It is not mere Sabbath preaching that will retain, or, far less, recal a people to the ordinances of Christianity. It is not even this preaching, seconded by the most strenuous week-day attentions, to hearers lying thinly and confusedly scattered over a wide and fatiguing territory. With such a bare and general superintendence as this, many are the families that will fall out of notice; and there will be the breaking out of many intermediate spaces, in which there must grow and gather, every year, a wider alienation from all the habits of a country parish; and the minister, occupied with his extra-parochial congregation, will be bereft of all his natural influence over a locality which is but nominally his. The reciprocal influence of his sabbath and week-day ministrations on each other, is entirely lost under such an arrangement. The truth is, that, let him move through his parish, he may not find so much as a hundred hearers within its limits, out of more than ten times that number who attend upon him. And, conversely, however urgent might be the demand in his parish for room in his church, which, under the existing practice, it is not likely to be, he has not that room that is already in foreign occupation, to bestow upon them. A parochial congregation would have, at the very outset, throned him in such a moral ascendency over his district of the town, as the assiduities of a whole life will not be able to earn for him. But, as the matter stands, he is quite on a level, in respect of influence, with his dissenting brethren; and the whole machinery of an establishment, in respect of its most powerful and peculiar bearings upon the people, is virtually dissolved. On the system of each minister feeding his church from his parish, he could not only have crowded his own place of worship, but stirred up such an effective demand for more accommodation, as might have caused the number of churches and the number of people to keep in nearer proportion to each other. But, under the paralyzing influence of the present system, it is not to be wondered at, that the urgency for seats should have fallen so greatly in the rear of the increasing rate of population; and that the habit of attendance on any place of religious instruction whatever, should have gone so wofully into desuetude—and that the feeble operation of waiting a demand, instead of stimulating, should be so incompetent to reclaim this habit; and that the labouring classes in towns, should have thus become so generally alienated from the religious establishment of the land—and, what is greatly worse than the desertion of establishments, that a fearful majority should be now forming, and likely to increase every year, who are not merely away from all churches, but so far away, as to be beyond the supplementary operation of all meeting-houses—a majority that is fast thickening upon our hands, and who will be sure to return all the disorders of week-day profligacy upon the country, because that country has, in fact, abandoned them to the ever-plying incitements and opportunities of Sabbath profanation.

Before setting forth those expedients for the alleviation of this mischief, which we shall venture to recommend, we shall offer numerical estimates of the extent of it, taken from the actual survey of small slips and portions of the territory, but which, we are confident, do not exceed a fair average reckoning for the whole.

Let it be premised, that, in a country parish, the number who should be in attendance upon church, is computed at one-half of the whole population. In towns where the obstacle of distance is not to be overcome, a larger proportion than this is generally fixed upon. We think it, however, overrated at two-thirds, and shall therefore assign the intermediate fraction of five-eighths, as the ratio which the church-going inhabitants of a town should bear to the total number of them.

The first result that we shall give, is the fruit of a larger survey, made in one of the extreme districts of Glasgow, and comprehending a population of 10304. The number of Sabbath-hearers ought, at the rate now specified, to have been 6240. The number of seats actually taken, in all the churches and meeting-houses put together, was only 2930. This survey becomes more instructive, when regarded in the separate portions of it. As it passes onwards to the limits of the royalty, where the people become poorer, and the space which they occupy is in contact with that enormous parish, the Barony, whose population, by a recent survey, is found to be 51861, the proportion of non-attendance becomes much greater. There are, along the line of separation between the city and the suburbs, contiguous populations of 377, 400, 500, 475, 469, and 468, where the numbers that ought to attend a place of worship, are 236, 250, 322, 297, 293, and 293, respectively; and where the sittings actually taken, which correspond to those numbers, are 76, 74, 131, 87, 103, and 113. Thus, in some instances, is it found, that the church-going population bear only the proportion of less than one-fifth to the whole, and than one-third to that part of the whole, who would, in a well-ordered state of things, be in a regular habit of attendance upon ordinances. It is remarkable, that in one of those spaces which comprised a population of 875, there were not above 4 individuals who had a sitting in an established church; so that, were it not for dissenters, who take up at least 148 out of the whole, and 38 in chapels of ease, there would have been a district of the city, with a larger population than is to be found in many of our country parishes, in a state nearly of entire Heathenism. The country, in fact, lies under the deepest obligation to the dissenting clergy; and let no petty jealousies interfere with the acknowledgments due to men who have done so much to retard the process of moral deterioration, and whose ability and zeal have carried onward to the limit of its utmost possible operation, the high function that they fulfil in the commonwealth.

This survey was not carried beyond the limits of the Royalty; but we are sure, if it had, that all the results would have been aggravated. In a parish of upwards of 50,000 people, where one church, and three subsidiary chapels, form the whole amount of accommodation provided by the establishment, we confidently aver, that not one-fifth of those who live in it, and not one-third of those who should have sittings, are in the habit of attendance upon any ordinances whatever; and that this computation holds, after dissenterism has put forth all its resources, and it has been free to expatiate over every neighbourhood of human beings for several generations. Such is the tried inefficiency of its mechanism. It will never, of itself, do the work of an establishment, however essential it may be in a country, to stimulate and to supplement an establishment. And when we contemplate the magnitude of those suburb wastes, which have formed so rapidly around the metropolis, and every commercial city of our land— when we think of the quantity of lawless spirit which has been permitted to ferment and to multiply there, afar from the contact of every softening influence, and without one effectual hand put forth to stay the great and the growing distemper—when we estimate the families which, from infancy to manhood, have been unvisited by any message from Christianity, and on whose consciences the voice of him who speaketh the word that is from heaven has never descended, we cannot but charge that country, which, satisfied if it neutralise the violence, rears no preventive barrier against the vices of the people, with the guilt of inflicting upon itself.a moral, if not a political suicide.

It is to be presumed, that, in the central districts of the city, the rate of attendance upon places of worship is not so deficient. It is observable, that the mere juxta-position of a church or a meeting-house, stimulates, to a certain degree, the attendance of those who live in its immediate vicinity. The very sight of a fabric for Christian instruction, is, in itself, an obtrusion of Christianity on the notice of the people. But this circumstance singly, will not do much. The mere erection of fabrics for the accommodation of the inhabitants of a town, will have no sensible effect, without an aggressive operation upon the inhabitants themselves. There are interior departments of population in Glasgow, where the amount of church-going is greatly less than all that we have yet specified. In that short street called the Goose-Dubbs, with the few lanes and closses which belong to it, there are 945 people, only 106 of whom have seats any where. The deficiency is as great in some of the sub-districts of the Saltmarket *. Dissenterism has done something for these families. It has done much more for them than the establishment has done, and yet but a humble fraction of what an establishment might do, and is best fitted to do. But the mere building and opening of a new church, will not attract them. They who are connected with the church, must go forth upon them. The sluggishness of the existing habit, will not be so easily overcome as those may imagine, who have only observed the readiness with which a place of worship is filled, where there is the glare of novelty, or the attraction of a little more eloquence than usual, or even the solid recommendation that attaches to him who is a firm and faithful expounder of the New Testament. All this will impress a preference and a locomotion on the part of those who have a pre-existent taste for

---

* In one district of the Saltmarket, there are 387 people, and only 61 of them who have seats in any place of worship. In Clay-Braes, there are 64 seats among 319 people. And in one continuous space of the Bridgegate, are there 209 people, only 7 of whom have seats any where.

Christianity; and thus a new congregation may
immediately be formed, out of shreds and detach-
ments from all the previous ones. But it will be
a mixed, and not a local congregation. There is no
portion of what may be called the outfield population, that will be sensibly reclaimed by it. And
little do they know of this department of human
experience, who think that it is on the mere
strength of attractive preaching, that this is to
be done.

An experiment may often be as instructive by
its failure, as by its success. We have here to
record the fate of a most laudable endeavour,
made to recal a people alienated from Christian
ordinances, to the habit of attendance upon them.
The scene of this enterprise was Calton and
Bridgeton—two suburb districts of Glasgow which
lie contiguous to each other, bearing together, a
population of above 29,000, and with only one
chapel of ease for the whole provision which the
establishment has rendered to them. It was thought
that a regular evening sermon might be instituted
in this chapel, and that for the inducement of a
seat-rent so moderate as from 6d. to 1s. 6d. a-
year, to each individual, many who attended no
where through the day, might be prevailed upon
to become the regular attendants of such a congregation. The sermon was preached, not by one
stated minister, but by a succession of such ministers as could be found; and as variety is one of
the charms of a public exhibition, this also might

have been thought a favourable circumstance.
But besides, there were gentlemen who introduced
the arrangement to the notice of the people, not
merely by acting as their informants, but by going
round among them with the offer of sittings, and,
in order to remove every objection on the score of
inability, they were authorised to offer seats gratuitously to those who were unable to pay for
them.   Had the experiment succeeded, it would
have been indeed the proudest and most pacific of
all victories.   But it is greatly easier to make war
against the physical resistance of a people, than
to make war against the resistance of an established moral habit.   And, accordingly, out of the
1500 seats that were offered, not above 50 were
let or accepted by those who had before been total
non-attendants on religious worship; and then
about 150 more were let, not, however, to those
whom it was wanted to reclaim, but to those who
already went to church through the day, and in
whom the taste for church-going had been already
formed.   And so the matter moved on, heavily and
languidly, for some time, till, in six months after
the commencement of the scheme, in September
1817, it was finally abandoned.

There were several ingredients of success, however, wanting to this experiment.   There was no
such reiteration of one minister, as would ripen
into familiarity or friendship between him and
his hearers.   There was no reciprocity of operation, between the duties of the Sabbath, and the

duties of the week. The most aggressive part of a minister's influence upon the people, lies in his being frequently amongst them; the recognised individual, whose presence is looked for at their funerals, and who baptizes their children, and who attends their sick-beds, and who goes round amongst them in courses of religious visitation. There was nothing of all this in the experiment; nor were the Christian philanthropists who did go forth upon the population, so firmly embodied under one head, or so strictly and officially attached to one locality, as fairly to represent the operation of a stated minister, and, where possible, a residing eldership. Above all, in so wide and dispersed a locality in question, it was not by the marvellous doings of one year, that a great or visible change in the habits of the people ought to have been expected. The descent of more than half a century, will not be so easily or so speedily recovered. Such an achievement as this, can never be done without labour, and without the perseverance of men, willing to plod and to pioneer their way through the difficulties of a whole generation.

This may serve to guide our anticipations, respecting the probable effect of new churches, built in places of the most crowded and unprovided population. A given territory ought, by all means, to be assigned to each of them; and, in letting the seats, a preference should be held out to the residents upon that territory. But we should not be sanguine in our hopes, of the preference being, to any great extent, actually taken by them in the first instance; and this, if the cause be not adverted to or counted on, may, for a time, damp and discourage the whole speculation. On our first entrance upon new ground, we must consider that there is a minority already in possession of sittings elsewhere, and that, nearly up to the existing taste for church-going; and that there is a majority in whom that taste must be formed and inspired, ere the church can be recruited out of their numbers. A congregation, out of these, may be looked for in time, as the fruit and the reward of perseverance; but it cannot be looked for immediately. The best rule of seat-letting, in these circumstances, is, to hold out a preference, in the first instance, to the inhabitants of the new parish, and then, in as far as that preference is not taken, to expose the remaining seats to the applications of the general public. It is of importance, however, that each of the extra-parochial sittings should be let in the name of one individual, instead of their being let by threes and fours in the name of the head or representative of a family; for, in this latter case, they may pass from one member of it to another, and, perhaps, descend to its next and its succeeding generations. The object of this last regulation is, to secure a more rapid and abundant falling in of extra-parochial vacancies, which should be rigidly and unviolably offered to parishioners from one year to another, as they occur. Under such a constitution, there may, at the outset of every new church, be but a small proportion of parish- ioners attending it; but, with the removal or the dying off of extra-parochial hearers, there will. be a certain number of vacancies to dispose among them annually. Meanwhile, the interest of the minister, in his new parish, will be gradually ex- tending, and, with very ordinary attention on his part, may so keep pace with the disappearance and decay of the exotics among his congregation, as will enable him to replace them by parish appli- cants; and thus, in the process of time, will a home be substituted in the place of a mixed con- gregation. It were laying an impossibility upon a clergyman, at once to call in from a yet unbroken field, fifteen hundred ready and willing attendants, upon his ministrations. But this, without any colossal energy at all, he might do at the rate of fifty in the year. So that though he begins him- self with a mixed auditory made out of hearers from all the parishes of the city, there may be such a silent process of substitution going forward during the course of his incumbency, as shall enable him to transmit to his successor an almost entirely parochial congregation.

This is the way, in fact, in which all our existing congregations might be at length parochialised. It should be done by an enactment of gradual operation. Were they now broken up, for the purpose of being new-modelled, and that instantly on the local principle, there would be violence done to the feelings of many an individual. But what is more, it would also be found that after the dispersion of our mixed congregations, there would be a very inadequate number of applicants in the poorer parishes ready to take the places which had thus been dispossessed. It is much better if the existing arrangement can be righted without the soreness of any forced or unnatural separations, and in such a way as that no actual sitter can, on his own account, personally complain of it. Though he retain his right of occupation till death, the substitution of a home for a foreign congregation, will yet go on, and as rapidly perhaps as the parochial demand for seats can be stimulated. So that the sure result will at length be arrived at, of the parish and congregation being brought within the limits of one influence, and reduced to the simplicity of one management.

There is a philanthropy more sanguine than it is solid, which, impatient of delay, would think an operation so tardy as this unworthy of being suggested, and refuse to wait for it. But it is the property of sound legislation, to look to distant results, as well as to near ones—to be satisfied with impressing a sure movement, though it should be a slow one—nor does the wisdom of man ever make a higher exhibition, than when apart from the impulse of a result that is either speedy or splendid, she calmly institutes an arrangement, the coming benefit of which will not be fully realised till after the lapse of our existing generation.

But it is not enough that the demand of each parish, for seats, should be stimulated up to the extent of its present accommodation. The truth is, that all our large towns have so far outgrown the church establishment, that though each church were crowded, and with local congregations too, and each meeting-house already in existence were also filled to an overflow, there would still be a fearful body of the people in the condition of outcasts from the ordinances of Christianity. The mere erection of additional fabrics will do nothing to remedy this, without an operation on the people who should fill them. It must be admitted that the Calton experiment looks rather discouraging. But still, we think that certain adverse ingredients may be removed from it, and certain favourable ingredients be substituted in its place. It was really not to be expected, that much could be done by an indefinite number of ministers, who each had the transient intercourse of a rare and occasional Sabbath evening with the people, without any week-day movement amongst them at all. But is there not a greater likelihood of success, when the same attempt is made by one minister in his own parish, in conjunction, perhaps, with an assistant equally bound to its locality with himself? And what the influence of a few private philanthropists, going forth on so wide and populous a district as the one we are alluding to, could not accomplish by a transient effort, may at length be accomplished by persevering and reiterated efforts on the part of

an official body, raised, perhaps, into existence for
the very object of calling out a parochial congregation, and animated with a sense of the importance of achieving it. Even with all these advantages, the strenuousness of an encounter with
previous and established habits will be felt, an encounter which will require to be as assiduously
met by moral suasion through the week, as by
preaching on the Sabbath. At the same time, it
is a very great mistake, to think that any other
peculiar power is necessary for such an operation,
than peculiar pains-taking. It is not with rare
and extraordinary talent conferred upon a few,
but with habits and principles which may be cultivated by all, that are linked our best securities
for the reformation of the world. This is a work
which will mainly be done with every-day instruments operating upon every-day materials; and
more, too, by the multiplication of labourers, than
by the gigantic labour of a small number of individuals. The arrangement now suggested, may
exemplify this. Let a Sabbath evening sermon be
preached in the church of a city parish, to a parochial congregation, distinct from the day-hearers
altogether. Let a moderate seat-rent be exacted,
and a preference for these seats be held out to
those in the locality, who have sittings no where
else. Some care and some perseverance will be
necessary to ensure the success of such an enterprise. But there is nothing impracticable about
it, and no such impediments in the way of its exe-

s

cution, as to stamp upon it the least degree of a visionary character. There need be no additional labour to the minister, who may, in fact, take full relief to himself, from an assistant. There may, at length, be no additional expense to the city, seeing that out of the produce of the seat-rents, all the charges of the evening arrangement will in time be defrayed. There will even be no additional fabrics to build, in the first instance, which the people are not yet in readiness to fill, were they erected in any sensible proportion to the existing deficiency. Thus, by a very cheap and simple arrangement, may the number of ecclesiastical labourers be doubled in every city of our land; and, with the distinctness of the day and evening congregations, the number of sitters belonging to the establishment, at length, be doubled also. We are not aware of a speedier method for reclaiming the outcasts and wanderers of a city population, to congregational habits; nor can we think how an approximation equally rapid, and, at the same time, equally practicable, can be made in towns to the parochial system. It would instantly improve the condition of the minister as to his relationship with the parish, who will gain more by it, in point of recognition, within his own locality, in a single month, than he could do by preaching to a mixed congregation for a whole life-time. And it would gradually extend a taste and a demand for the services of Christianity, among a people who had no taste and no demand for them before. It is altogether a chimerical apprehension, that it may only change day-sitters into evening-sitters, and cause those who have now a full participation of ordinances to be satisfied with less. It would change total non-attendants into attendants upon an evening service, who, at length, not satisfied with their deficiency from others, would have a demand for more. Instead of diminishing the taste which now is, it would create the taste which must still be called into existence. Instead of superseding the use of new churches for the people, it would prepare a people for the new churches, and turn out to be the most effectual nursery of their future congregations.

And here let it be remarked, how effectually it is, that Sabbath-evening schools subserve the prospective arrangement which we are now contemplating. It requires a much harder struggle than most are aware of, to prevail on grown-up people, who never have attended church, to become the members, either of a day or an evening congregation. But the compliance which cannot be won in manhood, for attendance on a church, we win in boyhood, for attendance on a school; and, when the boy becomes the man, a second effort is not necessary. It were, in fact, a far more congenial transition for him to pass from the evening school to the evening church, than if he never had attended school at all; and far more congenial for the member of an evening, to become the member of a day congregation, than if, brought up in the utter want of congregational habits, he never had attended either the one or the other. Thus it is, that the Sabbath school system, which many regret as a deviation from the regularities of an establishment, is the very best expedient for feeding an establishment, and making it at length commensurate with the moral and spiritual necessities of our population. It connects the susceptibility of youth with a result, which, but for the possession of an element so manageable, might never be arrived at. It appears like the first and the firmest step to a great moral renovation in our land. And a parochial system, which might never have been reared in towns, out of such stubborn materials as the depraved and inveterate habits of our older, is thus likely to be formed and extended out of the softer materials of our younger generation.

It is felt by many as a deduction from the good of the local system in towns, that the poorer among the families so frequently change their places of residence; and that there must not only be the same parish, but also the same parishioners, else the acquaintanceship which is formed, will be constantly liable to be broken up, by the constant dispersion of its members. The quantity of fluctuation is greatly over-rated. The district referred to in our last chapter, as having been assumed by a philanthropic individual, for the purpose of its moral and economical cultivation, contains 219 families, of which there were 23 removals at the last term, or about one-tenth of the whole. It will, speaking generally, be found not to exceed this fraction, in small contiguous districts of such a population; and even from this, there ought to be an abatement, in estimating the number of yearly removals from a parish: for many of the movements are internal, being from one small district of the parish to another. And besides, even though there were removals out of the parish every year, at the rate of one-tenth of all the families in it, we are not to infer, that, in ten years, there is a complete change of families; or that the old parish is thus scooped away by so many liftings of the people who live in it. The truth is, that the movement is far more a vibratory than a successive one. The families that leave a parish this year, are, in a great measure, the very families that came to it last year. There is a certain number, and those chiefly of the worse-conditioned of the population, who are constantly upon the wing; and they alternate from one parish to another, over the heads of a stable population. A locally parochial system would serve, in the long run, to retain even these; but, even in their present amount, they leave the great bulk of the inhabitants of every parish, in a fixed and permanent state for any species of cultivation that might be applied to them. We believe, indeed, that the families of a city parish are less given to change than those of an agricultural parish, from the expiry of leases, and, above all, the yearly fluctuation of farm-servants. So that, there is scarcely any department, however poor, of any city, however crowded, which would not, in the course of time, be turned into a home walk; and where the simple perseverance of such ecclesiastical attentions as are current in the country, would not, were the parishes sufficiently small, have the effect of binding the minister to the families, and of binding the families to one another. The new comers would soon catch the *esprit de corps* that was already formed in the neighbourhood of their new residence, and be soon so far assimilated by the overwhelming admixture of their superior number, to the tone and habit of the people who were there before them, as at least, to be accessible to all the attentions which are current in the parish, and be trained very shortly, to such a recognition of the parish-church and parish-minister, as, in our large towns at present, is nearly unfelt and unknown altogether.

There is nothing in the mere circumstance of being born in a town, or of being imported into it from the country, which can at all obliterate or reverse any of the laws of our sentient nature. That law, in virtue of which a feeling of cordiality is inspired, even by a single act of recognition, and in virtue of which it is augmented into a fixed personal regard by many such acts, operates with just as much vigour in the one situation as it does in the other. In towns, every thing has been done to impede the reiteration of the same attentions upon the same families. The relationship between ministers and their parishes has, to every moral, and to every civilising purpose, been nearly as good as broken up. Every thing has been permitted to run at random; and, as a fruit of the utter disregard of the principle of locality, have the city clergyman and his people almost lost sight of each other. It is the intimacy of connection between these two parties which has impressed its best and most peculiar features on the Scottish nation; and it were giving way to a mystic imagination altogether, did we not believe that the treatment of human nature, which leads to a particular result in the country, would, if transplanted into towns, lead to the same result on their crowded families. We have no right to allege a peculiar aptitude to moral worthlessness, in the latter situation, when we find that every moral influence, which bears upon the former, has, in fact, been withdrawn from our cities. The moral regimen in the one, is diametrically the reverse of what it is in the other; and, not till they are brought under the operation of the same causes, can we estimate aright the question, whether the town or the country is most unfavourable to human virtue.

It may be long before we are in fair circumstances for determining this question experimentally, because it may be long ere our enormous city parishes are so far subdivided, as that one church and one minister shall be commensurate to the population of each of them. But certain it is, that the mere act, either of building the churches, or of splitting down the parishes, will not suffice for the purpose of reclaiming the people to the habit of their Scottish forefathers. There must be a previous operation upon the people, ere the desire or the demand for Sabbath accommodation can guarantee to the builders of churches, that their churches shall be filled. For this purpose, we hold the strict, and, as nearly as may be, the exclusive union of churches with their parishes, to be indispensable; and, even with this advantage, do we think, that the existing habit of alienation from ordinances, instead of being altogether reclaimed by exertion, will, in part, need to be removed by death; and that it is mainly to an operation upon the young, and that through the medium of Sabbath schools, that we have to look for the coming in of a better order of things, with the coming up of another generation.

CHAP. IV.

THE EFFECT OF LOCALITY IN ADDING TO THE USEFUL
ESTABLISHMENTS OF A TOWN.

It were, perhaps, a sanguine anticipation to expect, that the gradual process, unfolded in the last chapter, for reclaiming the people of our cities, to a habit of attendance on the ordinances of Christianity, should be completed in the course of one, or even of two generations. For, what a rapid process of church-building would this imply? More would need to be done in this way in several of our towns, than has been done altogether, since the first erection of them. There are many of them, in fact, so unprovided with churches, that it were a great achievement, could these be built, and people be prepared for filling them, to such an extent, as that, out of each five thousand of the inhabitants, there might be a congregation belonging to the establishment. This would still leave greater room for dissenters than that which they have actually succeeded in occupying, and might, therefore, still leave unfinished, the great work of retrieving a habit which surely may be recalled, seeing that it once existed. The time once was, when, in virtue of the nearer proportion which obtained between a city population, and the places of worship that were provided for them, we saw nearly the present number of churches more

T

crowded than they are now, out of less than half the number of our present residenters.

This, by the way, holds out to us another view of the importance of dissenters, and of the increasing demand that may still obtain, through a very lengthened period of years, for their services. The process by which the establishment will gain ground, on the out-field population, that is, on those who at present neither attend church nor meeting-house, must be very gradual; and mean while, if it advance at all, it will not lessen the demand for seats from the dissenters, but rather increase it. There is a direct and arithmetical style of computation, which often fails when it is applied to the phenomena, or the principles of human nature. It is thus, for example, that many conceive an alarm, lest one benevolent society should suffer in its revenues, when another benevolent society is instituted in the same town, and among the same people. They calculate by a mere process of subtraction upon the money of subscribers; and they do not calculate on the moral impulse which every new scheme of philanthropy is fitted to send into their hearts. They seem not aware, that the mere habit of liberality, in behalf of one object, renders them more accessible to the claims of any new object, than if the habit had not been previously called into existence. The truth is, that after all which is given away in liberality, there still is left, in the fund for such luxuries as may easily be dispensed with, and in

the fund which goes to the loose and floating
expenses of pocket-money, an ample remainder
for meeting fresh and frequent applications. The
money is, of course, lessened by the amount that
has previously been given; but, if the habit and
disposition of giving be increased, this may secure
for an indefinite length of time, more than a full
compensation. And thus it is, that in starting
some new enterprise of philanthropy, one may
far more surely count on being liberally supported,
in a town teeming with previous charities, and
where the fund for benevolence has, therefore, to
a certain degree been impaired, but the feeling of
benevolence has been strengthened by exercise—
than in a town, where, as no encroachment has
yet been made upon the means, so no excitement
has yet been given to the motives of charity.

And there is a similarity to this, in the matter
before us. The new church which is opened, will
not so operate by a process of subtraction upon
those who hear in meeting-houses, as it will operate
by a process of fermentation upon those who hear
no where. It will increase the taste and the
demand for church-going. If rightly followed
up, by such local and aggressive operations as we
have already explained, it will leaven the dead mass,
and revive an appetite for the ministrations of
Christianity, beyond its own power to meet and
to gratify. The population is greater than, perhaps, with the most rapid process of church-building, which can rationally be counted on, will be

overtaken in the course of a century. And, meanwhile, it were no paradox to those who know the amplitude of the field that is yet unbroken, and who calculate on the power of a living excitement sent over the face of it, though, for many years to come, churches and meeting-houses were seen to spring up in frequency together, and both the dissenters and the establishment gained ground contemporaneously on the vast unoccupied extent that yet lies before them.

To make this plain by an example. The number of people in Glasgow and its suburbs is about one hundred and fifty thousand; of whom ninety thousand should be in a condition to attend church. Even though our chapels of ease were turned, as they ought to be, into parish churches, there is scarcely accommodation in our establishment for the one-fourth of this number; and, ere it can overtake the one-half, there must be no less than fifteen additional fabrics built; leaving, after all, as large a space for the energies of dissenterism, as the establishment shall itself have overtaken.

In repairing the defects of a great moral apparatus, it does harm to underrate the magnitude of the object. It is by so doing, that the advisers of public measures are often so sanguine in respect of anticipation, while the measures themselves are so slender in respect of efficiency. The grant, for example, of a million sterling for new churches in England, and the proposal of a hundred thousand pounds for the same purpose in Scotland, sound far more magnificently in the public ear, than they will be found adequate to the necessity which they are intended to meet. They have certainly been matters of gratulation to those who are friendly to our national establishments, and who, at the same time, regard Christianity as the alone specific for all the distempers of society. Yet it is not to be disguised, that, even when carried into full accomplishment, they will leave a vast extent of our population unprovided for. And, what is more, Government will positively have retarded the cause which it means to help, if, by its interference, it shall propagate this delusion—that, as the strength and wisdom of our great national council are now in motion upon the undertaking, all individuals, and all the subordinate bodies of the state, may now wait, suspended in a kind of respectful abeyance on that supreme body, whose function it is to oversee all, and to provide for all.

This is the precise mischief which is to be apprehended in the case of every wide and general superintendence. The more wide and the more general, the means will be *absolutely* greater, and the effort for the accomplishment of any given object will also be absolutely greater: and this is enough to fill and to satisfy the imaginations of all, who look no farther than to the measure itself, and have not patience nor arithmetic for computing the proportion which it bears to the evil it is meant to remedy. But, *relatively* to the whole amount of what ought to be done, will it come greatly short of what many individuals would do for their own local districts, and many corporations would do for their own townships. For the purpose, however, of calling out these latter to the full stretch of their means and energies, it is necessary that there should be no delusive expectation of aid from a higher quarter, so as that they should feel the full weight of the responsibility which lies upon them. It is thus, that we should like the principle of locality to be brought forth into operation, and directed to the object of multiplying both schools and churches over the face of our land. It works far more intensely and productively within its own limited sphere, than Government, we fear, will soon find itself able to do, over the whole country, or than a great city superintendence will do in the bulk, for its general population. And, therefore it is, that we contemplate a great national effect, not as the result of any corporate movement, or any legislative operation, but as the result of a slow accumulative process, helped forward mainly by the growth and expansion of Christian philanthropy in our land, and at length completed into a whole, by the simple apposition of parts done separately, and done independently.

But while it is to be feared, that the movement of our legislature, in behalf of Christian institutions, (far more showy than it is productive,) has lulled asleep much of the private liberality that else would have operated; it were also to be re-

gretted, as a very mischievous re-action, should
the zeal, and the bustle, and the adventure, of
individuals in the same cause, have the effect to
slacken, rather than to excite our tardy corporations. It is exceedingly desirable, that they too
should come forward, were it for nothing else than
the weight of their testimony, which is eminently
fitted to carry the public mind along with it.
Only, it were a salutary accompaniment, if, along
with their testimony, there also went forth the
lesson of their utter inability for more than a small
fraction of this great achievement. The resources,
in fact, for giving such a national extension to the
cause, as will work a national effect on the habits
of our people, must be provided in another way
than out of the present resources of any corporation. Nor can we expect that, with their existing
means, any more than a few rare and desultory
efforts will be made for an object which, after all
they shall do, will still appear to lie at a hopeless
and impracticable distance.

It is well, indeed, that both the council of a city
and the great council of a nation, should be told
what an arm of impotency it is that they often put
forward. It is altogether grievous to remark the
satisfaction, with which a magistracy will dwell on
the achievement of adding one church more to a
city, that stands in need of an additional twenty.
It is not the one church that is to be regretted. But
it is the repose, or even the triumph of a great ex-
ploit, which is evidently felt by many of our public

functionaries upon the occasion. It is not even the circumstance of one church only being built in the space of two or three years, that ought to be complained of. It were vain to expect any thing else than a very gradual movement, even though all the applicable energies of society were brought to bear upon it. But the thing to be mainly regretted is, the deceitful imagination that enough is doing, or enough is done, when we see put on their uttermost stretch, the feeble and inadequate energies of a ruling corporation. The glare of magnitude and publicity, which is attendant upon its proceedings, serves far more to blind the general understanding into the treacherous conclusion, that enough is doing, than it does to enlighten it upon the question, how much is to be done. After the slight and superficial enterprise is over, it may be made out arithmetically, that the former proportions of the outfield to the church-going population are not sensibly affected by it; that the elements of depravity are nearly in as great force as ever, and the counteractions which have been provided for it, nearly in as great feebleness as ever; and, in a word, that, thoroughly to fill up the neglected spaces, which have so widened and multiplied over the expanse of a town or of a kingdom, something far more gigantic must be done, than appears to lie within the means either of Government or of any inferior municipality in the land.

It is the misfortune both of a civic and of a national legislator, that he deals so much in generalities. He casts a hurried glance over the whole field of contemplation, and the influence of what he does, or of what he devises, is thinly spread along the face of the territory before him. He is seldom arrested by that dull and humbling arithmetic, which casts up to him the utter insignificance of all that he has attempted on the general mass and habit of society. He vainly tries, by his one enactment, to measure strength with the needs or the immoralities of a vast population. Nor will he submit to the mortification of being told, that though the sound of it has gone forth among all, the sensible and pervading influence of it is scarcely felt among any. It is the wideness of his survey which makes him overlook particulars: and with his habit of largely expatiating, does he neglect completely and minutely to fill up. This it is which accounts for the utter futility of many projects splendid in promise, and vanishing away into a meagre accomplishment. This it is which explains the abortive magnificence of many of our great national undertakings.

But all this is the natural effect of office and situation; nor can we well expect it to be otherwise, either with the members of a legislature, or with the members of a municipality. But it is to be regretted, of our private philanthropists, who are at liberty to begin their own work in their own way, that they should not have entered on the clear path of comfort and just calculation, and,

U

ultimately, of sure and complete success. The
prevailing tendency, hitherto, has been, to attempt
great things rather than to do small things thoroughly and well; to set up a mechanism which will
work for the whole city, rather than reduce the
city into manageable parts, and seek for the accomplishment that is proposed, by the mere apposition of these parts to each other; to aspire, and
that, by the energies of one grand association, after
some universal result, which never will be reached
but by the summing up of the separate achieve-
ments of many lesser associations. It may look a
strange way of proposing a universal good, either
for a city or for a nation, to bid our active philanthropists never admit the town as a whole, or the
nation as a whole, into any of their speculations.
But we are quite satisfied, that much of that effort,
which would else have been productive, is wasted;
and that, merely because of the insuperable magnitude of the object at which it aims. There
are many individuals, whose zeal for the good of
humanity is now dissipated and lost among vague
generalities that might be turned to a tenfold more
beneficial account, could they only be prevailed
upon to meddle not with matters that are too high
for them—many individuals who have worth enough
to live for the good of society, but who have not
wisdom enough for suiting their exertions to the
real mediocrity of their powers; and who, accordingly, come forth upon their enterprise, just as if
the whole burden of this world's benevolence lay

upon their shoulders. The best thing they can do
is, to gather in their ambitious fancies, and give
themselves, instead, to actual and living fulfilments
on the sphere which is immediately around them.
The eyes of a fool, says Solomon, are towards all the
ends of the earth. We cannot join in the hostility
that has often been expressed against missionary
operations; but certainly there is a vague and va-
grant philanthropy in our day, which loses much of
its energy in its diffusiveness, and which it were
far better to fasten, and to concentrate, and to
confine, within the limits of a small locality. We
leave to those more lofty and adventurous spirits,
whom Providence will certainly call forth, the task
of devising for the good of the world abroad; and
we trust that they will never fail to be supported
in this noble cause, by the liberalities of the people
at home. But our object, at present, is, to guide
to its highest productiveness, the benevolence of
him whose station and opportunities restrain him
more to his own vicinity; and to engage him, if possible, with the near and practicable realities which
lie within his reach. His best contribution to the
interest of the world, is, to do the humble and
practicable task which his hand findeth to do, and
to do it with all his might, till he has finished it off.
A single obscure street, with its few divergent
lanes, may form the length and the breadth of his
enterprise; but far better that he, with such means
and such associates as are within his reach, should
do this thoroughly, than that, merging himself in

some wider association, he should vainly attempt
in the gross, that which never can be overtaken
but in humble and laborious detail. Let him not
think, that the region which lies beyond the limits
of his chosen and peculiar territory, is to wither
and be neglected, because his presence is not there
to fertilise it. Let him not proudly imagine himself to be the only philanthropist in the world.
Let him do his part, trusting, at the same time,
that there are others around him who have zeal
enough, and understanding enough, to do theirs.
The example of a well-cultured portion of the territory, will do more to spread a beneficent influence over the whole, than is done by the misplaced
energies of men who cannot be tempted to move,
till some design of might and of magnificence is
proposed to them. The efficacy of this humbler
style of benevolence will, at length, come to be
witnessed; and the comfort of it to be felt; and it
will diffuse itself, by sympathy, over the contiguous spaces; and the local resources of each space
will be abundantly called forth on the near and
exciting object of its own cultivation; and the
result universal will be attained, not by the combination of all the powers into one effort, but by the
summation of many efforts done by these powers
apart from, and independent of, each other—not by
one stalking society lording it over the whole,
but by manifold associations, each assuming its
own distinct task, and fulfilling a work commensurate to its own separate energies.

The institutions which are most wanted in our great towns and populous villages are those, the object of which is, the christian education of our labouring classes. This object embraces schools for ordinary scholarship through the week, and churches for the delivery of gospel doctrine and exhortation upon the Sabbath. They who are friendly to the religious establishments of our country, can find their way far more immediately to the erection and endowment of the former, than of the latter. They who found a school, have the patronage of the school. They who build and endow a church for the establishment, cannot, without many forms, and the concurrence of many authorities, retain the patronage of the church. This is a peculiarity which leads us to postpone to the next Chapter, the most essential explanations that are connected with the multiplication of churches. And all we shall attempt at present, is, to instruct the friends of general education, in what appears to us the likeliest mode of equalising our schools to the necessities of our population.

We have already, in a little work which stands separately out from our present series of expositions, endeavoured to demonstrate the Scottish system of education, and to prove both the possibility and the great advantage of its application to large towns. We refer our readers to that small performance*; and shall be satisfied with a short

---

* Considerations on the System of Parochial Schools in Scotland, and on the advantage of establishing them in Large Towns.

recapitulation of as much of it as is necessary to our present argument.

It is with common, as it is with christian education. There is not such a native and spontaneous demand for it in any country, as will call forth a supply of it at all adequate to the needs of the population. If the people are left to themselves, they will not, by any originating movement of their own, emerge out of ignorance at the first; nor will they afterwards perpetuate any habit of education to which they may have been raised in the course of one generation, if, in all succeeding generations, they are left wholly to seek after scholarship, and wholly to pay for it. To keep up popular learning, there is just the same reason for an establishment, as we have already alleged in behalf of an establishment for religion. The article must be obtruded upon them, and, in some degree, offered to them; and if the best way of so obtruding it, is, that there shall be one fabric of general repair for the people of each distinct locality, to which parents, under the impulse of near and surrounding example, may send their children for the purposes of education—then let these fabrics be multiplied to a sufficient extent; and under a right management will the security be complete, both for the people attaining a right place in the scale of mental cultivation, and after they have attained it, for never again descending to the low state out of which they had been called.

We have, in the small work to which we have

just referred, attempted to expose the defects both of a wholly gratuitous, and of a wholly unendowed system of education; affirming that, under the one scheme, the article is undervalued, and that under the other, it is not sought after to the extent to which it would be beneficial. Almost all the education of our great towns is shared between these two methods, and a woeful decline from the habit and accomplishment of our Scottish country parishes, is the undeniable consequence. To restore the mass of our population in towns, to the degree of scholarship that has shed so proud a moral glory over the face of the country at large, there seems no other expedient than that of erecting Schools and School-houses, and salarying teachers for each little district of a town and suburb population; establishing a local connection between each fabric and a given portion of the vicinity around it; and announcing it as the privilege of all the families which reside within its limits, that in that fabric a good and a cheap education is to be had for their children*.

It is a moderate computation, that one-fifteenth of the whole population should be at school; and that a school, therefore, where a hundred children are taught, should serve the demand of a popula-

---

* We are aware that Lancastrianism undertakes a more economic plan of education. It may do very well at the first breaking up of a country, where there was no habit of scholarship before. But we hold it to be a bad substitute for the old Scottish method, which provides a local and residing schoolmaster, and brings such a number of scholars around him as do not exceed the range of his own minute and personal superintendence.

tion of fifteen hundred. It is an equally moderate computation, that permanently to provide for the endowment of such a school, would require the sum of a thousand pounds sterling; or, in other words, that ere such a system could be completed for Glasgow and its suburbs, the sum of a hundred thousand pounds behoved to be expended on it.

We are quite prepared here for the epithets of visionary and theoretical, as ready to fall in most impetuous denunciation on all those who should affirm, that, for the cause of popular education amongst us, a sum so mighty ever will be raised, or an object so vast ever will be overtaken. We are aware of the discredit which this charge has inflicted, and of the damp and discouragement which it has thrown over many of the best projects of benevolence; and we, therefore, count it worth while to pause a little here, and examine somewhat attentively what the grounds are on which a charge of this sort may be soundly preferred, and what the schemes are which most abundantly deserve it.

It does not bring down the imputation of visionary upon a man, when he simply affirms of any state or condition of things which has not yet been attained by society, that it were a desirable attainment. It were truly desirable that all men were virtuous. It were desirable that such were the providential habits of our poor, as that the country should not be liable, through any mismanagement of theirs, to the burden of an excessive population. It were desirable that such a

habit of education as would tend both to exalt
their individual character, and to raise them above
the influence of those delusions which might array
them in hatred and turbulence against the cause
of order, had a universal establishment among
their families. There seems to be no imputation
of the visionary, incurred by simply affirming all
these things to be desirable. There is full permis-
sion to express our wishes on the subject, whatever
ridicule or resistance may be awaiting our speculations. It is not the mere expression of that to
be desirable, which all men feel to be desirable,
that provokes the charge of visionary; and the
question still remains, what distinctly and precisely
the provocative is?

The imputation of visionary, then, seems specifically to fall on him, who affirms that to be
practicable, which they, who advance the imputation, think to be impracticable. Both parties may
equally feel the object in question, to be desirable.
The man of sanguine temperament, thinks that it
is not merely a thing to be desired, but a thing
that may be done. The man of slow and sober
reflection, thinks too, that it were a matter to be
desired, but that it cannot be done.

There is, at the same time, a distinction to be
attended to here. One may barely affirm an object
to be practicable, without specifying the means
that he has in contemplation. If no adequate
means occur to those who hear the affirmation,
he lays himself open to the imputation of being

a visionary. Or he may propose the means, and, if they appear to the others inadequate to the accomplishment, then, with a contempt which may be seen to leer under a front of conscious sagacity, will they again pronounce him to be a visionary.

Let us apply these very obvious preliminary remarks to the topic that is now before us.

All the friends of universal education will agree in thinking it very desirable that an apparatus were raised for providing it. It is quite obvious, that, in none of our great towns, is there such an apparatus; and the question simply is, what appears the likely and the practicable way of arriving at it?

We have heard, that, among the legal and constituted bodies of the place, various movements have been made towards such an object; but we never heard that more than one school was in contemplation for each of the parishes. Such an achievement we are sure would satisfy the great bulk of our practical men, and the signal effort that Glasgow had made for the education of her citizens, would be talked of and approven, and set the public imagination at rest upon the subject for half a century.

Now, to such a measure as this, and the anticipations that are connected with it, let us apply the test for determining whether it be of a visionary character. The test is, the inadequacy of proposed means to a proposed object. This measure, then, instead of providing a school for each fifteen hundred of our people, would only provide a school for about each twelve thousand of them. We doubt whether the advantage rendered to education, by such a proceeding, would not be more than neutralised by the disguise that it might serve to throw over the nakedness of the land. We fear, that it would operate for ages as a sedative upon a far more efficient philanthropy, than ever can be exerted through the medium of any corporation. The goodly apparatus of twelve established schools, with the usual accompaniment of a yearly examination, and a published statement of the appearance and proficiency of scholars, would so fill and satiate the eye of our citizens, that even the arithmetic of the subject, however obvious, might not disturb their complacency. To propose any thing, with the view of supplementing that which looked so ample already, would appear to be quite uncalled for, and thus might the holders of our wealth be lulled into a profounder apathy than before. Meanwhile, the people, with this fractional attempt upon their habits, would, to all sense and observation, exhibit about the same ignorance as ever. And the men who glowed with the fond anticipation of a more exalted and enlightened peasantry, and were confident of carrying it into effect by means so inadequate—these would turn out to be the visionaries.

We have also heard of various consultations upon this subject, with the Government of the country. There is one way, that we shall explain afterwards, in which we think that its interposition might in time be rendered effective. But we fear that any hand which it proposes to put forth at present, will be a hand of impotency. One school for each parish, and one parish for each ten or twelve thousand of many a city population, will be an apology for a good thing, but it will not be the good thing itself. And those who count upon a renovating influence on our people, from an apparatus so meagre as this, whether they be the public functionaries of the state, or the men whom the functionaries advise with, are indeed the most egregious of all visionaries.

There are certain of our mere operatives in public business, who, however plentiful their reproach of others as visionaries, never dream that they are visionaries themselves. They seem to regard it as their sufficient exemption from such a charge, that their hand is so wholly occupied in practice, and their mind so little, if at all, occupied with principle. It would look, as if to escape from being a theorist upon any given topic, it were altogether necessary to abstain from thinking of it; and that, to stamp a sound and experimental character on a man's notions, it is quite enough that he personally bustle and spend all his time among the mere matters of manipulation and detail. Such men never, perhaps, in the whole course of their lives, have given one hour of meditative solitude to the question at issue; and, perhaps, think that the whole effect of such a season of loneliness, would be to gather around them the spectres of vain imagination. They have no other conception of a student, than as of one who muses all day long, over the inapplicable abstractions of an ideal and contemplative region; nor do they see how, in calm and collected retirement, it is possible for the mind to calculate and to recollect, and to be altogether conversant among the realities of the living world, over which it may have cast a most observant regard, and the well known familiarities of which, it is able to turn into the materials of a just view, and a just anticipation. In these circumstances, it ought not to be wondered at, that practical men have engrossed the credit of all the practical wisdom that there is in society; and that they have missed the self-discernment which might have led them to perceive, that the possessor of a body, which moves its dull and unvarying round through the duties of public office, and of a mind that is either profoundly asleep to the rationale of public affairs, or catches its occasional view of them by rapid and confused glances—that he, with all the confidence which a kind of coarse and hackneyed experience· has given to him, may, very possibly, be the most blundering and bewildered of all visionaries.

The thing to be chiefly dreaded from the deed of Government, or the deed of a city corporation, in this matter, is, that it may overbear the public into the conclusion, that enough has been done, because they have done it. There is an imposing magnitude in the measures of a public body, which can only be reduced to its correct estimation, by being arithmetically compared with the magnitude of the subject over which it operates. It is seldom, when a boon is thus conferred upon a country, that it is accompanied with the proclamation of its insignificance, relative to the whole need of a country. But it were well, both in the case of schools and churches, that such a proclamation were made. In this way, the very partial endowment, instead of acting as a soporific, would act as a stimulus on the benevolence of individuals. If, when the rulers of the nation, or the rulers of a city, did something, (and it is most desirable that they should,) they made a full demonstration of its inadequacy to the object; this would effectually be leading the way to its full accomplishment. Such a high testimony would call forth the means and energies of many voluntary associations; which, instead of being superseded into downright inaction, as they else might have been, would be excited to follow the paternal example, that had thus been set before them.

But voluntary associations have come forward in the cause of education, without waiting for any such signal. And if, to look confidently forward to a proposed end, with feeble and disproportionate means, be to incur the character of visionary, then we fear that this imputation must be made to rest upon them also. They have all been greatly less efficient than they might have been, from their neglect of the principle of locality. There are many associations which, by their resources, could have done that permanently and substantially for a district of the town, which they have vainly attempted, and have, therefore, done partially and superficially for the whole. The money which could have built a local school, and emanated enough of interest for ever to have kept it in repair, and provided the teacher with a perpetual salary, has been dissipated in transient and ineffectual exertions for the accomplishment of a universal object. The error is, to have been led away, by the splendour of a conception, far greater than it was able to realise. It is this ambition, to plan beyond the ability to execute, which has involved in failure and misdirection, so many of the efforts of philanthropy. And they who have so precipitately counted on any general result, that would be at all sensible, from the proceedings of any one society, however magnificent in its scale, and however princely the offerings that were rendered to it, have evinced themselves well entitled to the character of visionaries.

The great mischief of any such society, is, that it blinds the public eye to the utter inadequacy of its own operations. It sends a feeble emanation over the whole city; which were doing an important benefit, had it only the effect of making the darkness visible. But, instead of this, we fear, that the light which it thus diffuses, imperfect as it is, is rated, not according to the intensity with which it shines upon our population, but according to the extent in which it is thinly and obscurely spread over them. The very title of a school for all, is enough to deceive a miscalculating public, into the imagination, that all are provided with schooling. If, instead of trying to engross the whole, the society in question had concentrated its means and its energies upon a part, and upon such a part, too, as it could overtake most thoroughly, there would have been no such pernicious delusion in the way of rendering a solid and entire benefit to the labouring classes. The very contrast it had produced between the district it so effectually brightened, and the total darkness of the surrounding or contiguous spaces, would have forced that lesson upon the public notice, which, under the generalising system, is thrown into disguise altogether. Instead of a semblance of education for the whole, let there be the substance of it in one part; and this will at length, spread and propagate its own likeness over all the other parts. It will serve like the touch of a flame to kindle the whole mass into a brilliancy as luminous as its own. It never would be permitted to stand a barren and solitary memorial. Other men would soon feel a responsibility in other quarters, who now feel none at all. Other societies would speedily arise in other districts; and the whole effect, which was so vainly looked for, as the result of one great organization, will at length be made out, by the apposition of successive parts to one another.

Our earnest advice, for these reasons, is, that no benevolent society for education shall undertake a larger space of the city than it can provide for, both completely and perpetually; by reclaiming its families to a habit of scholarship for ever, through the means of a permanent endowment, attached exclusively to the district of its operations. It is far better to cultivate one district well, though all the others should be left untouched, than to superficialise over the whole city. It is far better, that these other districts be thrown as unprovided orphans, upon a benevolence that is sure to be called out at other times, and in other circles of society. Instead of casting upon them a feeble and languid regard, it is infinitely better to abandon them to the fresh, and powerful, and unexpended regards of other men. Let none of us think to monopolise all the benevolence of the world, or fear that no future band of philanthropists shall arise, to carry the cause forward from that point at which we have exhausted our operations. If education is to be made universal in towns by voluntary benevolence, it will not be by one great, but by many small and successive exertions. The thing will be accomplished piecemeal; and what never could be done through the working of one vast and unwieldy mechanism, may thus be completed most easily, in the course of a single generation.

Let us now attempt to trace the character of the process that we have just recommended, from the first beginning of it, and along that line of conveyance, by which it is finally brought onward to the result of an adequate provision for the entire and universal scholarship of our city families. We see nothing of the visionary at its commencement. One society, that should propose to raise a hundred thousand pounds for a project so gigantic, may well be denounced as visionary; but not so the society that should propose to raise one or two thousand pounds for its own assumed proportion of it. There is many an individual, who has both philanthropy enough, and influence enough, within the circle of his own acquaintanceship, for moving forward a sufficiency of power towards such an achievement. All that he needs, is the guidance of his philanthropy at the first, to this enterprise. When once fairly embarked, there are many securities against his ever abandoning it till it is fully accomplished. For, from the very first moment, will he feel a charm in his undertaking, that he never felt in any of those wide and bewildering generalities of benevolence, which have hitherto engrossed him. To appropriate his little vicinity—to lay it down in the length and the breadth of it—to measure it off as the manageable field within which he can render an entire and a lasting benefit to all its families—to know and be known amongst them, and thus have his liberality sweetened by the charm of acquaintanceship with those who are the objects of it—instead of dropping, as heretofore of his abundance, into an ocean where it was instantly absorbed and became invisible, to pour a deep, and a sensible, and an abiding infusion into his own separate and selected portion of that impracticable mass which has hitherto withstood all the efforts of philanthropy—instead of grasping in vain at the whole territory, to make upon it his own little settlement, and thus to narrow, at least, the unbroken field, which he could not overtake—to beautify one humble spot, and there raise an enduring monument, by which an example is lifted up, and a voice is sent forth to all the spaces which are yet unentered on—this is benevolence, reaping a reward at the very outset of its labours, and such a reward, too, as will not only ensure the accomplishment of its own task, but, as must, from the ease, and the certainty, and the distinct and definite good which are attendant upon its doings, serve both to allure and to guarantee a whole host of imitations.

And, to redeem this initiatory step still further from the charge of visionary, it ought to be remarked, that even though not followed up by any imitation, it is not lost. A certain good will have been rendered to society, and a good too, fully proportionate to the labour and expense that have been bestowed upon it. If permanently to cover the whole city with education, be an enterprise worth a hundred thousand pounds, then, to cover a hundredth part of it, is an enterprise worth a thousand pounds. The purchase and the pur-

chase-money are equivalent to each other; and if
not a magnificent operation, it is, at least, not like
many of the magnificent projects of our day—it
is not an abortive one.

Viewed, indeed, in the light of one isolated
effort—of one single feat of liberality, there is
something altogether, independent of its being a
likely stepping-stone to many similar undertakings by other hands and in other places, that is
well calculated to engage the kindly affections of
our nature. It is vesting one's self with the noblest
of all property, when he can point to a certain
geographical district in a great city, on which he
has stamped a visible impress of his benevolence,
which it will wear to the end of time, and be a
blessing to its future families throughout all generations. Some may regard this more in the light
of a solace to the vanity of his constitution—but
surely it is fitted to soothe and to satisfy his better
feelings, that the objects of his liberality come so
distinctly under his notice; that the good he has
rendered, survives the exertion he has made in so
separate and visible a form; that the families he
has benefited, can be so specifically pointed to, and
the children, who, through him, are brought under
the wholesome ministration of a sound and a cheap
scholarship, may be met, as often as he will, to
witness the progress of his own experiment, and
cheer them on to the attainments which he himself
has provided for them. There is in all this, a concentrated charm, which were dissipated into thin

air, had the same cost and the same exertion been
incurred among some of the heartless and unproductive generalities of a more extended operation.

But more than this. It is felt by every man as
a stronger pull, both on his liberality and his exertion, when he sees the end of what he is embarked
upon, than when that end lies at an obscure and
indefinite distance from him. The moment that
an exhausted crew come within sight of land, a
new energy is felt to revisit and revive them. An
enterprise of charity may be so vast that this sight
may never be attained; or, it may be so circum-
scribed within distinct and narrow boundaries,
that it may never fail, from the very outset, to enliven the hope, and spirit on the progress of benevolent adventurers. Under the local system, this
principle comes into full play, and works a mighty
increment of good to society. Insomuch, that
even with the same number of philanthropists,
a greater amount both of money and of exertion is
rendered to the cause, by separate bands of them,
each of them expatiating on its own local and
limited province, than by the whole body of them
putting forth one gigantic effort on the whole field
of operation that lies before them.

And again. The very same system does call
forth a greater number of philanthropists. This
is due, not merely, to the superior practicability
of its object, but also to the strength of that local
interest with which it is associated. When the
good proposed to be done, is for the special behoof

of one city parish, or even one department of a city parish, this carries a far more forcible appeal than any general object would, to all those connected with it, either by office, or by property, or by residence. It is felt by all such, as a directly pertinent application, and so, both in respect of agency and of subscription, calls forth a host of latent capabilities, that, under a general system, would never have been reached, and never have been entered upon. There can be no doubt, that the more you subdivide a territory into districts, the more intense, and the more productive, will be the operation in each of them; so as to draw out a far greater number of supporters, and to raise a far greater sum than ever could have been raised out of the same district, for any scheme of universal education. Better that this scheme should never be entertained, than that it should so float in the imaginations of the sanguine, as to lead them away from the alone path of practical wisdom, which can conduct to its accomplishment. Better far, surely, that it should at length come out in exhibition as the actual result of each particular body labouring assiduously for its own particular object, than that, in the shape of an airy dream, to which the public eye is generally and collectively drawn, it should call forth the one ostentatious, but futile movement that will never realise it.

It is not known how precious and how productive a thing the operation of this local interest is, even in the very poorest of our districts. The capabilities of humble life are yet far from being perfectly understood, or turned to the full account of which they are susceptible. We certainly invite, and with earnestness too, the man of fortune and philanthropy, to assume a locality to himself, and head an enterprise for schools, in behalf of its heretofore neglected population. But little is it known to what extent the fund may be augmented by pains and perseverance among the population themselves. With a little guidance, in fact, may the poor be made the most effective instruments of their own amelioration. The system which could raise a single penny in the week from each family, would, of its own unaided self, both erect and perpetuate a sufficient apparatus for schooling over the whole empire, or over any part into which it was introduced, in about twelve years. This is a mine which has lately been entered upon, for the purpose of aiding those excellent religious charities that have so signalised our nation; and more is extracted from it than from all the liberalities of the opulent. In a cause so near and so exciting as that of home education, it could, by dint of strenuous cultivation, be made to yield much more abundantly. So that, should the rich refuse a helping hand to a cause so closely associated with the best interests of our country, we do not despair of the poor being at length persuaded to take it upon themselves, and of thus leaving the higher classes behind them in the career of an enlightened patriotism.

Yet it were well, that the rich did step forward and signalise themselves in this matter. Amid all the turbulence and discontent which prevail in society, do we believe, that there is no rancour so fiery or so inveterate in the heart of the labouring classes, but that a convincing demonstration of good will, on the part of those who are raised in circumstances above them, could not charm it most effectually away. It is a question of nicety, how should this demonstration be rendered? Not, we think, by any public or palpable offering to the cause of indigence, for this we have long conceived should be left, and left altogether to the sympathies of private intercourse; it being, we believe, a point of uniform experience, that the more visible the apparatus is for the relief of poverty, the more is it fitted to defeat its own object, and to scatter all the jealousies attendant upon an imaginary right among those who might else have been sweetened into gratitude by the visitations of a secret and spontaneous kindness. Not so, however, with an offering rendered to the cause of education, let it be as public or as palpable as it may. The urgency of competition for such an object, is at all times to be hailed rather than resisted; and on this career of benevolence, therefore, may the affluent go indefinitely onward, till the want be fully and permanently provided for. We know no exhibition that would serve more to tranquillise our country, than one which might convince the poorer classes, that there is a real desire, on the part of their superiors in wealth, to do for them any thing, and every thing, which they believe to be for their good. It is the expression of an interest in them, which does so much to soothe and to pacify the discontents of men; and all that is wanted, is, that the expression shall be of such a sort, as not to injure, but to benefit those for whom it is intended. To regulate the direction of our philanthropy, with this view, all that needs to be ascertained, is, an object, by the furtherance of which, the families of the poor are benefited most substantially; and, at the same time, for the expenses of which, one is not in danger of contributing too splendidly. We know no object which serves better to satisfy these conditions, than a district school, which, by the very confinement of its operation within certain selected limits, will come specifically home with something of the impression of a kindness done individually to each of the householders. It were possible, in this way, for one person, at the head of an associated band, to propitiate towards himself, and, through him, towards that order in society with which he stands connected, several thousands of a yet neglected population. He could walk abroad over some suburb waste, and chalk out for himself the limits of his adventure; and, amid the gaze and inquiry of the natives, could cause the public edifice gradually to arise in exhibition before them; and though they might be led to view it at first as a caprice, they would not be long of feeling that it

z

was at least a caprice of kindness towards them—
some well-meaning quixotism, perhaps, which,
whether judicious or not, was pregnant, at least,
with the demonstration of good will, and would
call forth from them, by a law of our sentient nature, which they could not help, an honest emotion
of good will back again; and, instead of the envy
and derision which so often assail our rich when
charioted in splendour, along the more remote
and outlandish streets of the city, would it be
found, that the equipage of this generous, though
somewhat eccentric visitor, had always a comely
and complaisant homage rendered to it. By such
a movement as this, might an individual, throughout a district, and a few individuals throughout
the city at large, reclaim the whole of our present
generation, to a kindliness for the upper classes
that is now unfelt; and this too, not by the ministration of those beggarly elements, which serve
to degrade and to impoverish the more; but by the
ministration of such a moral influence among the
young, as would serve to exalt humble life, and
prepare for a better economy than our present,
the habits of the rising generation.

We know not, indeed, what could serve more
effectually to amalgamate the two great classes of
society together, than their concurrence in an object which so nearly concerns the families of all.
We know not how a wealthy individual could work
a more effectual good, or earn a purer and more
lasting gratitude, from the people of his own se-

lected district, than by his splendid donative in the cause of education. Whatever exceptions may be alleged against the other schemes of benevolence, this, at least, is a charity whose touch does not vilify its objects; nor will it, like the aliment of ordinary pauperism, serve to mar the habit and character of our population. Here, then, is a walk on which philanthropy may give the rein to her most aspiring wishes for the good of the world; and while a single district of the land is without the scope of an efficient system for the schooling of its families, is there room for every lover of his species to put forth a liberality that can neither injure nor degrade them.

Every enlightened friend of the poor ought to rejoice in such an opportunity, amid the coarse invectives which assail him, when led by his honest convictions to resist the parade and the publicity of so many attempts as are made in our day, in behalf of indigence. It may sometimes happen, that selfishness, in making her escape from the applications of an injudicious charity, will be glad to shelter herself under some of those maxims of a sounder economy, which are evidently gaining in credit and currency amongst us. And hence the ready imputation of selfishness upon all, who decline from the support of associations which they hold to be questionable. And thus is it somewhat amusing to observe, how the yearly subscriber of one guinea to some favourite scheme of philanthropy, thereby purchases to himself the right of stigmatizing every cold-blooded speculator who refuses his concurrence; while the latter is altogether helpless, and most awkwardly so, under a charge so very disgraceful. In avowing, as he does, the principle, that all the public relief which is ministered to poverty, swells and aggravates the amount of it in the land, and that it is only by efforts of unseen kindness, that any thing effectual can be done for its mitigation—he cannot lay bare the arithmetic of private benevolence, and more especially of his own—he cannot drag it forth to that ground of visibility, on which he believes that the whole of its charm and efficacy would be dissipated—he cannot confront the untold liberalities which pass in secret conveyance to the abodes of indigence, with the doings and the doqueted reports of committeeship—he cannot anticipate the disclosures of that eventful day, when He who seeth in secret shall reward openly, however much he may be assured, that the droppings of individual sympathy, as far outweigh in value the streams of charitable distribution, which have been constructed by the labour and the artifice of associated men, as does the rain from heaven, which feeds the mighty rivers of our world, outweigh in amount, the water which flows through all the aqueducts of human workmanship that exist in it. From all this, he is precluded, by the very condition in which the materials of the question are situated; and silent endurance is the only way in which he can meet the zealots of public charity, while they push and prosecute the triumph of their widely blazoned achievement—even though convinced all the while, that, by their obtrusive hand, they have superseded a far more productive benevolence than they ever can replace; that they have held forth a show of magnitude and effort which they can in no way realise; and with a style of operation, mighty in promise, but utterly insignificant in the result, have deadened all those responsibilities and private regards, which, if suffered, without being diverted aside, to go forth on their respective vicinities, would yield a more plentiful, as well as a more precious tribute, to the cause of suffering humanity, than ever can be raised by loud and open proclamation.

The disciples of the Malthusian philanthropy, who keep back when they think that publicity is hurtful, should come forth on every occasion when publicity is harmless. That is the time of their vindication; and then it is in their power to meet, on the same arena, with those Lilliputians in charity, who think that they do all, when, in fact, they have done nothing but mischief. We hear much of the liberality of our age. But it appears to us to be nearly as minute in respect of amount, as much of it is misplaced in respect of direction; nor can we discover, save among the devoted missionaries of Serampore and a few others, any very sensible approximations to the great standard of Christian charity, set forth in the gospel for our imitation. The Saviour was rich, and for our sakes he became poor; and ere the world he died for, shall be reclaimed to the knowledge of himself, many must be his followers, who regard their wealth, not as a possession but as a steward-ship. We anticipate, in time, a much higher rate of liberality than obtains at present in the Christian world; nor do we know a cause more fitted to draw it onwards, than one which may be supported visibly, without attracting a single individual to pauperism, and which, when completed, perman-ently and substantially, will widen, and that for ever, the moral distance of our people, from a state so corrupt and degrading. Ere the apparatus shall be raised, which is able, not faintly to skim, but thoroughly to saturate the families of our poor with education, there will be room for large sums and large sacrifices; nor do we know on whom the burden of this cause can sit so gracefully and so well, as on those who have speculated away their feelings of attachment from all societies for the relief of indigence—and who are now bound to demonstrate, that this is not because their judgment has extinguished their sensibilities; but because they only want an object set before them which may satisfy their understanding, that, with-out doing mischief, they may largely render of their means to the promotion of it.

We are sensible, that, to look for a universal result, in the way that we have now recommended, is to presuppose a very wide extension of Christian zeal, seconded by an equal degree of Christian

liberality all over the land. If it be visionary to
look for this, then do we hold it alike visionary,
to look for any great moral improvement in the
economy of our national institutions without this.
We see not our way to any public or extended
amelioration, save, through the medium of greater
worth in the character of individuals, and a greater
number of such individuals in the country; and
but for this, would we give up in despair, that
cause on which both politicians and moralists have
embarked so many sanguine speculations. It is
not, we think, on the arena of state partizanship,
that a victory for this cause is to be decided; but
that, similarly to the growth of the small prophetic
stone, which at length attained to the size of a
mountain that filled the whole earth, will it gradually proceed onwards, just as the spirit and
principles of the gospel find a numerical way
through human hearts, and multiply their proselytes among human families. If it be here, that
a contemptuous scepticism discovers the weak side
of our argument, and proclaims it accordingly; it
is also here, that Prophecy lifts up the light of
its cheering countenance on all our anticipations.
Meanwhile, its best and brightest fulfilments are
not to be without human agency, but by human
agency; and even already do we see a rising
philanthropy in our day, which warrants our
fondest hopes both of the increase of learning and
virtue amongst our population. For a time, it
may waste a portion of its energies among the
bye-paths of inexperience. Ambition may be-

wilder it. Impatience may cause it to overrun itself. A taste for generalities may dazzle it into many fond and foolish imaginations; and the ridicule of an incredulous public may await the mortifying failures, which will ever mark the enterprise of him, whose aim is beyond the means of his accomplishment. But the spirit of benevolence will not be evaporated among all these difficulties: It will only be nurtured into greater strength, and guided into a path of truer wisdom, and sobered into a habit of more humble, and, at the same time, far more effective perseverance. Man will at length learn to become more practical and less imaginative. He will hold it a worthier achievement to do for a little neighbourhood, than to devise for a whole world. He will give himself more assiduously to the object within his reach, and trust that there are other men and other means for accomplishing the objects that are beyond it. The glory of establishing in our world, that universal reign of truth and of righteousness which is coming, will not be the glory of any one man; but it will be the glory of Him who sitteth above, and plieth his many millions of instruments for bringing about this magnificent result. It is enough for each of us to be one of these instruments, to contribute his little item to the cause, and look for the sum total as the product of innumerable contributions, each of them as meritorous, and many of them, perhaps, far more splendid and important than his own.

CHAP. V.

ON CHURCH PATRONAGE.

In the case of a district school, where the appointment of the teacher lies with those who built and
who partially endowed it, matters may be so ordered,
as that we shall not have much to fear from a corrupt
exercise of the patronage. It were well, we think,
for the purpose of securing a local and a residing
patronage, that a voice in the election of the teacher
should be given to two or three of the ecclesiastical
functionaries of the parish in which the school was
situated. These would feel a responsibility for their
choice to the district families with whom they stood
so closely associated. And should their propensity
to favouritism not be overruled by the force of public opinion, the patrons by subscription, by whom
they, in most instances, would be far outnumbered,
were enough to neutralize it. And lest there still
were an unity of disposition, among the majority of
electors, in behalf of an unworthy candidate, it
would go far to check this tendency, that the school,
though endowed to a certain extent, is endowed but
partially. The office, in fact, if it be rightly constituted, is only an object of ambition to those who are
qualified. The teacher may have a dwelling-house
and a salary, and still have his main dependence
on the scholars' fees. It will thus be an object of
keenest competition to those who hope most san-

guinely for a crowded attendance; and amid the quantity of known and aspiring talent that will come forth upon every vacancy, it is not to be conceived, that, in the face of a vigilant neighbourhood, and when parents, by the simple withdrawment of their young, could reduce the teacher to starvation, the patrons will disgrace themselves, and that without essentially benefitting their client, by a glaringly unfit nomination.

And, in the very same way, might not a district chapel be raised as well as a district school, and with still greater securities even, for a right exercise of the patronage? How often, for example, do we observe a meeting-house, built at the expense of so many adventurers, and with the prospect of such a return from the seat rents, as, after defraying the salary of the minister, and all other charges, will yield them a full indemnification? Here the effective patronage is as good as shared between the electors and the hearers, and the hold is in every way as strong as human interest can make it for a pure, or at least for a popular appointment. And, with such an appointment, all the expenses of the institution may be covered; so that though at first sight it looks a more arduous enterprise to found a chapel than a school, the truth is, that the latter may require a stretch of benevolence which the former may not. To make common education universal among the children of the operative class, it seems necessary that there should be a gratuitous erection, and a gratuitous salary; enabling the teacher to meet the whole population with scholarship on reduced fees: in which case a part only of the whole expense is laid upon the attendance. To meet the same class with Christian education, we have ample and repeated experience, that the whole expense may be charged upon the attendance; provided only, that right measures be taken to secure an attendance. This is done simply by a popular appointment; by holding forth instruction to the people from a man of acceptable doctrine, and of esteemed ability and character. That the house be well filled, the great and sufficient step is, that the pulpit be well filled. This, therefore, will be the first care of those who have a direct interest in the attendance: and it is a care which is often so abundantly repaid, as to make the chapel indemnify itself, and that out of a congregation chiefly made up of the families of labourers.

If, then, the process that we have already recommended for pervading a city with common education, through the week, be at all practicable, there appears to be a still smoother and more practicable way of pervading it as thoroughly with Christian education, on the Sabbath. By the simple and successive apposition of chapel-districts to each other, may a sufficient apparatus at length be reared in a town for the religious instruction of all its families; and such we conceive to be the efficiency of a wisely exercised patronage in drawing out the attendance of the people, that we think a system of this kind may at length be completed without any draught whatever on the liberality of the public. This great achievement lies, we think, within the power and scope of dissenterism; and if so little progress has yet been made towards it, it is only because dissenters have not localised. They have attracted a few scattered families towards them, but they have not sent forth an emanating influence upon the whole. They have not yet found their way to that strong reciprocal influence which lies between the weekday attentions of one man reiterating upon one neighbourhood, and the Sabbath instructions that are delivered by the same man in the heart of the same neighbourhood. They have not penetrated or transfused the mass of our population. They have only drawn together a few of its particles. That principle of locality, of the truth and power of which, the trial of a single month will give more satisfying evidence than the argumentation of many volumes, has not yet by them been proceeded on to any extent; and we know not how long it may continue to be regarded both by them and by the general public, as a mere imaginative charm of no force and no efficacy. Did an association of Christian philanthropists only try this experiment on any suburb and neglected portion of a city multitude, we are persuaded that they would soon find themselves in possession of a new power for calling forth the people to the ministrations of the gospel. Let them simply rear their taber-

nacle, and assume for it a locality, to the families
of which they might grant a preference for seats,
and restrict the week-day services of the minister
whom they have chosen. At first, in a rude and
heathenish district, the preference would not be
extensively taken; in which case the remaining
seats would be held forth to general competition.
Now, it is not yet known how surely and how
speedily the assiduities of the minister, within the
limits of his territorial district, would spread the
desire among its people to sit under him; nor
how readily the very obtrusion of his chapel upon
their notice, as a chapel appropriated for the use
of their little vicinity, would hasten forward their
attendance; nor how powerfully, by the force of
contiguous and increasing example, next door families would be drawn into the common relationship of parishioners and hearers with the man
who preached so near them every Sabbath, and
was daily observed to be plying amongst them,
during the week, the sacred and benevolent attentions of his office. There might, at the outset of
such an enterprise, be only a partial attendance
from the district, supplemented by hearers from all
parts of the city. But should the vacancies that
occur by the death or removal of these hearers, be
rigidly held forth, in the first instance, to local
applicants ; a single generation would not elapse,
ere this chapel-minister, though a dissenter, stood
vested with all that ascendency over his little
neighbourhood, which a parochial congregation

is fitted to give to a minister in the Establishment. He would soon ascertain the comfort and the power of operating within a locality, occupied by the people of his own congregation; and would find that in such a concentration of all his forces, there lay an efficacy tenfold greater than what lies in the diffuseness and variety of his present movements. It is thus that dissenters may gain by territorial conquest, upon an Establishment which either provides inadequately, or patronizes carelessly, for the religious welfare of a city population. They may not only draw people, but recover ground from the church, and bring, if they will, every inch of the domain they have thus wrested under a parochial economy. They might at length work themselves into an arrangement of high influence, which, by the existing practice of our cities, is still denied to the established clergy, who are compelled to sit loose to their parishes, from the influx of extra-parochial hearers upon their congregations. The ministers of the Establishment would thus become mere congregational teachers, whereas those of the dissent would attain, through the medium of locality, a close and intimate relationship with the great mass of our city families. Should the present wretched mode of seat-letting be perpetuated, it lies with the dissenters themselves to become, if they will, the stable and recognized functionaries of religion in our great towns; and, by a fair usurpation,

to change places with the Establishment altogether.

If it be possible to cover the face of a city
with district-schools, for the expense of which
there must be a draught on the liberality of the
public, it is surely as possible to cover it with
district-chapels, which, with the benefit of locality,
and a wise exercise of the patronage together,
may at all times be made to pay themselves. The
former advantage is little understood, and has
scarcely at all been acted on by dissenters. The
latter is far more palpable, though without the
aid of locality, it will never, for reasons that
have already been adduced, stay the moral and
religious deterioration of cities. Were dissenters
armed with both these advantages, it would give
them a might and a pre-eminence in large towns
which they have never yet attained. They would,
in fact, acquire for the apparatus they had reared,
all the homage and all the perpetuity of an establishment; and wield those very influences over
the population, for which alone a national church
is in any way desirable,

But an instrument that is ready made to our
hands should not be wantonly set aside; and it were
far better that the church should be stimulated
than that it should be superseded. It has already a great advantage over dissenters, in that locality, the full benefit of which, were it not for
the obtuseness of our civic legislators, might be
so soon and so easily restored to it. But there is

not the same hold upon it for a pure exercise of the patronage. The expense of its fabrics and its salaries is not in general derived from hearers, and therefore the taste of hearers may not be at all consulted in its appointments. Instead of a respectful deference to the popular opinion, on these occasions, there is often a haughty, intolerant, and avowed defiance to it—and we then see the longings of the public sorely thwarted by the resolute and impregnable determination of the patron. It may be easily conceived, therefore, how wide the disruption is between the ruling and the subject party, when a spirit altogether adverse to the prevailing taste is seen to preside over the great bulk of our ecclesiastical nominations. If power and popularity shall ever stand in hostile array against each other, we are not to wonder though the result should be, a church on the one hand, frowning aloof in all the pride and distance of hierarchy upon our population, and a people on the other, revolted into utter distaste for establishments, and mingling with this a very general alienation of heart from all that carries the stamp of authority in the land.

We should like, even for the cause of public tranquillity and good order, that there were a more respectful accommodation to the popular taste in Christianity, than the dominant spirit of ecclesiastical patronage in our day is disposed to render it. We conceive the two main ingredients of this taste to be, in the first place, that esteem which is felt by

human nature for what is believed to be religious honesty; and, in the second place, the appetite of human nature, when made, in any degree, alive to a
sense of its spiritual wants, for that true and Scriptural ministration which alone can relieve them.
Now, if these be, indeed, the principles of the popular taste, we know not how a deeper injury can be
inflicted, than when all its likings and demands, on
the subject of religion, are scorned disdainfully
away. There is a very quick and strong discrimination between that which it relishes and that which it
dislikes, in the ministrations of a religious teacher;
and, previous to all enquiry into the justice of this
discrimination, it must be obvious, that if instead
of being gratified by the compliances of patronage,
it is subjected to an increasing and systematic annoyance, this must gender a brooding indignancy
at power among the people, or, at least, a heartless indifference to all that is associated with the
government of the country, or with the matters of
public administration.

In every matter that is seen intensely to affect
the popular mind—that mind which is so loud in
its discontent, and so formidable in its violence—
that mind, the ebullitions of which have raised so
many a wasting storm in our day, and which, still
heaving, and dissatisfied, and restless, seems as if
it would roll back the burden of its felt or its fancied wrongs on the institutions from which they
have germinated—it surely is the part of political
wisdom to allay rather than infuriate the disorder,

by according all which it can, and all which it
ought, to the general wish of society. And the
obligation were still more imperious, should it be
made out that the thing wished for would add to
the public tranquillity, by adding to the public
virtue—that what is granted would not merely ap-
pease a present desire, but would shed a pure as
well as a pacifying influence over the future habits of our population—that, instead of a bribe
which corrupted, it were a boon to exalt and to
moralise them: thus combining what is rarely to
be met with in one ministration, the property of
calling forth a grateful emotion now, and the property of yielding the precious fruit both of national worth and loyalty hereafter.

We believe that there is no one subject on
which our statesmen are more woefully in the
dark, than the right exercise of church patronage. They apprehend not its true bearings on
the political welfare of the country. The whole
question is blended with theology: and this has
shaded it with such a mystery to their eyes, as one
profession holds forth to the eye and the discernment of another. They have not, in fact, steadily
looked to the matter, with their own understanding; and acting, as they often do, in the hurry of
their manifold occupations, on the guidance and
information of others, they have very naturally
reposed this part of their policy on the advice of
mere ecclesiastics. It is true, that, in many a
single instance, the nomination may be so over-

ruled by family interest and connection, as to bring patronage and popularity into one. But, with this abatement, there is a leading policy which presides over this department of public affairs; and we repeat it, that it is a policy mainly derived from the representations and the authority of churchmen. It is far more the interest of a government to be right than wrong; and we think, that in this, as in every other branch of their operations, they do what is honestly believed to be most for the civil and political well-being of the state. But, just as in questions of commerce, they may be misled by lending their ear to the political science of party and interested merchants; so, in questions of church countenance and preferment, they may be misled by lending their ear to the oracles of a spiritual partizanship. It is thus that the main force of their patronage may be directed to one kind of theology; and that may be the very theology which unpeoples the Establishment of its hearers. It is thus that their honours and rewards may, in the great bulk of them, be lavished on one set of ecclesiastics, and these may be the very ecclesiastics who alienate the population from the church, and so widen the unfortunate distance that obtains between the holders of power in a country, and the subjects of it.

It is manifest, therefore, that there must, on this subject, be a delusion somewhere, though it may not be easy to expose it. It is obviously for the interest of statesmen that there should be a

harmony of temper between them and the population; and never is this so forced upon our convictions as when, in a time like the present, a
slumbering fire is at work, which, if much further
irritated, will break out into fierce and open conflagration on the existing structure of society.
We know not what the political concessions are,
which would allay the tumults of the public mind;
nor are we sure that any concessions of that sort
would be at all effectual. But there is, at least,
one avenue by which our rulers might still find
their way to acceptance and gratitude all over the
land. There is, at least, one link of communication, to the fastening of which they have only to
put forth a friendly hand; and, by keeping hold
of which, they will be sure to retain a steady hold
on the affections of a now alienated multitude. It
must be quite palpable, even to themselves, that
there is one kind of church appointment which
sends a glow of satisfaction abroad among the families of a parish; and that, by a boon so cheap
and simple, as a mere habit of acceptable patronage, they may bring in as many willing captives
to the Establishment, as there is room in the
Establishment to receive. Little as they may
know of the theology of the question, they must,
at least, know that which so much glares upon
the observation of all, as that, with a certain style
of ecclesiastical patronage, they may, when they
will, turn the great current of the population into
the national church, and again replenish the emp-

ty pews and spacious but deserted edifices of the
their great hierarchy, with willing and delighted
hearers from all the ranks of society. And the
question recurs, what is the might and the mystery of that spell which has so bewildered our men
of power from the path that would lead to a result
so desirable? Or, if not the effect of an infatuation, but of a principle, what are the weighty reasons of vindication for a policy that has so severed
the church from the common people, and reduced
to naked architecture one-half of that costly apparatus, reared by a former age, for upholding
the Christian worth and virtue of the commonwealth?

There seem to be three distinct grounds, on
which the popular taste in Christianity is so much
held at nought by the dispensers of patronage.
First, on the ground of the contempt that is felt
for it, as a low, drivelling affection; secondly, on
the ground of the moral reprobation in which it is
held as being inimical to human virtue; and,
thirdly, on the ground of the suspicion that it is
in close alliance with a factious and turbulent
disposition, and that, therefore, every encouragement which is awarded to it forms an accession
of strength to the cause of democracy in the land.
On one or other of these grounds is there an array of
contempt and resistance against the popular taste;
and men of the highest ascendency in the kingdom are often to be seen among the foremost in
this array. Tre chy of, down with fanaticism,

ascends from the bosom of the church; and the
dignitaries of the state may be observed in firmly
leagued opposition with the dignitaries of religion,
against the warmest likings of the multitude.

I. First, then, the popular taste in Christianity
is often treated by the holders of patronage, as if
it were a perverse appetite for absurdity and error. It is looked to as a thing of whim, and a
thing of imagination; and there can be no doubt
that it has its occasional whims and absurdities—
its squeamish dislike to what is in itself very innocent—and its fanciful and extravagant regards
to what in itself is very insignificant. Among
these we would remark its puling and fantastic
antipathy to all the visible symptoms of written
preparation in the pulpit*,—and its jealousy of all
doctrine that is uttered in any other than the current phraseology,—and its sensitive recoil from
such innovations of outward form, as might sim-
plify or improve any of the services of the church,
—and its appetite for length and loudness, and
wearisome occasions, and other puerilities, which
have made it appear an utterly weak and con-
temptible thing, in the eye of many a scornful
observer. The popular taste, even in its pur-

---

* We must, however, earnestly recommend to all the readers of sermons,
that they shall try to attain the habit of reading them freely and impressively,
and in such a way as marks the direct communication of personal feeling
from the speaker to those whom he addresses.

est and most respectable form, will still be a subject for caricature. But it has supplied additional features for such a sketch out of its own follies, and its own excrescencies; insomuch, that, to the eye of many, and those too among the most powerful and enlightened of our land, does it hold forth the general aspect of a freakish and wayward propensity, which it is quite fair to trample upon, and, at all events, no outrage on any worthy feeling of our nature, utterly to thwart and to disregard.

And here one reason at least becomes manifest, why, on the part of clergymen, the mere whimsies of popular feeling ought not to be complied with; and that between favourite preachers and their doting admirers such a spectacle should never be held out, as that of servile indulgence upon the one side, and weak, trifling, senseless conceits of taste and partiality, on the other. It is this which, more perhaps than any other cause, has degraded the popular opinion into a thing of no estimation, and has thrown circumstances of ridicule around it, which have given an edge to satire, and furnished a plea of extenuation for the policy that holds it at nought. If it be grievous to observe the demand of the people about frivolities of no moment, it is still more grievous to behold the deference which is rendered thereto by the fearful worshippers at the shrine of popularity. It is a fund of infinite amusement to lookers on, when they see, in this interchange of little minds,

how small matters can become great, and each
caprice of the popular fancy can be raised into a
topic of gravest deliberation. It were surely better that Christian people reserved their zeal for
essentials; and that Christian teachers, instead of
pampering the popular taste into utter childish-
ness, disciplined it, by a little wholesome resistance, into an appetite, at once manly, and rational, and commanding. Every thing that can
disarm the popular voice of its energy will be la-
mented by those who think as we do, that it is a
voice which, in the matters of Christianity, is
mainly directed to what is practically and substantially good; and that it is just the despite which
has been done to it that has so paralyzed the ministrations of our Establishment. And, therefore,
do we hold it so desirable that the popular taste
were chastened out of all those vagaries which
have just had the effect of chasing away the homage that else would have been rendered to it. We
know that it has its occasional weaknesses and extravagancies; but we believe that these are in no
way essential to it, and that, by the control of the
ministers of religion, acting wisely, and honestly,
and independently, they could all be done away.
Though these were lopped off from the affection,
it would still subsist, with undiminished vigour,
and it would then be seen what it nakedly and
characteristically is—not that mere fantastic relish
which it is often conceived to be, but the deep and
strong aspiration of conscious humanity, feeling,

and most intelligently feeling, what the truths, and who the teachers are, that are most fitted to exalt and to moralise her.

In proof of this we may, with all safety, allege that let there be a teacher of religion, with a conscience alive to duty, and an understanding soundly and strongly convinced of the truths of the gospel; let him, with these as his only recommendations, go forth among a people, alive at every pore to offence from the paltry conceits and crotchets in which they have drivelled and been indulged for several generations; let them be prepared with all the senseless exactions which a dark and narrow bigotry would often bring upon a minister; and let him, disdainful of absurdity in all its forms, whilst zealous and determined in acquitting himself of every cardinal obligation, only labour amongst them in the spirit of devotedness: and it will soon be seen that the general good will of a neighbourhood is far more deeply and solidly founded, than on the basis of such petty compliances as have made popularity ridiculous in the eye of many a superficial observer. The truth is, that there is not one irrational prejudice among his hearers, which such a teacher would not be at liberty to thwart and to traverse, till he had dislodged it altogether. Grant him the pure doctrine of the Bible for his pulpit, with an overflowing charity in his heart for household ministrations—and the simple exhibition of such worth and such affection on the week, from one who preaches the truths of Scripture on the Sabbath, will, without one ingredient of folly, gain for him, from the bosoms of all, just such a popularity as is ever awarded to moral worth and to moral wisdom. This, indeed, we believe to be the main staple of that popularity which is so much derided by the careless, and often so unfeelingly trampled upon by the holders of patronage. And thus it is fearful to think that, in the systematic opposition which has been raised upon this subject against the *vox populi*, government may, unknowing of the mischief, have been checking, all the while, the best aspiration that can arise from the bosom of a country—may have been combating, in its first elements, the growth of virtue in our land—and, in wanton variance with its own subjects about the principles of religion, may have been withering up all those graces of religion, which would else have blessed and beautified our population.

II. But this brings us to the second imputation that has been brought against the popular taste, in matters of Christianity—far graver than any that is uttered in the mere playfulness of contempt, and in virtue of which it has often been reckoned with, as a pernicious delusion that unsettles the morality of the people, as if, in its preference for doctrine, it loathed and neglected duty, and could only relish that ministration, which, instead of acting as a stimulus, acted as a soporific to human virtue. This we believe to be

a very prevailing conception among the enemies
of popular Christianity; and hence there are not
a few who may resist its inroads as conscientiously
as they would the inroads of any moral pestilence,
—regarding the character of the population as exposed to hazard from the currency of a favourite
and high-sounding mysticism, that made no account of ordinary practice, and left the conduct
of its disciples without restraint and without regulation. There is the imagination of a seducing An-
tinomianism, in the creed of the vulgar, that enters
into all this hostility against their opinion and their
will in matters of religion, and often gives the tone
of serious indignant principle to a distinct class of
antagonists from the former—who, more disposed
to fasten on the alleged follies of the popular taste,
regard it rather as a topic of light and airy ridicule, than as a topic of earnest, solemn, and em-
phatic denunciation.

Now what we affirm is, that the very peculiar
economy of the gospel, devised as it has been for
the recovery of a sinful race from a great aberra-
tion into which they have wandered, exposes its
most honest and intelligent disciples to precisely
these aspersions—and that, therefore, the mise-
steem in which the popular taste is held may be
due to a misunderstanding of this economy. The
gospel, in the first instance, proclaims so wide an
amnesty for transgression, that the most gross and
worthless offenders are included; and there is
none so far sunk in the depths and atrocities of

moral turpitude, but that still the overtures of redeeming mercy may be brought down, even to
his degraded level, and he be told of an open
gate and a welcome admittance to heaven's sanctuary. That blood of atonement which cleans-
eth from all sin is proclaimed of virtue enough to
cleanse him from his sin; and he, without any deduction whatever, on the score of his former ini-
quities, is not barely permitted, but entreated and
urged to enter, through a great propitiation, upon the firm ground of acceptance with God.

Now, it is not merely that such encouragement,
held forth in the gospel to the most profligate
of our species, has suggested the idea of an impunity held forth by it to moral evil. But what
serves still more, perhaps, to stir the imputation,
that it makes no account of moral distinctions
whatever, is, that it appears to reduce the purest
and most profligate to the same level of worthlessness before God, and, in pointing to the avenue
of reconciliation, addresses both of them in the
same terms. It looks as if, under this new system,
all the varieties of character were to be superseded; and it is, indeed, a very natural conclusion
from the doctrine of the efficiency of faith without works, that works are henceforth to be in no
demand and of no estimation. The man who is
deemed by society to have no personal righteousness whatever, is told to link all his hopes of acceptance with the righteousness of Christ; and
the man to whom society awards the homage of a

pure and virtuous character, is likewise told that
it is a fatal error to ground his security on any
righteousness of his own; but that he also must
place all his reliance before God on the righteousness of Christ.   This is very like, it has been
said, to the entire dismissal of the personal virtues from religion, and the substitution of a mere
intellectual dogma in their place.   It is certainly
a dogma, that glares upon us as the most promi-
nent feature of the popular or evangelical system;
and we ought not to wonder if, on a partial and
hurried contemplation, it should be apprehended
that, instead of amending the people, its direct
tendency is to vitiate and demoralise them.

For the purpose of arriving at truth in this
matter, it were well to reflect under what kind of
moral impression it is, that a believer, who hopes
for acceptance through the Mediator, renounces
all trust in his own righteousness.   They who
would malign his system, affirm it to be, that it
is because his moral sense is so far obliterated,
that the distinction between right and wrong has
become a nullity in his estimation; insomuch that
he looks on a man of double criminality to be no
further, on that account, than his neighbour, from
the friendship of God.   But might it not rather
be, because his moral sense is so far quickened
and enlightened, that the differences between the
better and the worse among men are lost in the
overwhelming impression that he has of the fearful deficiency of all? The man whose conceptions

have been enlarged upward to the high measure-
ments of astronomy, may know that though one
earthly object is nearer to the sun than another,
yet the distance of both is so great as to give
him the impression of a nearly equal remoteness
with each of them. And the man whose conscience has been informed upon heaven's law,
may know that though one of his fellows has, by
an act of theft, receded further than himself, who
never stole, yet that both are standing in their
common ungodliness at an exceeding wide distance of alienation from the spirit and character
of heaven. When one man's righteousness is
placed by the side of another, it would argue a
moral blindness, not to perceive the shade of difference that there is between them. When the
better righteousness of the two is placed by the
side of the Saviour's, it would argue a still more
grievous defect both of moral sight and moral
sensibility, not to perceive the contrast that
there is between the sacred effulgency of the one,
and the shaded earthly ambiguous character of
the other. And if, in the New Testament, the
alternative be actually placed within the reach of
all, of either being tried according to their own
righteousness, or of their being treated according
to the righteousness of Christ—it may not be from
a dull, but from a tender and enlightened sense of
moral distinctions, when one renounces the former,
and cleaves to the latter, as all his defence and
all his dependence.

It seems to be on this principle that the publi-
cans and the sinners, in the gospel, are stated to be
before the Pharisees, in coming to the kingdom of
heaven. The palpable delinquencies of the former
seem to have forced more readily upon their apprehension the need of another righteousness than
their own. The plausible accomplishments of the
latter served to blind their consciences against this
necessity. They were alive to the difference that
obtained between themselves and others. But,
they were not alive to the deficiency of their own
character from the requirements of God. And
it is thus, perhaps, that the doctrine of human
worthlessness still finds its readiest acceptance
among the lower orders of society. Their beset-
ting sins are of easier demonstration than either
the voluptuous or ungodly affections of the rich,
blended as they often are with so much honour,
and elegance, and sensibility. Still, it is not from
the dulness, but from the delicacy of the moral
sense, that it can penetrate its way, through all
these disguises, to the actual character of him who
is invested with them: and it is not because this
power of the human mind is steeped in lethargy,
but because it is of quick and vigorous discernment, that man renounces his own righteousness,
and betakes himself to the righteousness of faith.

And what is true of the acceptance of this righteousness on the part of man, is also true of the
proposal of it on the part of God. It is not because he under-rates morality, that he refuses the

morality of man as a plea of confidence before him—but, because sensitive of the slightest encroachment on a law, the authority of which he holds to be inviolable, he will not admit the approach of sinners, but in a way that recognizes the truth of the Lawgiver, and thoroughly reconciles it with the exercise of his mercy. Throughout the whole economy of the system of grace, there is not one expression which so thoroughly and so legibly pervades it, as the irreconcileable variance that there is between sin and the nature of the Godhead. It would almost look as if it were for the purpose of holding forth this expression, that the whole apparatus of redemption was instituted. Every circumstance that can give weight to such a solemn demonstration is made to accompany the overtures of forgiveness to man in the New Testament. It is not a simple assurance of pardon that is there exhibited, but of pardon linked with the atonement that has been rendered for iniquity. This, in truth, is the leading peculiarity of the gospel dispensation, that while mercy is addressed to all, it is addressed in such terms, and through such a line of conveyance, as to magnify ·all the other attributes of Deity. So that man cannot enter into peace but through the medium of such a contemplation as must obtrude upon his mind the entire and untainted purity of the divine nature. The avenue of reconciliation is inscribed on each side of it with the evil of sin, and with the sacred jealousy against it of a most high and holy God.

And, if it be God's intolerance of sin, and a high sense of the authority of his law, as inviolable—if it be these that modelled the gospel economy at the first—it were strange, indeed, should these principles fall out of sight, or be, in any way, traversed and given up, in the subsequent progress and application of the gospel among men. It were strange, indeed, if those principles which originated this system should be abandoned, or even so much as impaired in its forthgoings through the world—if the moral expression it bears so decisively, as it comes out of the hands of God, should be dissipated into nothing, when making its way through the hearts and the habitations of men—if that which so strongly marked, at its outset, God's abhorrence of sin, should, in any of its future developements, have the effect of encouraging sin—or, if a method of salvation so peculiarly devised, and that, for the express purpose of guarding and demonstrating the honours of virtue, should, after it is brought out to the notice, and has gained the concurrence of those for whom it was instituted, obliterate, in their minds, the distinction between right and wrong, or reduce virtue to a thing of no demand and no estimation.

The gospel, in the meantime, maintains a most entire consistency with itself. It unfolds that provision by which atonement has been made for the guilt of sin; but it never ceases announcing as its ulterior object, to exterminate the being of

z

sin from the heart and the practice of all its dis.
ciples. Its office is not merely to reconcile the
world, but to regenerate the world; and there is
not an honest believer, who rejoices in pardon,
and does not, at the same time, aspire after all
moral excellence; knowing, that to prosecute a
strenuous departure from all iniquity is his ex-
pressly assigned vocation, and that he who, from
Christ as a redeemer, has obtained deliverance
from the punishment of sin, must, under him as
a captain, hold an unsparing war with the power
and the existence of it.

Here, then, would appear to lie the misconception which we are endeavouring to combat.
The advocates of the evangelical system affirm
the nullity of human righteousness, when regarded
in the light of its founding any claim to reward
from the great Moral Governor of our species.
And this affirmation of theirs hangs upon the
principle, that by admitting the validity of such
a claim, the character of heaven's jurisprudence
would be degraded beneath that standard of high,
inflexible, and uncompromising purity, from which
God will not consent that it shall be brought
down, in accommodation to human frailty and human sinfulness. But the same August Being, who
is thus prompted by the holy jealousies of his nature to lay an interdict on the claims of sinfulness,
must, on the very same prompting, be equally
bent on the utter extirpation of it from the character of all whom he takes into reconciliation.

If the presumption of sin be hateful in his sight, the existence of sin must be hateful to him also. He who, of purer eyes than to look upon sin, can have no tolerance for its claims, can have as little tolerance for its wilful continuance in the sinner's bosom. The entire nullity of human righteousness viewed as a plea for reward from a God of such surpassing holiness, so far from being at variance is altogether of a piece with the entire necessity of this righteousness, viewed as a personal accomplishment for the kindred society of One whose character is so lofty. There is no inconsistency whatever, but the directly opposite, in that the obedience of man should be inadmissible as his personal claim to heaven, and yet indispensable as his personal qualification for it. And thus it is that while, in the doctrine of justification by faith alone, the virtue of a human being is not admitted as an ingredient at all into that title-deed which conveys to him his right of entry into paradise, it is this virtue and nothing else, which making constant progress in time, and reaching its consummate perfection in eternity, that renders him fit for the blessedness, and the employments, and the whole companionship of paradise.

And perhaps the most plain and direct vindication of the evangelical system, as being altogether on the side of morality, is that morality forms the very atmosphere both of the happiness which it offers here, and of the heaven to which it points hereafter. In the service of an earthly superior, the reward is distinct from the work that is done for it. In the service of God, the main reward lies in the very pleasure of the service itself. The work and the wages are the same. It is not *after* the keeping of the commandments, but *in* the keeping of the commandments, that there is a great reward.* Even from the little that is made known to us of the upper paradise, it is evident that its essential blessedness lies not in its splendour, and not in its melody, and not in the ravishment of any sensible delights or glories— but simply in the possession and play of a moral nature, in unison with all that is right, and in the rejoicing contemplation of that Being from whose countenance there beams and is imprest upon all the individuals of his surrounding family the moral excellence which belongs to him.† The gate of reconciliation, through the blood of Christ, is not merely the gate of escape from a region of wrath—it is the gate of introduction to a field of progressive and aspiring virtue; and it is the growth of this virtue upon earth which constitutes its full and its finished beatitude. The land to which every honest believer is bending his foot-steps is a land of uprightness,‡ where the happiness simply consists in a well attempered soul rescued from the tyranny of evil, and restored to the proper balance of principles and affections

---

* Psalm xix. 11.   † 1 John iii. 1, 2, 3.   ‡ Psalm cxlvii. 9, 10.

which had gone into derangement. It is the happiness of a moral being doing what he ought, and living as he ought. It were a contradiction in terms, to aver of such a system that it is unfavourable to the interests of virtue. The doctrine of justification by faith is not the absorbent of all human activity, but the primary stimulant of that busy and prosperous career, in which the soul, emancipated alike from fear and earthly affection, rejoices in the acquirement of a kindred character to God, and finds the work of obedience to be its congenial and best loved employments. This is the real process of effort and mental discipline that is undergone by every honest believer, though hidden from the general eye under the guise of a phraseology that is derided and unknown by the world. He is diligent that he may be found without spot and blameless, on the great day of examination. It is the business of his whole life to perfect holiness in the fear of God.

And for effecting this moral transformation on the character of its disciples, does this system of truth provide the most abundant guarantees. It holds forth the most express announcement that, without such a transformation, there will be no admittance into the kingdom of God. And it reveals an influence for achieving it, which is ever in readiness to descend on the prayers of those who aspire after the habits and the affections of righteousness. And, along with the call of faith, does it lift the contemporaneous call of repentance. And it marks out a path of obedience, by the urgency and the guidance of precepts innumerable. And, so far from lulling into inaction, by its free offer of forgiveness, does it only thereby release its disciples from the inactivity of paralysing terror, and furnish them with the most generous excitements to the service of God, in the love, and the gratitude, and the joy of their confident reconciliation. And, finally, as if to shut out all possibility of escape from the toils and the employments of virtue, does it make known a day of judgment, wherein man will be reckoned with, not for his dogmata, but for his doings; and when there will be no other estimate of his principles than the impulse which they gave to his practical history in the world—they who have done good being called forth to the resurrection of the just, and they who have done evil unto the resurrection of damnation.

Now, all this truth has full recognition and occupancy among the articles of the evangelical creed; and the doctrine of justification by faith alone, so far from laying any arrest on the practical influence of it, is felt by every genuine believer to give all its spirit and all its scope to the new obedience of the gospel. Without this doctrine, in fact, there can be no agreement between God and man, but by a degrading compromise between the purity of the one and the imperfection of the other; and the point at which this compromise should be struck is left undetermined, and at the discretion of each individual, who will, of course, accommodate the matter to the standard of his own performances; and thus, under all the varieties of moral turpitude, as well as of moral accomplishment, will there be a fatal tranquillity of conscience, in a world where each may live as he lists; and heaven's law, once brought down to suit the convenience of our fallen nature, may at length offer no disturbance to any degree either of ungodliness or unrighteousness in our species. But, with the doctrine of justifica_ tion by faith there is no such compromise. The rewards of the divine government are still granted in consideration of a righteousness that is altogether worthy of them. The claims of the Godhead. to the perfect reverence, as well as the perfect love, of his creatures, are kept unbroken; and when he proclaims his will to be our sanctification, the disciple, as he feels himself released from the vengeance of an unbending law, also feels himself to be placed in a career of exertion that is quite indefinite; where he will stop short at no degree of moral excellence—where he can be satisfied with no assignable fulfilment whatever—where his whole desire and delight, in fact, will lie in progress, and he will never cease aspiring and pressing forward, till he has reached his prize, and stands upon the summit of perfection.

It is only under the impulse of such principles as these, that the mighty host of a country's population can be trained either to the virtues of society, or to the virtues of the sanctuary. The former may, to a certain extent, flourish of themselves, among the children of this world's prosperity. But, saving in conjunction with, and as emanating from the latter, they never can be upheld amid the workshops and the habitations of industry. It is a frequent delusion, that the evangelical system bears no regard to the social virtues, because, in the mind of an evangelical Christian, they are of no religious estimation whatever, but as they stand connected with the authority of God. But he cannot miss to observe that the sanctions of this authority are brought, in every page of the Bible, most directly and abundantly to bear upon them; and thus, in his eyes, do they instantly reappear, strengthened by all the obligations, and invested with a full character of deepest sacredness. The integrity of such a creed as he professes is the best guarantee for the integrity of his relative and social conduct. And it is only in proportion to the prevalence of this derided orthodoxy, that the honesties and sobrieties of life will spread in healthful diffusion over the face of the country. That system of doctrine which is stigmatized as methodism; and against which government are led to array the whole force of their overwhelming patronage; and on the approaches of which ecclesiastics are often seen to combine as they would against the inroads of some pestilential visitor; and which, when it does appear within

the well-smoothed garden of the Establishment,
is viewed as a loathsome weed that should be cast
out and left to luxuriate in its rankness, among the
wilds and the commons of Sectarianism;—what a
quantity of undesigned outrage must be inflicted
every year on the best objects both of principle
and patriotism, should this, indeed, be the alone
system that has the truth of heaven impressed
upon it, and the alone system that can transform
and moralise the families of our land!

If, then, evangelical Christianity be popular
Christianity—if its lessons are ever sure to have the
most attractive influence upon the multitude—if,
whatever the explanation of the fact may be, the
fact itself is undeniable, that the doctrine of our
first Reformers, consisting mainly of justification
by faith, and sanctification through the Spirit of
God, is the doctrine which draws the most crowded audiences around our pulpits, and this doctrine
is, at the same time, the most powerful moralising
agent that can be brought to bear upon them—
then does it follow that the voice of the people
indicates most clearly, in this matter, what is best
for the virtue of the people—that the popular
taste is the organ by which conscious humanity
expresses what that is which is best fitted both to
exalt and to console her—and that, by the neglect and the defiance which are so wantonly rendered to its intimations, are our statesmen withholding the best aliment of a people's worth, and
therefore the best specific for a nation's welfare.

III. But we now proceed to the third great prejudice which requires to be combated. In the mind of many of our politicians there is a conceived alliance between the fervour of the popular demand for that religion which is most palateable, and the fervour of the popular demand for those rights which form the great topic of disaffection and complaint among the restless spirits of our community. It is quite enough to decide their impressions upon this subject, that the voice which they hear in favour of a certain style of Christianity, is the voice of a great assemblage, made up chiefly of the vulgar; and that when it reaches them, it is in the shape of a cry or a challenge from the multitude. This will instantly remind them of the vociferation and the menace that arise from the factious on a political arena, and they will feel inclined to deal with it accordingly. Let there be but the sympathy of the same impassioned feeling among a number of people, and, whatever be the topics of it, this is quite enough to conjure up to the apprehensions of many a distant observer the imagery of riot, and resistance, and the sturdiness of dissatisfied plebeianism. When Bishop Horsley said in Parliament, that the popular zeal which had gone so extensively abroad, in behalf of missionary objects, was but another expression of the revolutionary spirit, or a new direction which it had now taken, after the overthrow of its clubs and associations, we doubt not he said what he honestly believed to be the truth. A bare inventory of names, however, had he actually taken it, might have convinced him that the missionary cause was altogether another enterprise, supported by another set of individuals, and animated, too, with a spirit which would not only have lent no re-inforcement to the turbulence that he dreaded, but if fostered through the country to the uttermost, would most effectually have neutralised it. To be blind on a matter like this, is to be in blindness, if not of the first, at least of among the most important elements of political wisdom. Nor can we conceive how a government may be misled more grievously, than when the character and views of a great and growing body of their own subjects are thus misapprehended.

But there are other causes for the delusion that we are now attempting to expose; and, perhaps, the most powerful of them is, that insignificance in which a spiritual and devoted adherent of the evangelical system will generally hold all the common objects of partizanship. He cannot, with a heart pre-occupied by eternal things, let himself down to a keen interest in the rivalry of this world's politics. Like a man intent on the prosecution of a journey, and with a mind absorbed by the objects of it, he cannot mingle any great earnestness or intensity of feeling with the disputes of his fellow travellers; and especially if they relate to matters connected with the mere comfort and accommodation of the few days in which they are to keep together. He is otherwise taken up, and he finds no room in his bosom for the eager and busy emulations of a combatant upon an arena, where he is comparatively so little affected by all that is going on. The ruling party of the State can see no use for such an individual, and can place but a small reliance upon him; and what will confirm their whole sense of hopelessness about his services is, that, as indifferent to the rewards as he is to many of the aims and objects of political adherence, he appears to stand beyond the possibility of being purchased by them. As contrasted with the man whom they can at all times count upon, he will, indeed, be felt as of little or no estimation for any of their purposes. And thus it is fearful to contemplate, by how direct and natural a process the whole of the Church patronage that is vested in the hands of Government may be employed in rearing a careless and worldly priesthood all over the land—how the men who sit loose to time are the surest to be overlooked and neglected in the dispensation of benefices; and those who, by the very zeal and indiscriminateness of their party attachment, betray the earthliness of the element they breathe in, may, on that single account, be raised to those places of highest ascendency, from which the weightiest and most abundant influence could be made to descend on the character of the population.

And here we may remark how readily the want

of a very devoted regard to the special interests of a reigning and existing Administration may be confounded with the want of loyalty. They who honour not the king's immediate servants lie open to the imputation that they bear no great honour to the king himself. Thus it is that the man who simply feels himself in a state of unconcern about the stability of a present Administration, may come to be likened to those radically disloyal, who vent forth asperity and menace against all Administrations. It is surely possible to link the utmost reverence with the solid and abiding pillars of the Constitution, and, at the same time, to feel but small interest in the changes of that more shifting and moveable part of its apparatus which is termed the Cabinet. But neither is this enough for the full vindication of those who cannot embark their zeal in the affairs and the contests of partizanship. Now, this a man whose zeal is all pre-engaged on higher objects cannot do. And, accordingly, in this part of our kingdom, at least, there does exist a very general imagination, among the upper classes, that, with the more serious and spiritual clergy of our Establishment, there is a sort of hollowness of principle, in reference to the Government of the land —a certain suspicious cast of democracy about them; and altogether an ambiguity of political sentiment, on which no dependence could be laid, in the crisis of national danger—in the dark and turbid hour of a people's violence.

And the man who cannot bring himself to take a keen concern in the affairs of partizanship, will fare no better with the resisting than he does with the ruling party of the State. It is altogether of a piece with the general habitude of his feelings, that as he does not much care, on any ground of interest, at least, whether those who are in place shall retain it, so he does not much care whether those who are out of place shall succeed in acquiring it. In this apparent contest, indeed, between place and patriotism, he can see no more of the ravenous in the firm hold of the one party upon that which they have, than in the eager grasping of the other after that which they have not; and so, if in Parliament, he will sit and vote like a conscientious juryman on the specific merits of every question that comes before him. We believe that, acting on the guidance of such a principle as this, he will, under every successive change of the Cabinet, vote generally with Ministers, and occasionally against them. It is so much more the interest of every Administration to be right than wrong, that it were strange, indeed, if they blundered the matter so systematically as to be wrong in any thing like a majority of instances. And, hence, this man of simplicity, who sits loose to the profit, and is only alive to the principle, of our domestic politics, while, by his incidental deviations from Ministry, he forfeits all confidence as a stedfast and thorough-going adherent of theirs, will, by his more habitual dissent from the measures of Opposition, call down from the other party, a far severer weight of reprobation.

And, indeed, it may be seen of every such individual, that, while only perhaps slighted or the object of playfulness to the former party, he is often, to the latter, the object of a keen and impassioned virulence. The very circumstance of their exclusion from office holds them forth to the public eye as the martyrs of political integrity,—and it is beyond all endurance, when the voice of censure descends upon them from one who stands so evidently posted on a ground of independence still higher than their own. This they could bear from the servile adherents of Ministry; but when it comes down upon them from the eminence of accredited honesty and of worth unimpeachable, it is unsufferably galling. They know that the main ingredient of their popularity is the imagination of their disinterestedness; and it is not to be forgiven, that one who neither cares that he is out, nor wishes to be in, should, ever and anon, from the platform of a disinterestedness far more unquestionable than theirs, be blasting this imagination, and so neutralising the very charm in which their great strength lies. To stand in the ranks of Opposition is like standing in the ranks of a sturdy and self-denying patriotism; and when thwarted at every turn by one more pure and obviously more patriotic than them all, nothing can more cruelly disarm of all its force an exhibition so imposing, and so fitted to maintain a party

in public confidence and estimation. This may
serve to explain the angry intolerance of the minority in Parliament against every man in it of true
independence, and also why it is upon such that
the anti-ministerial press is sure to lavish the whole
strength and bitterness of its acrimony.

And here, for the purpose of marking still more
specifically the men whom we are attempting to
describe, let them be brought into comparison
with another set of men, who, in some of their
features, may be thought to resemble them.
Among the political characters of our age, there
are certain mal-contents who are altogether unap-
peasable; and who speak despairingly alike, and
contemptuously alike, of both the great parties in
the State; and who, if not yet seated within the
territory of Radicalism, are at least standing on
the very borders of it; and with whom the passions
of the multitude are the favourite weapons which
they employ, as instruments of annoyance against
all the existing authorities of the land. They
are like the others in this, that they cohere not
either with the one side or the other of that great
regular partizanship which obtains in our legislative bodies; and yet how diametrically opposite
are they, in the whole spirit, and principles, and
temper, of their public conduct. Loud, and in-
flammatory, and seizing, with most congenial ea-
gerness, upon every topic of fermentation, the
only element they can breathe in with comfort is
that of uproar and discordancy; and whether they

meditate in earnest an overthrow of government or not, there is no spectacle which they more evidently enjoy, than when they see the fabric urged and played upon by the undulations of popular violence. Such a furious denouncer of both the parties in the State as one of these, stands contrasted, in almost all his lineaments, with him who is the hireling or the devotee of neither; but whose calm, reflecting, independence is altogether in the spirit of that wisdom which is pure, and peaceable, and gentle, and full of mercy and good fruits, without partiality and without hypocrisy. And if any thing be wanting to establish the total diversity of principle that there is between the two sorts of independence, we have only to observe the aspect which the champion of radicalism bears to the champion of Christian consistency in Parliament, and gather, from his invective and his scorn, its most satisfying illustration.

But after all, it may be asked, of what possible use are such men of simplicity and godly sincerity in Parliament?—men, of whom you are never sure on what side to find them, and whose whole line of proceeding is a constant mockery on the expectations of party. And, were there no higher principle in politics than those which characterise and mark off the distinctions of party, the question were altogether called for. But there are higher principles. The cause of order and general government is a higher cause than the cause of any Administration; and often, in periods of turbu-

lence and national distress this cause is endanger-
ed; and it is not the suspected testimony of the
partizan, but the testimony of the patriot, that is
of any power to still the commotion. It is not
the man of thorough-paced devotion to his party,
under all the fluctuation of its principles; but the
man of stedfast devotion to principle, under all
the fluctuations of party—it is he, and he alone,
who can lift a voice of authority that will be listened to, amid that deafening noise which, at
times, is heard to rise, in one appalling outcry of
menace and discontent, from all quarters of the
land. He sits loose to both parties, but, in such a
crisis as this, he stands at the distance of the anti-
podes from him who reviles both parties; and
while the one does what he may to thicken the
disorder, does the other rally, at the simple lifting
up of his voice, all the right-hearted men of the
nation around the standard of loyalty. Were this
his solitary service, it were enough to stamp upon
him a character of far higher value than any unvarying adherent either of Ministry or Opposition
can lay claim to. But the truth is, that his presence in the Legislature is of daily and perpetual
benefit. He bears with him, at all times, an unseen force of control over the motions of Government; and each of the parties, though they may
be ashamed to acknowledge it, are yielding him a
constant homage, and rendering to his principles
and views a constant accommodation. The man
who is ever to be found on a higher walk of con-

sistency than the consistency of mere partizanship, cannot be disregarded with impunity. There is both a moral compulsion in the worth of his own character; and a still more palpable compulsion in the weight of his opinions, over the best and most wholesome part of the community. It is thus that he obtains an unknown ascendency in Parliament, not visible, in nearly its full extent, to the public eye; but most distinctly and powerfully felt in all those modifying processes under which every bill is shaped and prepared, ere it is brought ostensibly forward. If parties be indispensable to the business of a large deliberative assembly, if the machinery will not work without them, if there be no going on, unless a certain number of hands on each side of the vessel keep stedfastly by the tackling at which they are respectively stationed—let the many be enlisted into this needful service, if needful it really be; but let us never want the men of purer and loftier character, who bring thought, and conscience, and moral principle, into contact with each specific movement of this great national engine,—who make the freshness and simplicity of their own individual worth to bear on all its operations—and who, taking no part in the game of competition between the two parties, but often derided as anomalous by them both, are, nevertheless, of mighty influence in staying both the corrupt encroachments of the one, and the factious extravagance of the other.

It may now be perceived what a pure (which

we have already endeavoured to prove is mainly synonymous with a popular) exercise of Church patronage will do for the political well-being of a country. It would, generally speaking, fill the Establishment with clergy who, detached from the world, on that account sat loose to partizanship; but who, thoroughly imbued with the spirit of the Bible, on that account were the staunch and honest devotees of general patriotism. To them no one Administration could look for effective aid against their rivals in the contest of power. But on them every Administration would have reason to count for the most effective aid, in the contest of disaffection and disloyalty against the regular authorities of the land. The minister who had earned the confidence of his people, by urging the faithful exposition of all Scripture upon them, stands on a high and secure vantage ground, when, out of that indelible record, he bids them honour the king, and obey magistrates, and meddle not with those who are given to change, and lead a quiet and a peaceable life, in all godliness and honesty. These accents would fall utterly powerless from the lips of one who, on an arena of partizanship, had manifested the heat or the worldliness of a mere political clergyman. But they would carry another influence along with them, when recognised as the effusions of the same honest principle which took the whole round of Scripture, and brought forth of its treasury all the truths and lessons that are to be found in it.

It may thus be seen, how possible it is, by one style of ecclesiastical patronage, to sacrifice the permanent tranquillity of the kingdom to the ephemeral views of an existing Administration; while, by another style of it, a secure and everlasting barrier may be raised against all the surges of insurrectionary violence. A church filled with the zealous friends and retainers of one leading political interest can have no authority over a population whom the very character of its priesthood has alienated from its services. A church teeming with zealous, and holy, and well-principled evangelists, that has drawn largely of its hearers from the multitude, and won largely on their veneration and regard—such a church, without one offering at the shrine of any party whatever, but mixing her lessons of loyalty with all the other lessons of the Christian law, will be found, in the fiercest day of a nation's trial, to be its best and surest palladium.

But the partizanship of clergymen is just as hurtful, on the one side of politics, as the other. The spirit of their office should raise them above this arena altogether, and lead them to refrain from taking any share in the contest at all. We believe that the fancied alliance between the party of Whiggism in the State, and the Evangelical party in the Church, has tended, in Scotland, to the discouragement and depression of the best of causes. It has helped to direct the whole power and patronage of government against the more acceptable clergy of our land, and so multiplied the topics of heartburning and irritation between the people and their rulers. A few political clergy standing prominently forth, on either side of the church, will suffice to fasten a political imputation on the whole body that is represented by them—and it is ever to be regretted, either that Government should thus have been blinded into the indiscriminate opposition of all that would make most for the Christian worth and eventual loyalty of the population; or that the zealots of Ministry should have been betrayed into the imagination that they were fighting the battles of order, when, mistaking sound faith for tumultuous fanaticism, they were ever thwarting those ecclesiastical measures which were best fitted to harmonise as well as morally to elevate the lower orders of the country. A priesthood strictly devoted to their own professional objects, and keeping aloof from the contest of this world's politics, and neither servile in their loyalty, nor boisterous in their independence, and ardently prosecuting the literature of their order, or the labour of love in their parishes—the intent and engrossing aim of such a priesthood is to rear a generation for eternity. But still the blessings which they would scatter along the path of time are also incalculable. The promise of the life that now is, as well as of the life that is to come, is attendant upon all their exertions. And it is deeply, indeed, to be regretted, that the voice of party should have so marred and transformed

the whole of this contemplation, as to have alienated the Government of the land from the alone
instrument that can be at all effectual in forming either a moral or a manageable population.

CHAP. VI.

ON CHURCH PATRONAGE, CONTINUED.

WE are not aware that law has provided any limitation whatever to the right of patronage in the English Church, which, for ought we know, may be exercised in a way altogether absolute and uncontrolled, and without any power of counteraction or restraint vested in the people. So that, however obnoxious a presentee to a living may be, in the parish that has been assigned to him, he, by holding a deed of presentation, holds a title to the benefice which cannot be wrested from him by any earthly power. The concurrence of the Bishop of the diocese is, perhaps, indispensable to the completion of this right; and if he be not responsible to any power out of the Church for the principles upon which he either grants or refuses this concurrence, we can see that, however little it may have been exercised of late, there virtually lies a veto among ecclesiastics on every nomination to an ecclesiastical office. Still, however, should there be the same regardlessness of the popular taste among the dignitaries of the Church, that we fear there still is among the great majority of the holders of patronage, the practical security would appear as feeble as is the legal one, against the likings of the multitude on the subject

of Christianity being, in the greater number of instances, thwarted and overborne.

In these circumstances, the most direct method
for restoring the Establishment to efficiency and
acceptance among the people, is to conciliate the
regard both of the patrons and of the dignitaries
to the evangelical system, which is the only one
that can attract the multitude, because the only
one, the application of which to their condition, or
their conscience, is at all felt by them. This,
however, is not the work of a day; and whether
we look to the High Church intolerance that so
evidently scowls from the Episcopal bench, or to
the jealousy of all popular interference with the
right of Church nomination that has recently been
evinced in the Legislature of these kingdoms, we
must still reckon ourselves at a fearful distance
from a right adjustment between patronage, on
the one hand, and popularity, on the other. This
distance, however, we conceive to be lessening.
A more just estimation of popular Christianity is
now making ground in the walks of property and
political influence; and a more respectful deference to the popular voice will be sure to follow in
its train. It ought now to be well understood
among them, that the moral reprobacy of the
lower orders, as well as their political restlessness
and discontent, emanate from popular infidelity,
and not from that which has been ignorantly and
injuriously aspersed as popular fanaticism. When
the whole truth becomes evident to them, it will

2 c

then be perceived, that by the latter of these two
elements alone will the former ever be neutralised.
It is not by a haughty defiance to the taste or the
tendencies of the multitude; or by declamatory
charges against sectarianism; or by a remote and
lofty attitude of withdrawment, on the part of her
superior ecclesiastics, from all those Christian institutions which are at once the ornament and the
blessing of our country; or by the strict and jea-
lous guardianship of bishops, in alarm for the im-
portation of an enthusiastic spirit into their dio-
ceses: it is not thus that the Church of England
ever will acquire a religious and rightful ascendency over its population. Under such a process
her arm will wither into powerlessness; and an
instrument, else of greater might and efficacy than
dissenterism, with the putting forth of all her energies, can ever hope to attain to—will lose its
whole force of moral and salutary control over the
character of the nation. The alienation of the
people will widen every year from the bosom of
the Establishment—and the Establishment, reft of
all spiritual virtue, will at length be reduced to a
splendid impotency of noble edifices, and high
gifted endowments, and stately imposing ceremo-
nial. We plead not for the overthrow of this magnificent framework; for, if animated with the
breath of another spirit, as it stands, we conceive
it fitted to wield a far more commanding influence on the side of Christianity than were likely to
come from the ashes of its conflagration. But ne-

ver will it recover this influence, till the spirit of the olden time be recalled—never, till what is now dreaded by the majority of that Church as fanaticism come again to be recognized and cherished as the sound faith of the gospel—never, till what they now nauseate as methodism be felt as the alone instrument that can either moralise the people in time, or make them meet for eternity.

Our reason for affirming a jealousy of the popular voice in the appointment of clergy, on the part of the British Legislature, is founded on an examination of their recent Act for building, and promoting the building, of additional churches, in populous parishes. Though the Parliamentary grant for this object is so small that, for a great national effort, it must be extensively aided by the voluntary subscriptions of the people, yet the will of the people is admitted to no authority in the nomination of the minister. Their contributions are looked for, without any such equivalent, either in whole or in part, being provided to encourage them. When the erection is a chapel for an ecclesiastical district, the patronage is vested either in the incumbent of the parish, or the chapel is to be patronised in such a way as may be agreed upon by the patrons of the parish where it is situated, in conjunction with the commissioners for carrying the act into execution. When the erection is a new parish church, then its patronage is vested in the patron of the original parish from which it is detached. In other words, patronage is to have as great an ascendency, and the popular will to be of as little legal force in counteracting it, with the new churches, as with the present ones; and so sensitive is the aversion to any limitation upon the former element, by the encroachment of the latter, that when a clause was proposed in the House of Commons, for vesting the patronage of new churches or chapels in the twelve highest subscribers, where the edifices were raised wholly by subscription, this clause, though supported by the whole evangelical interest in Parliament, and advocated by the chiefs of Administration, called forth a prompt and overbearing majority, who instantly put it down.

Now this is certainly not the way to promote the building of new churches; neither is it the way to secure an attendance upon them, after they are built. And the only hopeful circumstance in the whole of this national provision is, that the stipend of the minister is paid out of the pew-rents which are raised from the hearers. This will compel an accommodation to the popular taste at least in the first instance. But we cannot fail to remark how utterly helpless every speculation of our Legislature is, about the revival and the growth of public virtue in our land, when thus impeded by their own groundless alarms; and by their utter misconception of what that instrument is, by which people can be drawn to an attendance on the lessons of Christianity, or of what that Christianity is which emanated pure from the mouth of revelation, and which,

by its adaptation to human want and human consciousness, is sure to meet with a responding
movement from the multitude, whenever it is addressed to them.

There is one evil that has ensued upon this
movement of the Legislature. It has tended to
fill and to satisfy the public imagination, and thus
laid an arrest upon the zeal of private adventurers, who are friendly alike to the cause of the
Establishment and to the cause of Christian education. Previous to the passing of this Act, Mr.
Gladstone of Liverpool erected two new churches
in that town, after having negotiated for himself, not the permanent right of patronage, for
this could not be obtained, but the three first nominations of a minister to each of them. There
was, in this instance, every security for a popular
exercise of the right of patronage. The zeal which
prompted the undertaking was, in itself, a guarantee for the appointment of acceptable and effective clergymen. And, besides, as the seat-
rents were to form the revenue both for the stipend of the minister, and for the repair and upholding of the fabrics, there was all the power of
a veto conceded, by the arrangement itself, to the
popular voice. It is gratifying to know that this
patriotic and enlightened gentleman, after having
so materially strengthened the interests of the
Establishment, and added to it two flourishing
congregations, in that great commercial town,
where his philanthropy and public spirit have so

much distinguished him, has just been indemnified for the expenses of his most benevolent speculation, by its actual returns. This is a most important fact, in as far as it indicates a safe and likely career for the multiplication of religious edifices in our most populous and unprovided cities. And would magistrates or patrons, on the one hand, concede a liberal allowance of patronage to subscribers, we doubt not that wealthy individuals, on the other, both ready to hazard and even willing to lose in a good cause, would, in imitation of this fine example, come forth in sufficient strength, to second the designs and greatly to outrun the power of Government, in forwarding an enterprise so closely allied with the very highest objects after which either statesman or philanthropist can aspire.

And here it occurs to us to say, that had Mr. Gladstone obtained the perpetual patronage of his two churches, in return for having erected and endowed them, the right would have descended, by inheritance, to his family, and, like any other property, been transferable by sale. The right would have originated most legitimately, and been transmitted most legitimately; and long, perhaps, after the purely Christian object which it subserved at first had passed out of remembrance, would it be assimilated, in its character and in its exercise, to any other private right of church patronage in the country. We know not in how far the actual patronage in our land has taken its origin and its descent from the liberality of pious and benevolent founders; or been rendered to great proprietors, as an equivalent for the burden of church expenses which was laid upon them. But when we think for what essential purposes this right may be acquired, and how fairly it may be appropriated and handed down in families, from one generation to another, we are led to look to its guidance and not to its overthrow, for any great Christian reformation of the churches in our land. The holders of this important right will, at length, participate in the growing spirit and illumination of the age; and while others regard patronage as the great instrument of the corruption and decline of Christianity, we trust that, under the impulse of better principles, it will, at length, become the instrument of its revival.

It is not to any violent demolition in the existing framework of society, that we look for the impulse which is to regenerate our nation. The actual constitution, whether of Church or State, is a piece of goodly and effective mechanism, were the living agents who work it animated with the right zeal and the right principle. And sorry should we be, in particular, were a rashly innovating hand laid upon the venerable Hierarchy of England. Even the affluence of its higher dignitaries, so obnoxious to the taste of some, could be made subservient to the best of causes; and through it, the principle of deference to station, which, in spite of all his assumed sturdiness, every man feels to be insuperable within him, may be enlisted on the side of Christianity. We envy not that dissenter his feelings, who would not bless God and rejoice, in the progress of an apostolical Bishop through his diocese. But it is not from this quarter, at present, that the glance of disapprobation and disdain is made to fall upon him. It is from his own brethren, we fear, on the episcopal bench, who if, instead of lifting upon him the frown of a hostile countenance, were to go and do likewise, would throne their Establishment in the affections of the whole population, and, by the resistless moral force which lies in the union of humble worth and exalted condition, would cause both the radicalism and infidelity of our land to hide their faces, as ashamed. Wherever the good Bishop of Gloucester assumes, for a day, the office of humble pastor, in one of the humblest of his parishes, he leaves an unction of blessedness behind him; and the amount of precious fruit that springs from such an itinerancy of love and evangelical labour is beyond all computation. Such a mingling with the people as this would not confound ranks, but most firmly harmonise them. It would sanctify and strengthen all the bonds of society. And it is wretched to think not merely of sound principle being thrown aside, but of sound policy being so glaringly traversed by the derision and the discouragement which are laid on all the activities of religious zeal—or, that they who preside over the destinies of the English Church, as

well as they who patronise her, should have been
misled into the imagination that her security lies
in her stillness—and that, should the warmth of
restless sectarianism be, in any semblance or measure, imported into her bosom, it will burn up and
destroy her.

In Scotland, too, there is a law of patronage
now firmly established, and now almost entirely
acquiesced in; and there are few belonging to our
Church, who ever think of disputing the right of
the patron to the nomination. But there seems
to be a great diversity of understanding about the
line which separates his right from the right of the
Church. He can nominate; but it would startle
the great majority of our clergy, were they told,
that the Church can, on any principle which seem-
eth to her good, arrest the nominee. The Church
can, on any ground she chooses, lay a negative
on any man whom the patron chooses to fix upon.
It is her part, and in practice she has ever done
so, to sit in judgment over every individual nomination. There are a thousand ways, in which
a patron might, through the individual whom he
nominates, throw corruption into the bosom of
our Establishment; and we would give up our best
securities, we would reduce our office as constitutional guardians of the Church, to a degrading
mockery, were we to act as if there was nothing
for it, but to look helplessly on, and to lament that
there was no remedy. The remedy is most com-

pletely within ourselves. We can take a look at the presentee; and if there be any thing whatever, whether in his talents, or in his character, or in his other engagements, or in that moral barrier which the general dislike of a parish would raise against his usefulness, and so render him unfit, in our judgment, for labouring in that portion of the vineyard, we can set aside the nomination, and call on the patron to look out for another presentee. It is the patron who ushers the presentee into our notice; but the fitness of the person for the parish is a question which lies solely and supremely at the decision of the ecclesiastical courts.

For the purpose of limiting the Church in the exercise of this right, it has been contended that her judgment on the fitness of the presentee is restricted to the mere question of his moral and literary qualifications. But she has often taken a far wider range of cognizance than this, and there is nothing to prevent her from widening that range to any extent she will. Previous to the enactment of that law which, with all the formalities, has recently been established, and by which a Professor in a university is declared incapable of holding a country parish, there was the case of a Professor, who had received a presentation to such a parish, brought up for the decision of the General Assembly. It is true that, by a majority of five, he was found a competent person for the charge; but, had three of these five voted differently, the holder of the presentation would have given it up as a lost cause; nor would it ever have entered into the conception of the patron that any thing remained for him but to issue a new presentation in behalf of some other individual. The incompetency of the presentee would thus have been declared, and on a ground altogether different from that of moral or literary qualification. The truth is, that the Church is not at all limited to particular grounds. She is at liberty to decide on any principle she may; and, instead of departing from her character, will, in fact, dignify and adorn it, by admitting every principle connected with the religious good of the people into her deliberations. She can set aside any presentee, and that generally on the principle that it is not for the cause of edification that his presentation should be sustained. More particularly she has often, in the course of her bygone history, judged it inexpedient to settle a presentee, in the face of violent dislike and opposition from the people; and, on this principle, alone, has laid her veto upon his presentation, without any reference to the moral or literary qualifications of the holder of it.

There is, with many, a confusion of principle upon this subject, that has been a good deal aggravated by a case which occurred twice in the history of the Church, in which, after that the General Assembly had set aside a presentee nominated by one claimant to the patronage, and authorised the settlement of one who was nominated by another, the former was found entitled, by the civil court, to retain the fruits of the benefice. But this decision of the civil court, it must be remarked, was founded solely and exclusively on the legal right of the claimants to the patronage. The minister who was actually inducted was deprived of the stipend attached to his office, but just because his presentation was found to be invalid. It is no exception whatever to the principle which we have just affirmed, that a case can be quoted of a clergyman not having a right to the emoluments of his charge, who had the authority of the Church for his settlement, but had not, at the same time, a good presentation. The only case, in point, against it would be that of a clergyman having a good presentation, and, at the same time, not having the authority of the Church for his settlement, and enjoying, nevertheless, the fruits of the benefice. And if no such case can be alleged, saving, perhaps, in days of persecution and violence, it would appear that the authority of the Church, not responsible certainly for her decisions to any power existing without the limits of her ecclesiastical jurisdiction, is just as indispensable to the valid settlement of a minister, as is a deed of presentation.

The truth is, that there are two essential circumstances which must meet together, ere a preacher can be ordained to the charge of a parish. He must have a presentation from the legal holder of the patronage; and he must have the concurrence of the Presbytery to which the parish belongs, or of its superior church judicatories. As the matter actually stands, the first circumstance is indispensable; nor can we proceed to ordain a preacher to the charge of a parish, till he come to us with a valid presentation; and few are the members of our Establishment who would hold it advisable to oppose the right of patronage. But what we contend for is, that the other circumstance is equally indispensable—that as the matter has ever stood, from the infancy of our being as a Church, and as the matter stands at this very hour, there must, previous to his ordination, be the concurrence of the Church; and if we know not a single instance, in our day, of a minister being suffered by law to officiate and to draw the emoluments of his living, in the face of the right of patronage exercised against him; so, neither do we know a single instance of a minister being forced upon a parish, we shall not say in the face of the people, but in the face of the ecclesiastical power; nor are we aware of any settlement where the preacher did not enter upon his charge with the sanction of our votes, and under the canopy of our majorities.

The right of a veto by the Presbytery on every presentation, when they judge there is a defect in the moral or literary qualifications of the presentee, is conceded on all hands. When they pass a veto on any other plea, however, their sentence, it would appear, must be borne upwards by appeal to the General Assembly, and may be decided there, on any principle which shall seem good unto that venerable Court.* They may put their conclusive veto on any presentation, for any reason, or, if they choose, for no reason at all. Even though there should be manifest injustice in their decision, there exists not, without the limits of the Church, any one legal or constitutional provision against such a possibility. The only security, in fact, is that a Church so constituted as ours will not be unjust. At all events, the matter could not be mended, by carrying the question without the limits of the Church's jurisdiction, and so carrying the chance of, at least, as great error and injustice along with it, when the ecclesiastical reasons on which the General Assembly passed sentence were brought under the review of a civil judicatory. But in truth there is and can be no such transition. The power of a veto on every presentation, and without responsibility at any bar but that of public opinion, is by all law and practice vested in the supreme ecclesiastical court of this country. And in these circumstances, is it to be borne that, with a power so ample, we are tamely to surrender it to the single operation of another power not more firmly established,

---

* Appendix to Sir Harry Moncrieff's Life of Dr. Erskine, p. 424. The reader will find, in this Appendix, an able and luminous exposition of the whole question, done by the masterly hand of the Reverend Baronet, whose talents and force of character have shed a brightness over that Church, of which he is so distinguished a minister.

and not more uniformly indispensable than our own? Are we, whose business it is to watch over the interests of religion, and to provide for the good of edification, and who, if we would only make use of the rights with which we are invested, could, in fact, subordinate the whole machinery of the Establishment to our own independent views of expediency—are we, as if struck by paralysis, to sit helplessly down under the fancied omnipotence of a deed of patronage? So soon as the majority in our Church shall revert to the principle of its not being generally for the good of edification, that a presentee, when unsupported by the concurrence of the parish, shall be admitted to the charge of it, there is no one earthly barrier in the way of our nullifying his presentation, and making it as absolutely void and powerless as a sheet of blank paper. We are not now contending for the right and authority of a call from the people, but for the power of the Church to admit the will or taste of the people as an element into her deliberations on the question, Whether a given presentation shall be sustained or not? and of deciding this question just as she shall find cause. And therefore it is, that in the lengthened contest which has taken place between the rights of the patrons and of the people, the Church, by giving all to the former and taking all from the latter, and in such a way, too, as to establish a kind of practical and unquestioned supremacy to a mere deed of presentation, has, in fact, bartered

away her own privileges, and sunk into a state of
dormancy the power with which she herself is essentially invested, to sit as the final and irrevers-
ible umpire on every such question that is submitted to her.

But the Church has given away nothing that
she cannot recal. If there be, at this moment,
an entire independence of patrons upon the people,
this is a temporary grant, at the will and pleasure
of an authority that can, at any time, rescind it.
In the struggle between the right of patronage
and a principle of deference to the popular taste,
what was the theatre of the contest?—the General
Assembly. Where was it that patronage won her
victory?—in the supreme Court of our Establishment. To what do the holders of patronage owe
the practical sovereignty which, for half a century, has been conceded to those rights by which
they proudly think to overrule the deliberations
of clergymen?—why, to the votes of clergymen.
The vote of such an unrestricted supremacy to
the right of patronage was not extorted from us
by any legal necessity, but was the fruit of our
own voluntary deliberations ; and the good of the
Church was or ought to have been the principle
which influenced them. Other views of the good
of the Church may again lead to other conclusions.
And, in the exercise of her undoubted right to
sustain or to refuse, upon ecclesiastical grounds,
any presentation that is offered, we may again
come to regard, as of old, the acceptable talents

of the presentee, and the number of signatures to his call, and the station or character of those who have thus testified their concurrence in his appointment, to be just as essential elements of the question before us, as either his moral or literary qualifications.

It is on these principles that there are not a few of the clergy who cleave to the Establishment, in spite of all the partial corruptions that Sectarianism has alleged against her. They see in the bosom of their own church an open avenue to every desirable reformation. They honestly believe that there is not a better range of Christian usefulness to be found, over the whole face of the country, than within her walls—and that a man of principle and zeal, when backed by the independence which she confers, and shielded about by the amplitude of her securities and her power, stands on the highest of all vantage ground, for the work of honest and faithful ministrations. They trust that she is the destined instrument for the preservation and the revival of Christianity in our land—and would tremble for her overthrow, as the severest blow that, in this quarter of the island, could be inflicted on the cause of the gospel. And when either patrons or people are in the wrong, let us never see the day when the cause shall be committed to any but to those whom the wisdom of the country has raised above the temptations of dependence; and who can clear their unfaultering way, alike unmoved by the smile of grandeur, or by the frown of a sometimes deluded population.

But we forget that, after all, it will not be primarily by any triumph gotten on the field of public controversy, that an accommodation will at length be brought about between the measures of the patrons and the wishes of the people. Ere the majority of our Church be desirous of such an accommodation, there must be a great revolution of sentiment among them, about the deference that is due to the popular understanding; and this will imply a similar revolution among men of power and intelligence, in the country at large. Should it come at length to be a general recognition with the clergy, that, bating a few excrescencies, popular Christianity is indeed the Christianity of the New Testament, and the only system of doctrine which can either regenerate the people for heaven or reform them into the sober and patriotic virtues of the present world—this will also be a general recognition with the reading and reflecting classes of the community. And thus it will not be upon an arena of litigation that the *vox populi* will struggle its way to that ascendency which, in matters of religion, we conceive to be altogether due to it. It will arrive more surely and more pacifically at this result, by the silent progress of a common and harmonising sentiment among those various classes who wont to set themselves in battle array, and debate their conflicting pretensions, with all the keenness which opposite views and opposite interests could inspire. Patrons will come at length to see that the most acceptable offering at the shrine of popularity is also the best offering at the shrine of patriotism: and government will not fail, in time, to understand that the quick and sensitive tact of the people, in theology, to which so little indulgence has hitherto been given, so far from being, in any degree, allied to that appetite for disturbance which endangers a nation, is, in fact, the longing of man's diseased moral nature for that doctrine which brings, in its train, the righteousness that exalteth a nation.

With the great majority of dissenters, the appointment of ministers is by popular election. The right of suffrage is more or less extended, however, being sometimes vested in the sitters of a congregation; at other times, restricted to the members of it, or those who have been admitted to the ordinances; and, in no small number of instances, being exclusively in the hands of proprietors, or trustees, who own the chapel, and bind themselves to defray, from the proceeds of it, all the expenses of the concern.

We do not hold the last of these arrangements to be different, in point of effect, from either of the two former. It affords, no doubt, the example of a patronage shared among so many individuals, but still of a patronage controlled by the hearers, and in a state of dependence on the popular will. It is the obvious and direct interest of the electors to fix on the man who, by his talents and doctrine, shall secure a full attendance upon his ministrations; and so secure, at least, a sufficient rental for meeting all the engagements.

This state of things is tantamount to a right of patronage vested in the few, with the power of a veto on each nomination vested in the many—a power which will be exercised on each successive appointment, till that one individual is brought forward, in whom the patronage and the popularity come to an adjustment with each other. This, perhaps, is a simpler and better process for arriving at the result of an acceptable minister, than where the power of originating each his own candidate is spread over the whole multitude, and the proceedings may come at length to be marked with the turmoil and confusion that often attend the business of a large popular assembly. And we apprehend, that with a patronage under this kind of influence, the business of each appointment may not only be conducted in a style of greater smoothness and facility; but that as zealous, and able, and faithful ministers would be provided, as under a constitution of things where each individual sitter had a direct and personal share in the positive nomination.

And after all, it must often happen that, even under the most democratic economy of a congregation, the minister virtually obtains his office by the appointment of the few, and only with the acquiescence of the many. In every assemblage of human beings, this is the method by which all their proceedings are really carried forward. The ascendency of worth, or talent, or station, or some other natural influence, is ever sure to vest the power of originating in the few, and to leave no-

thing with the many but the power of a veto;
nay, even, n many instances, to disarm them of
that power. The work of choosing their minister,
in a dissenting congregation, is, we doubt not, in
the great majority of instances, most wisely and
most peaceably conducted. But, on looking to
principles as well as to forms, we have as little
doubt that, in very many instances, the appointment is the result of a harmonized meeting beween
what may be called a virtual deed of patronage,
on the one hand, and the power of a negative, on
the other. And, amid all the sturdy opposition
there is to the Church, on the score of what has
been felt, as the most corrupt and pernicious of
her grievances, it is curious to observe how the
method of proceeding, even under the most popular constitutions of a chapel, resolves itself effectually into a modified patronage.

And there are many ways in which the Establishment may be in circumstances of as great advantage as dissenterism, for having her Church
patronage so modified, as that the popular voice
shall have its right degree of ascendency, in the
appointment of ministers. Whensoever the holders of patronage shall come to appreciate aright
the character and tendencies of the evangelical
system, this of itself will answer all the purposes
of a modified patronage. And whensoever the
Church shall resume the exercise of the authority
which belongs to her, of giving effect to the expression of the popular will, on every individual
nomination, this will re-instate that negative, in

all its force, which would restrain patronage, as far as we hold it to be desirable. And, in all cases where the revenue from seat-rents is of importance to the patron, as in great towns, this forms a strong security for the popular exercise of the right. And, as in the building of new churches, it is revenue derived from this source which furnishes the means for the endowment of them, we cannot extend the Establishment, without extending the cause of popular Christianity, by adding to the number of instances in which we shall have an accommodation between the choice of the patrons and the wishes of the people.

Upon this last circumstance, indeed, we hold ourselves entitled to found the following observation. Let the patronage of the existing Churches in our Establishment be as corrupt as it may, every additional Church that is built and endowed, on the produce of its seat-rents, has, by its very constitution, a security for the right and popular exercise of its patronage. However the right of nomination may be vested, there is a virtual control with the hearers, which will necessitate the patrons towards acceptable and evangelical clergymen. Whatever disadvantages may be alleged on the side of the Establishment, when brought into comparison with the Dissent, in respect of the state of its patronage, they vanish altogether, in reference to new erections; and, standing upon equal ground, in this one particular, the only remaining question is, Which of the two is most fitted to overtake the necessities of our unprovided population? We have already endeavoured to point out the reason why, after that dissenterism has lavished all her resources on the task, for upwards of a century, the population have so grown and multiplied beyond her, that, in our large cities, one half, at least, of the labouring classes are, in respect of the ordinances of the gospel, in a state of practical heathenism; and why no expedient appears so likely to provide, for this sore destitution, as Established Churches, with local territories having a preference for seats assigned to them. And we do not feel restrained from urging this expedient by any alleged corruption respecting the patronage of the Establishment; for, in as far as the new erections are concerned, there will necessarily be a popular influence to over-rule the nomination. And for this, therefore, as well as for other reasons, do we look to the Establishment, in both countries, as the likeliest instrument for recalling a degenerate people to the faith and habits of a Christian land.*

---

* In addition to all the argument that we have alleged for the influence and utility of religious establishments, on the ground of locality, we shall subjoin a reason that comes with greater delicacy from the mouth of a dissenter. The following is a quotation from Baxter, who, if second to any, was only second to Dr. John Owen, among the English Non-conformists of the seventeenth century—a race of men who contributed so much to the glories of what may be termed the Augustan age of Christianity in our island:—

" If you love the common good of England, do your best to keep up sound and serious religion in the public Parish Churches; and be not guilty of any thing that shall bring the chief interest of religion into private assemblies of men merely tolerated, if you can avoid it.

" Indeed, in a time of plagues' epidemical infection, tolerated churches may be the best preservatives of religion, as it was in the first 300 years, and in the Arrian reign, and under Popery. But when sound and serious religion is owned by the magistrates, tolerated churches are but as hospitals for the sick, and must not be the receptacle of all the healthful. And, doubtless, if the Papists can but get the Protestant interest over into prohibited

Still, it is well for a country that dissenters do
their uttermost. They are right to extend their
interest and their ascendency as far as they can;
and to make as deep an impression on the outcast and alienated mass of our population as possible. The very jealousy that they awaken among
the fiery and alarmed bigots of our Establishment
is, of itself, a salutary principle. And we doubt
not that, to the good of their own direct exertions,
they have added a most important contribution to
the cause of Christianity, by the wholesome re-action to which, through them, the Church has
been stimulated. It is our part to rejoice that
Christ has been more preached in the Church,
by their means, even though, in some instances,
it may have been of contention. They have
poured a fresh zeal into the bosom of our Establishment, and done something to guide and to
purify the exercise of its patronage. It were well,
if, in every portion of the land, they could supplement all that is corrupt or defective in our national churches. Could such an arm of intole-

---

or tolerated conventicles (as they will call them), they have more than half
overcome it, and will not doubt to use it next as they do in France, and by
one turn more to cast it out. The countenance of authority will go far with
the vulgar against all the scruples that men of conscience stick at, and they
will mostly go to the allowed churches, whoever is there. Let us, therefore,
lose no possession that we can justly get, nor be guilty of disgracing the
honest Conformists, but do all we can to keep up their reputation for the
good of souls. They see not matters of difference through the same glass
that we do. They think us unwarrantably scrupulous. We think the matter of their sins to be very great. But we know that before God the degree
of guilt is much according to the degree of men's negligence or unwilling-
ness to know the truth, or to obey it. And prejudice, education, and converse, maketh great difference on men's apprehensions. Charity must not
reconcile us to sin, but there is no end of uncharitable censuring each
other."

rance be lifted up, in any country, as to crush
the energy of non-conformists, that would be the
country where the purest Establishment on earth
were sure to languish into indolence, or to gather
upon it the mould of spiritual decay. And, therefore it is, that we hold the best ecclesiastical system for a kingdom, to be a publicly endowed
Church, on the one hand, keeping pace, in its
extent, with the growth of the population; and
an altogether free, unshackled dissenterism, on the
other, without one civil disability, or one stigma
of degradation, however light and lenient it may
be, affixed to the profession of it.

And, we have only one word more to our political rulers upon this subject. We are most thoroughly aware of the association that obtains in
the minds of many of them between dissent and
democracy; and that, under this feeling, they not
only look with a hard and suspicious eye upon non-
conformity, but would resist every assimilation to
any of its features, on the part of the Establishment. The evidences are innumerable, that the
association is, in the main, unfounded. Among
others we appeal to the charges issued in Novem-
ber, 1819, by the Methodist body, against political disaffection, when Radicalism was at its height;
and to the known fact, that individuals were excluded from the membership of their churches,
for the single offence of attending the meetings
of the seditious. But the most satisfactory proof
of all, and one that comes immediately under the
eye of our statesmen, is that, which may be ob-

tained from an investigation into the habit and condition of those who are apprehended for seditious practices. We understand that, about three years ago, when such apprehensions were numerous, there was not among them the case of one individual, who was a member of any of the great dissenting bodies in our kingdom. And it will be found, we venture to say, in every season of political alarm, when such apprehensions are called for, that, with a very few exceptions, indeed, neither the guilt of disaffection, nor even the suspicion of it, has brought down this kind of visitation at least on a regular member of any of the evangelical denominations of Christianity. The great majority, in fact, belong to those outcasts from the word and ordinances, who associate themselves with no body of worshippers at all; and the question comes to be, Why were they not to be met with in the empty churches of the Establishment? This matter suggests whole volumes of argument and reproof to statesmen. And it is right that they should know the real origin of those troubles which most embarrass them. It does not lie with dissenters, who are innocent of it all; but it lies with their own careless and corrupt patronage. Were the Church of England rightly extended and rightly patronised, there would be neither sedition nor plebeian infidelity in the land. And thus, in the eye of one who connects an ultimate effect with its real though unseen cause, the whole host of Radicalism may have been summoned into being by the very Government that sent forth her forces to destroy it; and fierce ministerial clergymen, though they mean not so, may, each from his own parish, have contributed his quota to this mass of disaffection; and, ascending from the men of subaltern influence, that Bishop, whose measures have alienated from the Church the whole popular feeling of his diocese, instead of a captain of fifties, may virtually though unwittingly be a captain of thousands, in the camp of that very rebellion which would sweep, did it triumph, the existence of his order from the kingdom; and, to complete the picture of this sore and infatuating blindness, if there be one individual in the Cabinet, whose pernicious ascendency it is, that has diverted away the patronage of the Crown from the only men who can Christianise and conciliate the people, he, in all moral and substantial estimation, is the generalissimo in this treasonable warfare against the rights and the prerogatives of the monarchy.

But we believe that, in the majority of instances, they are the city rulers, who are the patrons of city churches; and the post they fill is, therefore, one of great responsibility for the well-being of the empire. It is under them that there exists the most fearful deficiency in the means of religious instruction; and it is, of course, throughout the mighty hosts over which they preside, that violence, and profligacy, and all the elements of moral and political mischief are ever sure to be most copiously engendered. They have the pow-

er, however, of counteraction in their own hands;
and were their eyes once opened to the influence
of locality, when combined with a reduction in
the size of parishes, and a pure exercise of patronage, they could not fail to perceive that, under a
steady and well-principled course of management,
the neglected myriads of a city might come, at
length, to change the ferocity of their aspect for
the moral and pacific cast of a country population.
There is the very same nature on which to operate
with both; and there is not one district, however
wild and outlandish at present, and though teeming with families in the coarsest style of dissipated
and worthless plebeianism, that would not experience a speedy transformation, were certain practicable facilities opened for admitting them to the
church of a laborious minister, on the Sabbath,
and securing for them, through the week, the
unwearied and ever-plying attentions of the same
individual. When he once found his way to a residing eldership, he would find himself elevated to
a tenfold ascendency over them; and without ro-
mantic effort (for if this were requisite, the whole
were fruitless Utopianism) might he bring his
densely peopled vineyard under all the blandness
of a village economy. They are the principle of
locality which has been so little adverted to, and
the preference of the parishioners to the sittings
of their own church which is still so provokingly
disregarded by our administrators, and the moderate extent of parishes which may at length be
attained by terms of liberal encouragement held

out to the subscribers for new churches, on the part of magistrates—these are the simple elements out of which a sufficient mechanism may be reared for regenerating even the most unwieldy metropolis; and, lastly, to animate this mechanism with a right spirit and principle of vitality, let our city patrons be no longer disdainful of conceding their favours to the expression of the popular will; and, on the side of religious honesty, as it in general is, will it almost always be sure to direct their regards to the most zealous and devoted labourers.

We have already said enough of locality and patronage, and the preference for seats to parishioners; but, on the topic of lessening the extent of parishes, by new erections, we would again recur to the example at Liverpool, as a proof how much may be done, without putting to hazard the funds of the corporation. If, for the encouragement of private adventurers, magistrates will not allow a perpetual right of patronage, they may, at least, allow that right for a certain term of years, or for a certain number of successive nominations. In this way, without expense to the town, may they obtain an immediate extension of churches, and an ultimate extension of their own patronage. It is not to be expected that subscribers will pay for the erection and endowment of a new church, if others are forthwith to patronise it. But should they be permitted to hold, for a time at least, in their own hands, a security for popular appointments, they would not only feel themselves prompted to this enterprise of benevolence, by a hope of indemnification from the seat-rents, but also by the hope of a fulfilment to their own wishes, in the increase of useful and acceptable clergy. If one individual has done so much in Liverpool, what may not be expected from the efforts of a great Christian public, in the cause? And we are not aware of any expedient, by which so speedy and effectual an enlargement of church accommodation, in populous towns, can be arrived at.

And there is one circumstance which may dishearten this process, at the outset, and which it were, therefore, well to understand and be prepared for. The people of every new parish should have the preference for seats in their own church. But there will generally be a disappointment, if it be thought that this preference is to be extensively taken. The truth is, that the great object of extending the church accommodation in cities is, not to meet the demand that already exists, but to create a taste and a habit which have now fallen into desuetude. It is altogether a reclaiming process; and more for the inspiration of a right appetite that is. not yet felt, than for the gratification of one which is already astir, and in quest of instruction. It is, therefore, very possible that, at the outset, there may be a very meagre demand for the sittings of the new fabric, in the appropriate district itself; in which case, after the preference has been held out for a sufficient length of time, the competition should be thrown open to the inhabitants of the town at large. And here lie the charm and the might of locality—that the minister, by concentrating his attention upon the families that reside in it, will soon stir up a re-action among them towards the place of his Sabbath ministrations; and he will excite a growing demand for seats that will soon press hard upon the vacancies which occur; and, by the simple regulation of continuing the rule of preference to the parishioners for these vacancies, a parochial will come, in the course of years, to be substituted for a general congregation; and, triumph enough for one incumbency, will the people of a given geographical section of a town, at one time alienated from Christianity and all its ordinances, be translated into the general habit of church-going; and, trained to the recognitions and the regularities of a country parish, will it be found that they are capable of exemplifying all its virtues, and of exhibiting the same aspect of kindliness and sobriety, which many think can only be kept inviolate in the more retired provinces of our empire.

With plain fabrics, and moderately endowed, a most useful class of evangelical labourers may be had, and on such seat-rents as could be afforded by the great bulk of the people. Indeed, in all the new churches, the utmost economy should be observed, else the system will never be carried forward to a right or adequate degree of extension. If our city rulers shall ever propose, in good earnest, to have an ecclesiastical apparatus, at all commensurate to their population, they must bethink themselves of churches altogether secondary to the present ones, both in architectural

splendour and in the salaries of clergymen. It is
right that a certain number of the livings should
be upheld in such a degree of superiority, as to
hold out an allurement to men of professional eminence, from all parts of the country. But should it
be reckoned necessary, so to hold up all the livings,
then this were an impracticable barrier in the way
of multiplying the parishes. And, therefore, the
best arrangement for a town that has only ten
churches, and would need thirty, is, in supplementing the deficiency, to descend from spires to
belfries, and, besides observing the utmost simplicity in the buildings, to assign such an income to
the clergyman, as that the whole expenses, both
of the erection and endowment, may, as nearly as
possible, be met by the proceeds of the attendance. This would give confidence, and call forth
a much more productive effort, in the way of private subscription for the cause, or even enable
magistrates to take the cause into their own hands.
But, in every possible way, it is a cause which
ought to be carried forward: and those are the
most patriotic and enlightened rulers, who, laying
aside the prejudices which have hitherto kept popularity and patronage at so heartless a distance
from each other, shall now give their promptitude
to the great object of so multiplying churches, as
to meet the necessities of the people, and of so
appointing churches, as to draw them to a willing
attendance on the ministrations of Christianity.

CHAP. VII.

ON CHURCH OFFICES.

BY the constitution of the Church of Scotland, it
is provided that, in each parish, there shall be, at
least, one minister, whose office it is to preach
and dispense the ordinances of Christianity, on the
Sabbath, and to labour in holy things among the
people, through the week; and elders, whose office it is to assist at the dispensation of sacraments, to be the bearers of religious advice and
comfort among the families, and, in general, to
act purely as ecclesiastical labourers for the good
of human souls; and, lastly, deacons, to whom it
belongs, not to preach the word, or administer the
sacraments, but to take special care in administer-
ing to the necessities of the poor.*

In the course of time, the last of these three
offices has fallen into very general desuetude.
The duties of it have been transferred to the eldership, the members of which body have thus
been vested with a plurality of cares; it being
both their part to labour in matters connected
with the religious good of the people, and to share
in the administration of those funds which the law

---

* See the Form of Church Government, agreed upon in the Assembly
of Westminster Divines, and ratified afterwards by an act of the General
Assembly, in the year 1645.

K

or custom of the country has provided for meeting the demands of its pauperism.

The moral effect upon the people of such a conjunction as this seems very much to have escaped observation. And, indeed, it is only under certain rare and peculiar circumstances, where this effect is very broadly or very strikingly exemplified. The truth is, that, in the great majority of our Scottish parishes, the sum expended on pauperism is raised by voluntary collection, and still maintains the character of a ministration of kindness. It is, besides, so very small in amount, as not to have come very sensibly or extensively into contact with the lower orders of society, who, in those parts of the country where the method of legal assessments for the poor has not been established, still retain the veteran hardihood and independence of their forefathers, and among whom the condition of known and public dependence is still regarded in the light of a family misfortune, or a family degradation.

It is not, therefore, in such Scottish parishes as these where we can see to greatest advantage the effect of such a combination of duties as that which we have now adverted to. Neither are we sure that any very decisive exhibition of this effect is to be met with, in the whole of England. There, it is true, the funds for pauperism are enormous, and they are spread in distribution over a very large proportion of the labouring classes in that country. But we are ignorant whether the

work of distribution is at all vested in men who
have the office, besides, of sharing in any religious
superintendance over the people. We rather
think that overseers, and others employed in the
dispensation of the legal aliment, hold out an exclusively civil and secular aspect to the eye of
the population; and that there is no such incon-
gruity among them as the one in question; and in
virtue of which the same individual is called upon, by one of his offices, to evince a concern, and
exercise a care, over their eternal interests, and,
by another of his offices, to enter the lists with
them on the arena of clamorous assertion, and
loudly proclaimed discontent, and stout or surly
litigation.

But there are a good many parishes, in Scotland, now in progress towards the English system
of pauperism, in as far as respects a compulsory
provision by assessment; and where, too, in the
amount of the sums expended, they are making
rapid advances towards the habits and economy
of our Southern neighbours. That which wont to
be applied for, with shame and humility, and to
be taken with gratitude, is now demanded in the
tone of a rightful or peremptory challenge; and
all the heart-burnings or jealousies of a legal contest are beginning to be infused into the ministrations of parochial charity. That which was before diffused among a very few of our families,
and had to them the feeling of an element of
kindliness, is now gathering a dark and malignant

tinge—and, what makes it still worse, is spreading itself over so many of our families as to threaten a bad impression on the general habit and character of our population. The people, at large, are becoming more closely associated with pauperism; and pauperism itself is fast transforming from its olden aspect of kind and gentle humanity, and putting on a countenance of grim attorneyship. Meanwhile, there has not been a sufficient corresponding change in the old bodies of administration; and thus both ministers and elders, whose joint office it is to woo the people to Christianity, have, in many of our larger towns, been implicated in a most unseemly warfare with them, on another ground altogether. It is in such transition parishes as these, from an old to a new system of things, that the phenomenon in question is in its best possible state for observation; and where we may catch such an evolution of our nature as shall not only serve to demonstrate a present evil, but as shall also bring out to view those general principles on which the charities of human intercourse ought to be conducted.

Conceive, then, an individual to be associated with a district in the joint capacity of elder and deacon, and that, at the same time, its pauperism has attained such a magnitude, and such an establishment, as to have addressed itself to the desires and the expectations of a large proportion of the families. The argument must suppose him to be equally intent on the duties of each office, without which there is a defect of right and honest principle, on his part, and this of itself is a mischievous thing, though no exception whatever could be alleged against the combination of these two offices. It will, therefore, serve better to expose the evils of this combination, to figure to ourselves a man of zeal and conscientiousness, on whom the burden of both offices has been laid, and who is uprightly desirous of fulfilling the duties of both. There are many who are but elders in name, while deacons alone and deacons altogether in practice and performance; and this, of itself, by the extinction, as far as it goes, of the whole use and influence of the eldership among the people, is, of itself, a very sore calamity. But let us rather put the case of one who would like religious influence to descend from him, in the former capacity, and, at the same time, would like to acquit himself rightly among the people, in the latter capacity: and we hope to make it appear that a more ruinous plurality could not have been devised, by which to turn into poison each ingredient of which it is composed—and that it is indeed a work of extreme delicacy and difficulty for an individual, on whom duties of a character so heterogeneous have been devolved, to move through the district assigned to him, without scattering among its people the elements of moral deterioration.

He goes forth among them as an elder, when

he goes forth to pray with them, or to address them on the subject of Christianity, or to recommend their attention to its ordinances, or to take cognizance of the education of their children. There are, indeed, a thousand expedients by which he may attempt a religious influence among the people; and, in plying these expedients, he acts purely as an ecclesiastical labourer. And, did he act singly in this capacity, we might know what to make of the welcome which he obtains from the families. But they recognize him to be also a dispenser of temporalities; and they have an indefinite imagination of his powers, and of his patronage, and of his funds; and their sordid or mercenary expectations are set at work by the very sight of him; and thus some paltry or interested desire of their own may lurk under the whole of that apparent cordiality which marks the intercourse of the two parties. It were a great satisfaction, to disentangle one principle here from another; and this can only be done by separating the one office from the other. It were desirable to ascertain how much of liking there is for the Christian, and how much for the pecuniary ministration with which this philanthropist is charged. The union of these two throws an impenetrable obscurity over this question, and raises a barrier against the discernment of real character, amongst the people with whom we deal.

But this combination does more than disguise the principles of the people. It serves also to deteriorate them. If there be any nascent affection among them towards that which is sacred, it is well to keep it single—to defend it from the touch of every polluting ingredient—to nourish and bring it forward on the strength of its own proper aliment—and most strenuously to beware of holding out encouragement to that most subtle of all hypocrisies, the hypocrisy of the heart; which is most surely and most effectually done, when the lessons of preparation for another world are mixed up with the bribery of certain advantages in this world, and made to descend upon a human subject in one compound administration. There is a wonderful discernment in our nature evinced by the Saviour and his Apostles, throughout their whole work of Christianising, in the stress that is laid by them on singleness of eye—and in the announcements they give of the impossibility of serving two masters, and of the way in which a divided state of the affections shuts and darkens the heart against the pure influence of truth. Simplicity of desire, or the want of it, makes the whole difference between being full of light and full of darkness. It is thus that Christ refuses to be a judge and a divider; and that the Apostles totally resign the office of ministering to the temporal wants of the poor; and that Paul, in particular, is at so much pains both to teach and to exemplify, among his disciples, the habit of independence on charity to the very uttermost—denouncing the hypocrisy of those who make a gain of godliness, and even going so far as to affirm, that the man who had joined their society, with a view to his own personal relief, out of its funds, from the expense of maintaining his own household, was worse than an infidel. On the maxim that " my kingdom is not of this world," it will ever be a vain attempt to amalgamate Christianity with the desires of any earthly ambition; and this is just as applicable to the humble ambition of a poor man for a place in the lists of pauperism, as to that higher ambition which toils, and aspires, and multiplies its desires, and its doings, on the walks of a more dignified patronage. We are not pleading, at present, for the annihilation of pauperism, but for the transference of its duties to a separate class of office-bearers. We are for removing a taint and a temptation from the eldership, and for securing, in this way, the greatest possible efficacy to their Christian labours. We are for delivering the people from the play and the perplexity of two affections, which cannot work together, contemporaneously at least, in the same bosom. On the principle that there is a time for every thing, we should like a visit from an elder to be the time when Christianity shall have a separate and unrivalled place in the attention of those with whom, for the moment, he is holding intercourse; and that when the impression of things sacred might be growing and gathering strength from his conversation, there shall not be so ready and palpable an inlet as there is at present, for the impression of things secular to stifle and overbear them.

There are two different ways in which an elder may acquit himself of his superinduced deacon-ship: either in the way of easy compliance with the demands of the population, or in the way of strict and conscientious inquiry, so as to act right-ly by the fund which has been committed to him. Take the first way of it, and suppose him, at the same time, to have the Christianity of his district at heart, and what a bounty he carries around with him on the worst kind of dissimulation! Like a substance, where neither of the ingredients taken singly is poisonous, and which assumes all its vi-rulence from the composition of them, what a power of insidious but most fatal corruption lies in the mere junction of these two offices! There is many a pluralist of this sort, who never can and never will verify this remark, by any experience of his own; because he has virtually resigned the bet-ter and the higher of his functions, or rather has not once from the beginning exercised them. But let him go forth upon his territory, in the dis-charge of both, and what a sickening duplicity of reception he is exposed to! What a mortifying in-difference to the topic he has most at heart, under all the constrained appearance of attention which is rendered to it! With what dexterity can the language of sanctity be pressed into the service, when their purpose requires it; and yet how evi-dent, how mortifyingly evident, often, is the total absence of all feeling and desire upon the subject, from the hearts of these wily politicians! How often, under such an unfortunate arrangement as this, is Christianity prostituted. into a vehicle for the most sordid and unworthy applications—all its lessons no further valued than for the mean and beggarly elements with which they are conjoined —and all its ordinances no further valued than as stepping-stones, perhaps, to a pair of shoes. It is this mingling together of incompatible desires— it is this bringing of a pure moral element into contiguity with other elements which vitiate and extinguish it—it is this compounding of what is fitted in itself to raise the character, with what is fitted, in itself, and still more by its hypocritical association with better things, to adulterate and debase it—it is this which sheds a kind of withering blight over all the ministrations of the pluralist, and must convince every enlightened observer, that, till he gets rid of the many elements of temptation which are in his hands, he will never expatiate, either with Christian comfort, or with Christian effect, among the population.

And here we may remark another argument against this plurality, which ought to address itself with great effect to all those who think that an increase of profligacy among the people is the sure attendant on an increase of pauperism. There may be no great harm done by putting this administration into the hands of an eldership, so long as the money is raised in the shape of a free-will offering from the giver, and it is made to descend in the shape of unconstrained kindness upon the receiver; or so long as they have only to deal with moderate sums among moderate expectations. But, when the fund is raised in a legal and compulsory way by assessment, and when that which wont to be petitioned for, in the shape of charity, is demanded in the shape of justice, and when the people are thus armed with the force and impetus of an aggressive legality, upon the one side, and are not met in the firm and resolute spirit of a defensive legality, upon the other, there will, in time, be amongst us a far more rapid acceleration of pauperism than ever has been exemplified in England. That old apparatus which would have sufficed under the old system, will be a feeble defence against the weight and urgency of applications that are sure to be engendered by the new. A kirk-session may do for an organ of distribution, while the expression of good will may be held forth, on the one side, and the feeling of gratitude may be called back, on the other. But when, from an administration of charity, it is transformed into a warfare of rights, it becomes altogether an unseemly contest for such parties as these—and a contest, in which the cupidity, and the love of pleasure, or of indolence, that characterise our nature, will mightily prevail over that unpractised simplicity which we should ever like to characterise our eldership; whose proper business it is to officiate among sacraments, and to exert a Christian superintendence over the families that are assigned to them. The exemption of Scotland from an oppressive pauperism is not at all due to the ecclesiastical form of that machinery under which it is administered. It is to be ascribed simply to the absence of a compulsory provision; and it will be found that, after this is introduced, then, so soon as it is fully understood and acted on, all that is ecclesiastical, in our courts of administration, so far from being a safeguard to the independence of our people, will, in fact, smooth, and widen, and encourage, their transition to pauperism. Scotland has not yet had time to overtake England, in the amount of her expenditure. But it will be found that, in the great majority of those parishes where a compulsory provision for the poor has been established, she is moving onward, at a faster rate of acceleration. The pauperism of Manchester is still greater, in its present amount, than that of Glasgow. But the proportional increase in Glasgow, during the last twenty years, is very greatly beyond that in Manchester.*

---

* It grieves us to remark, here, that there have lately sprung up, in Scotland, some strenuous advocates for a legal and compulsory provision, and that, on the ground of a few isolated cases, where there has been no increase of expenditure consequent on the introduction of this method into some of our Scottish parishes. The habit of the people may certainly survive the pernicious influence of this system for perhaps half a generation. It is certainly not all at once that a national spirit, or a national habit, can be overthrown. But it will at length give way to the force of new institutions; and it must for ever be regretted, if the wholesale experience of England, together with

Let us now conceive a pluralist to be aware of
this mischief, and, by way of guarding against it,
to put himself forth in an attitude more characteristic of deaconship—firm in resistance to every
claim that is capable of being reduced, and most
strict and resolute in all his investigations.   In this
case the only fit and effectual attitude of eldership
must be given up.   He may as well try to look two
opposite ways, at the same moment, as think of
combining the one with the other, and of keeping
the people at bay by his resistance to them, on the
ground of his lower, and, at the same time, drawing their regard, on the ground of his better and
higher ministrations.   He will find it utterly impossible to find access for the lessons of Christianity, into hearts soured against himself, and, perhaps, thwarted in their feelings of justice, by the
disappointments they have gotten at his hand.   It
is thus that, by a strange fatality, the man who has
been vested with a religious superintendence over
the people, has become the most unlikely for gaining a religious influence over them—and all his
wonted powers of usefulness, now worse than neutralised, have, by the positive dislike that has been
turned against him, been sunk far beneath the level of any private or ordinary individual.   There

---

that of the *vast majority* of those Scottish parishes where the English practice has been admitted, shall not countervail the argumentations of certain
able men, on a subject in which their powers of logic have certainly far out-
stripped their powers of observation.

cannot, surely, be a more complete travesty on all
that is wise and desirable in human institutions,
than to saddle that man, whose primitive office it
is to woo the people to that which is spiritually
good, with another office, where he has to war
against the people, on the subject of their temporalities. There may, at one time, have been a
compatibility between these two functions, under
the cheap economy of the old Scottish pauperism;
but it is all put to flight by the shock which takes
place between the rapacity of the one party and
the resistance of the other, under a system of English pauperism. The people will listen with disdain, or with shrewd and significant contempt, to
the Christian conversation of that elder who stands
confronted against them, on the ground of his deaconship: and they will expect an easy unresisting
compliance with all their demands from that deacon who has plied them with the affectionate
counsels of Christianity, on the ground of his eldership. They will dexterously work the desirous-
ness that he must feel, in the one of these capaci-
ties, against the duties that he would like to fulfil,
in the other of them. They will tell him that they
have no time and no heart for religion, while under the pressure of alleged difficulties that he will
do nothing to relieve. He, in the meantime, will
perceive that, unless he complies with the demand, he can find no acceptance; and that, though
he should comply, acceptance gained through the
medium of bribery will lead to no pure or desir-

able influence on the character of the population.
In this unfortunate contest, each will, in all likelihood, believe the other to be a hypocrite; the one
incurring this suspicion because of the way in
which the legal hardihood of the deacon stands in
awkward and unseemly conjunction upon the same
individual, with the apparent zeal and sincerity of
the elder; and the other incurring this suspicion,
because of the way in which a sordid desire after
things secular is mingled, in the same exhibition,
with a seeming deference to things sacred. It is
thus that the pluralist feels himself paralysed into
utter helplessness: and never was public function-
ary more cruelly hampered than by this association of duties, which are altogether so discordant.
There is no place for the still small voice of Christian friendship, in such an atmosphere of recrimi-
nation, and heart-burning, and mutual jealousy, as
now encompasses the ministration of charity, in
our great towns. To import the English principle
of pauperism among the kirk-sessions of Scotland
is like putting new wine into old bottles. It so
mangles and lacerates an eldership, as to dissipate
all the moral ascendency they once had over our
population. It is ever to be regretted that such a
ministration as this should have been inserted between the two parties. No subtle or Satanic ad-
versary of religion could have devised a more
skilful barrier against all the usefulness and effect
of these lay associates of the clergy: and, as the
fruit of this melancholy transformation, a class

of men, who have contributed so much to build up and sustain our national character, will be as good as swept away from the land.

And the clergy themselves have received a vitiat-ing taint from this pernicious innovation. They too have been implicated among the stout legalities of a business, now turned from an affair of the heart to an affair of points and precedents, where every question must be determined with rigour, and every determination be persisted in, with uncom-plying hardihood. The minister feels himself translated into a new and strange relationship with his people, and is in inextricable difficulties about the character he should assume; for whether he moves in the style of an affectionate pastor, or puts on the stern countenance amongst them of a litigant with their claims, corruption will be sure to attend upon his footsteps; and he will either call forth the fawning hypocrisy of expectants, on the one hand, or be met, in soreness and sullenness of spirit, by the disappointed candidates for parochi-al aliment, on the other.

In the late ferments of the popular mind which took place at Glasgow, one of the earliest move-ments was a combined application to each of the kirk-sessions, for an extension of the system of parochial aid. Whether the refusal of this was the pretext, or the principle, of the disturbances that followed, it ought at least to be quite palp-able that our ecclesiastical courts ought never to be involved in the whirl of any such political agi-

tations; and we have reason to believe that, from
the Church having been implicated to such a degree, in what was once a charitable, but is now
regarded as a legal ministration, there has a ran-
corous infidelity been spreading among the people
—a contempt for religion itself mingling with all
the odium and irritation that have been incurred
by its ministers.

There are two ways of decomposing this mischief. There may be a reversion to the old system of Scottish pauperism, so that its expenses
shall be wholly defrayed, as before, by voluntary
collections, and it shall regain the character of a
purely ecclesiastical ministration. We believe
this to be practicable, and that too with a speed
and a facility of which no adequate impression
can be given by argument. This is a subject in
which the result of experience, upon actual trial,
will far outstrip the anticipations even of the most
sanguine economist. If the existing cases of pauperism are suffered to die out, on the legal fund
raised by assessment, and the new applications
are met by the gratuitous fund gathered at the
church doors—the former fund would, in a few
years, be left unburdened, and be no longer called for; and the latter fund be found, in every
way, as adequate to the then existing demand
for relief, as the whole of the present revenue,
both legal and gratuitous, is to the present demand. It were interfering with a future part of
our argument, were we to enter now into the

M

question, why it is that a happier state of things, and a more diffused comfort and sufficiency among our people will follow upon the reduction, or even the total abolition of public charity, for the relief of indigence, than can ever be brought about, either by its most skilful or its most abundant ministrations? But, in the meantime, let the thing be tried, instead of argued; let separate parishes just throw themselves fearlessly on an experiment which, to many an eye, looks so hazardous; let the excess of their actual pauperism over their present collections be taken off, and provided for out of the sum raised by assessments; and let all future cases be attempted, at least, upon the produce of future collections :—and ere one year has rolled over this new system of things, there are many of our public and practical men, who have resisted to the uttermost all theoretical conviction upon the subject, that will, if they simply engage in the matter with their own hands, be sure to work their way to a most firm experimental conviction about it. Should this plan be entered upon, we would feel less earnest about the separation of our eldership from the work of public charity. There would still, it is true, after the abridgment had taken place, in the extent of its operation, be a remainder of the mischief that we have attempted to expose; but far more innocent, in point of effect, just because far more insignificant than before, in point of magnitude. Perhaps, however, a deaconship might be of tem-

porary use, in helping to conduct the pauperism
back again to its original state. It would, in the
meantime, relieve the eldership of all apprehension of personal fatigue and difficulty to themselves, while the experiment was going forward.
It would extend that most desirable of all operations—a frequent intercourse between the lower
and higher orders of the community. By this
widening of the public agency, too, there would,
at least, be a widening of the amount of practical
observation, on a matter that is grossly misunderstood by many reasoners and declaimers, and that
requires only the light of a close and familiar ex-'
perience to be thrown upon it. We may, afterwards, attempt to bring forward the reasons, why
a deaconship, however good as a temporary expedient, need not be insisted on as a part of the permanent or essential machinery of any parish;
however important their services may be, throughout the whole period of transition, from the present corrupt and modernised system of pauperism, in our large towns, back again to the old
and healthful economy of our Scottish parishes.

But should this plan not be adopted, it were
greatly better that the Church should be altogether
dissevered from the ministrations of public charity.
We shall never cease to regret the introduction
of a legal spirit into the work of human benevolence; and to regard the establishment of a com_
pulsory provision for the poor as one of the worst
invasions ever made on the olden habit of our

country, and as one of the deadliest obstacles to its
moral regeneration. But if this curse is to be
perpetuated upon our land, let elders and deacons
and all who hold any ecclesiastical character
amongst us, cease, from this moment, to be implicated in a business so mischievous. It is quite
enough that, in their strict official employment,
of sustaining the principle and character of the
country, they have the whole adverse influence
of this vitiating dispensation to contend with.
But, in the name of all Christian and all political
wisdom, let not such a dispensation be put into
their hands; nor let these labourers in the cause
of Scotland's piety and Scotland's worth be
charged with any distribution of a quality so poisonous, and, at the same time, so alluring, that
they can neither withhold it, without alienating
many hearts from them, nor spread it freely
around, without insinuating corruption into these
hearts, and scattering the seeds of a great and
pernicious distemper over the land.

It is our confident expectation, however, that
our towns will take the better way of it, and reduce their separate parishes to the economy from
which they have departed. In this case, there
will be a gradual diminution of the evil to which
our eldership is, at present, so much exposed.
Or if, to aid the process, an order of deacons
shall be instituted, then the members of the
former body, relieved altogether from the public
charge of the poor, may be left free to expatiate

among the people purely as their Christian friends, and with the single object of promoting the spirit and the observations of the gospel among their families.

When the work of an elder is thus disembarassed from the elements by which it was before vitiated, he will feel a sad'burden of perplexity and discomfort cleared away. He may, at times, be received with distaste, by families that would have welcomed him, on the ground of his secular ministrations. But surely it is better that there be a distinctly visible line of demarcation between these families, and those which still receive him with cordiality on a higher ground, and about the principle of whose cordiality, therefore, there can be no mistake and no misinterpretation. He who has felt the delight of genuine Christian intercourse with the poor, will feel all the charm of a deliverance, when the sordid and the sacred are thus separated the one from the other; and he, freed from the suspicions which, at one time, harassed and distressed him, can now expatiate, at least over a certain portion of the territory, with the animating thought that so many doors and so many hearts are open to him; and that, on the single score of such religious or such respectful attentions as he may be disposed to render to the population. He will feel himself as if elevated into a more etherial region, when borne in pleasantness along on the pure play of such feelings and such friendships as are called forth by simple

goodness, on the one side, and that simple gratitude, on the other, which is ever sure to be attracted by goodness, even when it has no gift to
bestow. In truth, the very purity of such a ministration adds prodigiously both to the pleasure
and to the power of it: and, whereas no cheering
inference could be drawn from the extended acceptance of an elder among the people, so long
as he stood charged with the elements of a beggarly dispensation—should that charge be given
up, we shall then, from every additional house,
where he is hailed as the acquaintance and the
respectable friend of the inmates, be able to infer
the authentic progress of a right and peaceful influence among our families.

There is a delusive fear to which inexperience
is liable upon this subject, as if there was a very
general rapacity among the families of the poor,
which, if not appeased out of the capabilities of a
public fund, would render it altogether unsafe
for any private individual, in the upper walks of
society, to move at large among their habitations.
It is not considered how much it is that this rapacity is whetted by the imagination of a great
collective treasure, at the disposal of this individual. An elder who is implicated with pauperism, or the agent of a charitable society who is
known to be such, will most certainly light up
a thousand mercenary expectations, and be met
by a thousand mercenary demands, in the course
of his frequent visitations among the people. But

let him stand out to the general eye as dissociated
with all the concerns of an artificial charity; and
let it be his sole ostensible aim to excite the religious spirit of the district, or to promote its education—and he may, every day of his life, walk
over the whole length and breadth of his territory, without meeting with any demand that is at
all unmanageable, or that needs to alarm him.
The truth is, that there is a far greater sufficiency
among the lower classes of society than is generally imagined; and our first impressions of their
want and wretchedness are generally by much
too aggravated; nor do we know a more effectual
method of reducing these impressions than to cultivate a closer acquaintance with their resources,
and their habits, and their whole domestic economy. It is certainly in the power of artificial expedients to create artificial desires, and to call out
a host of applications, that would never have
otherwise been made. And we know of nothing
that leads more directly and more surely to this
state of things, than a great regular provision for
indigence, obtruded, with all the characters of
legality, and certainty, and abundance, upon the
notice of the people. But wherever the securities which nature hath established for the relief
and mitigation of extreme distress are not so tampered with, where the economy of individuals,
and the sympathy of neighbours, and a sense of
the relative duties among kinsfolk, are left, without disturbance, to their own silent and simple

operation;—it will be found that there is nothing so formidable in the work of traversing a whole mass of congregated human beings, and of encountering all the clamours, whether of real or of fictitious necessity, that may be raised by our appearance amongst them. So soon as it is understood that all which is given by such an adventurous philanthropist is given by himself; and so soon as acquaintanceship is formed between him and the families; and so soon as the conviction of his good will has been settled in their hearts, by the repeated observation they have made of his kindness and personal trouble, for their sakes;—then the sordid appetite which would have been maintained, in full vigour, so long as there was the imagination of a fund, of which he was merely an agent of conveyance, will be shamed, and that nearly into extinction, the moment that this imagination is dissolved. Such an individual will meet with a limit to his sacrifices, in the very delicacy of the poor themselves; and it will be possible for him to expatiate among hundreds of his fellows, and to give a Christian reception to every proposal he meets with; and yet, after all, with the humble fraction of a humble revenue, to earn the credit of liberality amongst them. We know not, indeed, how one can be made more effectually to see, with his own eyes, the superfluousness of all public and legalised charity, than just to assume a district, and become the familiar friend of the people who live in it, and to do for them the thousand nameless offices of Christian regard, and to encourage, in every judicious and inoffensive way, their dependence upon themselves, and their fellow-feeling one for another. Such a process of daily observation as this will do more than all political theory can do, to convince him with what safety the subsistence of a people may be left to their own capabilities; and how the modern pauperism of our days is a superstructure altogether raised on the basis of imposture and worthlessness—a basis which the very weight of the superstructure is fitted to consolidate and to extend.

It is fully admitted, that an elder, to be at all useful to the people, must approve the genuineness of his Christianity amongst them; and this he cannot do if he carry to their observation the hard and forbidding aspect of one that has no feeling for the poor. It is the necessity of maintaining such a defensive aspect among the numerous applications which are gendered by an artificial system of charity, that renders it so desirable to rescue all ecclesiastical men from the work of its distributions. But should charity cease to be artificial, and the cause come, at length, to be confided to the operation of sympathy, and a sense of duty, among individuals, then, let an elder associate himself with the families of any city district, and it is certainly his part, as one of these individuals, to exemplify, in his person, all the virtues of that gospel, for the interest of which he professes to

N

be a labourer. But he will soon ascertain the difference, in respect of pressure and urgency of application for those alms which are dispensed by public and associated charity, and those alms which are done in secret. What is still better, there will be a charm of gratitude and of moral influence in the one ministration, which he never felt in the other: and, when the year has rolled over his head, and he computes all the expenses of that season of kindness and of enjoyment which is past, he will find in this, as in every other department of Christian experience, that the yoke of the Saviour is, indeed, easy, and his burden is light.

But it is not the *materiel* of benevolence, given to those few of his families who may require it,— it is not this that will bind to him the population he has assumed. This may be necessary to indicate the honesty of his principles. But it is the *morale* of benevolence,—it is the unbounded and universal spirit of kindness felt by him for all the families, and expressing itself in numberless other ways, besides the giving of alms,—it is this which will raise him to his chief and useful ascendency over them. It is seldom adverted to, how much a simple affection, if it be but authentically manifested in any one way, is fitted to call forth affection back again. It is little known how open even the rudest and wildest of a city population are to the magic of this sweetening influence. There is here one precious department of our nature which seems not to have been so overspread as the rest of it, by the ruins of the fall. Perhaps, vanity and selfishness may enter as elements into the effect; but, certain it is, that if one human being see, in the heart of another, a good will towards himself, he is not able, and far less is he willing, to stifle or to withhold the reciprocal good will that he feels to arise in his own bosom. This is a phenomenon of our nature which the hardy administrators of a poor's house have little conception of; and they may be heard to predict, that if you disjoin an elder from all the patronage which he shares with them, you take away from him the only instrument by which he can ever hope to conciliate his families. The truth is, that it is in virtue of being associated with them, that there is so wide a distance, and so many heart-burnings, between him and his families. And he never will be able to make ground amongst them, till that which letteth is taken out of the way. The hostility of the people, or the hypocrisy of the people, may be abundantly nourished out of the elements of the present system; but it is by the play of finer elements altogether, that the hearts of the people are to be won. We are quite aware of the incredulity of practical men upon this subject; but it is just because they are not practical enough, that they are blind to the truth, and cannot perceive it. This is a subject on which the faithful delineations of experience are, at the same time, so very beautiful, that they impress an indiscriminating mind with the suspicion of a fancy picture, on which the glare, and the tinsel, and the warm colouring, of an artist have been abundantly employed. We are quite confident, however, that, in the progress of the system of locality, there will be a speedy and a satisfying multiplication of facts, more than enough to verify that what has been affirmed upon this topic are, indeed, the words of truth and soberness.

It has never been enough adverted to, that a process for Christianising the people is sure to be tainted and enfeebled, when there is allied with it a process for alimenting the people—that there lies a moral impossibility in the way of accomplishing these two objects, by the working of one and the same machinery—and that if a combined operation has been set up, in behalf of the former, then its individual agents do wrong, by joining their counsels and their energies together, in behalf of the latter; for the duties connected with which they should simply resolve themselves into private Christians, each acting separately, and in secret, within his own sphere, and each eventually finding how much more remarkable that sphere becomes, when charity is again restored to its natural aspect, and all artifice, and all publicity, are done away from it.

Still, however, there is the impression among many, of a flowery and unsubstantial romance, in all that has been said about the charm of private kindness, when unassociated with such gifts as can only be supplied out of the treasures of public liberality. They regard it as a dream of poetry, which is never realised, even in a country parish —a scene more favourable, it is thought, to all sorts of sentimentalism—and which, therefore, lies at a still more hopeless distance away from us, among the rude and rugged materials of a city population. So that it still remains the obstinate conviction of by far the greater number of our municipal rulers, that, without a copious distribution of the material of benevolence, there is no making way among the crowded families of a town; and that the simple affection of benevolence, however intense in its feeling, and however obvious and sincere in all its indications, will not suffice for the acceptance of a mere Christian philanthropist, in the humble walks of society.

This is a question, too, which it were better to try than to argue. And yet it ought to be a palpable thing, even with our most every-day observers, that humanity is so constituted as to derive a sensation of pleasure from another's love, as well as from the fruit of another's liberality. When humanity, indeed, is brought up to its perféction, it will be the former, and not the latter, that will minister the highest gratification. There is to be treasure, we are told, in heaven; and yet there will neither be silver nor gold there, which the apostle Peter ranks among corruptible things; for, according to the report of our Saviour, there is nothing in that place of blessedness which either moth or rust can corrupt, or which thieves can steal. And there will also be benevolence in heaven—a communication from one to another, of such treasure as belongs to it—a mutual transference of enjoyment, which will heighten the enjoyment of each of the parties—a fulness of gratification arising not merely from the tide of kind and pleasurable emotion which passes and repasses between God upon his throne, and the holy and happy family around him, but arising also from the reciprocal conveyance of reverence and regard, and all that is righteous, and affectionate, and true, between the various members of that family. So that, even in a state of things where poverty is altogether excluded—where silver and gold cannot enter, as they do now, into that expression of good will, which is often rendered here by one human being to another—where, though materialism do exist, it is not such a corrupt and deranged materialism as that by which we are surrounded, and in virtue of which, the claims of want, and sickness, and suffering, are incessantly calling forth a supply of this world's wealth, from those who have it to those who have it not—in a state of things where those miseries which draw upon the ordinary beneficence of our species are unknown, and where almsgiving is impossible;—will there still, in some way or other, be a rich and blessed dispensation of good falling from those who have neither gold nor silver to give, and yet who, by giving such things as they have, will so elevate the raptures and the felicities of heaven, as to cause its joy to be felt.

In this world the poor shall be with us always; and, under the imperative duty of giving such things as we have, all who do have the silver and gold are under the obligation of being willing to distribute, and ready to communicate. And yet this is a world where the principles of heaven ripen into perfection. This is a world where the affections of heaven take their birth, and rise into maturity, and operate, in the midst of much to thwart and to discourage them, and find in the peopled scenes of humanity the objects of constant and manifold indulgences. This is a world too which gross and sensual as the general nature of its inhabitants may be, and keenly directed as their appetites are towards silver and gold, or such materials of enjoyment as these can produce, it is still a world, where, through all its generations the charm even of simple kindness is not unfelt, even when it has nothing to bestow; it is a world where Christian love, even though it do not possess the elements of liberality, is no sooner recognised in our bosom, than it causes another bosom to respond and to rejoice along with it; it is a world where the cordiality of man to his fellow, in its passage from one heart and from one habitation to another, is ever sure to carry along with it the truest and

most touching of all gratifications; it is a world
where we affirm, that good will, though unaccompanied with wealth, can spread a higher and more
permanent felicity, even among its poorest vicinities, than ever wealth can, in all its profu-
sion, unaccompanied with good will. So that
though a time be coming, when the world shall
be burned up, and all its silver and gold, and other
materials for the grosser desires of our body, are,
like the dross of some worthless residuum, to be
utterly consumed and cast away; yet, if the pure
and prompting benevolence of the soul, with all
its ardours upon the one side, and all its honest
gratitude upon the other, shall survive this process of destruction, and be transplanted into heaven, there will be enough to regale, and that for
ever, its immortal society; enough, out of the mere
interchange of its moralities and its feelings, to
sustain all its fondest delights, and all its highest
and most abiding ecstacies.

Now, though these moralities are here imperfect, yet are they not even now, in their present
measure, and according to their present degree,
convertible to the purpose of diffusing upon earth
a certain proportion of the blessedness of heaven?
When unaccompanied with the possession of gold
and silver, they will of course give to their instruments of benevolence, the aim and the direction of benevolence. But they are not always
thus accompanied. The poor in this world's
goods are often rich in faith, and heirs of the

everlasting kingdom. They may possess the elements of the character of heaven, though they do not possess the earthly means of earthly gratification. With this character, and its emanating influences, they will shed a lustre and a blessedness around the mansions of the city which hath foundations. And though the earthly be unlike to the heavenly nature, in its active principles, yet it is not so unlike, in its experience of passive enjoyment, but that with this character a poor man may shed a degree of the same lustre and the same blessedness around his present dwelling-place. It holds true, even of the most profligate of our kind, that attentions can soothe them, and the expression of civility can reconcile them, and the courteousness which is due from one human being to another can soften and draw them out to a return of courteousness back again; and the friendship which has positively nothing to offer, but its moral and affectionate regards, can waken in their minds a sensation of enjoyment; and good will, with those minuter services, which, of no moment in respect of their material benefit, go only to indicate the principle from which they spring, can, on the strength of its own bare and unassociated existence, subdue them into a reciprocal tenderness—and that all these, when obviously emerging out of a Christian heart, from a deep and a sacred fountain struck out there, and forming a well of water which springeth up into life everlasting, can give such an unequivocal charac-

ter of religiousness to all that its possessor either
doeth or saith to his neighbours who are around
him, as, though he has neither silver nor gold to
give away, may, in fact, render him their most
important benefactor. In that crowded obscurity of human beings where God hath fixed his habitation, he may be a light, and send forth a moral sunshine into the surrounding darkness; he
may be a leaven, and by the fermenting operation of his example and advice may leaven the
whole of his little neighbourhood; he may be a
salt, nor will it be known, perhaps, till the disclosures of another day, how far the influence of
his presence went to preserve from utter dissolu-
tion the putrid mass of wickedness around him;
or how much the recurring melody of his evening
psalms served to mitigate the uproar of its noisy
and turbulent dissipation. But the fact which
now calls our attention is, that even the most depraved of nature's children own the power and
the graciousness of those simple ministrations
which form the all that a humble Christian can
bestow—that his professions of kindness, and his
pleadings of earnestness, and his advices of piety,
to themselves and to their families, and his little
surrenders of time and of trouble, have an impression upon them—and that, even in spite of their
own unregenerate hearts, it is, upon the whole,
an impression of kindliness—that, giving only
such things as he has, and without either gold or
silver to give, he has wrought a benefit for them,

and for himself a gratitude, and a cordial remembrance, surpassing all that takes place in the more
common dispensations of charity: insomuch that,
whether we compute the good that has been rendered, on the one hand, as made up of moral
influence, and friendly admonition, and the nameless offices of a humble but honest regard; and the
return it calls out, on the other, as made up of a
heart-felt graciousness which even the sternest of
our kind cannot withhold from the man who
unites, in his person, the worth of Christianity
with the gentleness of Christianity;—we will positively find, in this simple play of the pure and
abstract feelings of benevolence, unassociated
as it is with what may be called the materialism
of benevolence, more of the ethereal character of
a higher and holier region, than in the mere intercourse of such a generosity as evinces itself only
by a gift, and of such a gratitude as evinces itself
only by the pleasure of receiving it.

It is surely a position, the truth of which may
be demonstrated to human experience, that the
simple existence of kind affection, on the one
hand, and the simple recognition of it, with its
influence in calling forth a corresponding return,
upon the other, are enough, of themselves, to
augment, and that too in a most substantial and
satisfying degree, the happiness of each of the
parties; and that, therefore, the man who has nothing to give but the expression of his friendly
regard may, in fact, be dealing out among his fel-

lows the materials of real enjoyment. It will not be difficult to convince of this truth the members of an affectionate family, in the transference of whose kindly feelings from one to another they intimately know that there is a sensation far more precious to the heart, than can be wrought there by the transference of gold or silver. Neither will it be difficult to convince the man of ever-flowing cordiality, in the walks of social intercourse, who, whether at the festive board, or even in his hurried passage through the bustle and throng of a street teeming with acquaintances, is most thoroughly conscious of the pleasure that is both given and received by the smile, and the rapid enquiry, and even the most slight and momentary token of deference and good will. Neither will it be difficult to make the truth of this lesson be recognised by him who has had frequent experience and fellowship among the abodes of poverty, and who can attest how pure and how delicious that incense is which arises from the simple acknowledgments of those who, save their regard and the expression of their honest attachment, have positively nothing to bestow. And neither will it be difficult to make this whole matter plain to the reflection of the poor themselves, upon whose humble vicinities the wealthy have seldom or never entered, and who know well that, within the narrow compass of their own intercourse, a bright and a gladdening influence may be conveyed from one humble tenement to another;

and that if the next door neighbour bear an affection to them, it throws a light into their bosoms which would not be there, if he bore against them a grudge or a displeasure; and that the difference, in point of feeling, between an atmosphere of kind agreement and an atmosphere of fierce and fiery contention is just as distinct as will be the difference between heaven and hell: insomuch that, after all, it is not so much the occasional liberality of him who makes the transient visit, and leaves behind him some token of his abundance,—it is not this which so cheers and alleviates the lot of poverty, as that more stedfast and habitual blessedness which, by the kindness of immediate neighbours, may be made to shine and to settle around its habitation. All this is abundantly obvious among the various conditions of society, in the bosom of a family, or among the rich, in all that regards their intercourse with each other; or among the rich, as to the sweetness which they have themselves experienced, in a simple offering of affection from the poor; or among the poor, in all that they know and feel of the relationship in which they stand with the members of their own neighbourhood. And the only difficulty, in completing this proof, which we have to contend with, is when we attempt to convince the rich that, while it is their duty to give of their gold and silver to those who stand in need of them, it is their kindness which, if actually perceived to be genuine, is more valued

and more enjoyed by the poor than even the fruit
of their kindness—it is the principle which
prompted the offering that, after all, affords a
truer relish to their feelings than the offering itself—it is the community of hearts which raises
and delights them more than even the community
of goods. If the one be established between the
various classes of society, it will no doubt bring
the best and fittest proportion of the other along
with it. But the thing of importance to be remarked just now is, that nature, even when sunk
in abject poverty, and, therefore, relieved in her
more pressing wants by an act of alms-giving, is
still more soothed and conciliated by an exhibition of good will, on the part of the giver, than
by the whole material product of the beneficence
that he has rendered—that it is a gross, and, in
every way, an injurious misconception of the poor
to think them beyond the reach of those finer influences which reciprocate between pure sympathy, on the one hand, and a simple sense and
observation of that sympathy, on the other. In
other words, that the rich are not aware of what
that is which gains the most effective influence
over the hearts of the poor, if they think that fortune has given them a power which belongs only
to the principle of generosity that is within, and
not to the mere fruit of generosity that is without; or if they think that money descending, by
the law of the land, in the shape of an unwilling
or extorted ministration, has any portion in it of

that higher control which only belongs to the law of love written in the heart, and evincing its operation in unwearied attentions, and engaging affabilities, and willing services.

Conceive, then, an individual who has been in the habit, for years, of going round among an assigned population as the agent and the distributor of relief, out of a public treasury. Should he transfer his office to another, and simply go round among them, in the new capacity of a friend and a Christian adviser, he may still have a certain proportion of silver and gold to dispose of, out of those private means which he, in common with all other men, should lay out on charitable uses, as God hath given him the ability. The gold and the silver may not, therefore, be totally withdrawn from his ministrations; but, in virtue of such an arrangement, the gold and the silver would, at least, be very much reduced, and he would be left without any thing to substitute in their places, but the attentions of kindness and the attentions of Christianity. We are not supposing this old office to be abolished, but only to be laid on another; and the question is a very plain one, Will the attentions which we have just now specified be, in themselves, enough to maintain him in the place which he formerly held over that neighbourhood of human beings, where he wont to expatiate? The practical solution of this question would lead us to determine whether the account, which we have now given, of our nature be of an experimental or of a visionary character. If there be other tokens of affection than the one act of giving money, and these tokens be exhibited; if there be other marks of good will than the distribution of a gold and a silver which he no longer has to bestow, and these marks be authentically seen and read of all men, upon his person; if, without the means of his former liberality, his present love be only verified in its naked existence, or if it announce its reality by such signs as nature has annexed to the feeling, and as every partaker of that nature knows well how to interpret; if, by the perseverance of months, he has schooled away every suspicion of hypocrisy, and, in the toils and the services of an unwearied assiduity, he has, at length, earned the conviction that all their hopes and all their anxieties are his own; if, when he knocks at their doors, it should only be on the simple errand of a cordial enquiry, or an imploring advice, either to themselves or to their children;—the man may positively have nothing but his heart to give, but, in giving that, he has touched the very principle of our nature which brings all its hidden machinery under his power. This ascendency of the moral over the material part of our constitution is no romance and no fabrication of poetry. It is exemplified every day, in the living and the ordinary walk of human experience. There is not, on the face of our world, one neighbourhood of contiguous families, either

so poor or so profligate as to withstand these repeated demonstrations; and that sullenness of
character which no bribery could reduce, and
which gathers a deeper and more determined
gloom, when the hand of authority is applied to
it, has been rendered tractable as childhood, under the mighty and the magical spell of a meek,
and endearing, and undissembled charity.

The law of reciprocal attraction between one
heart and another is a law of nature as well as
of Christianity; insomuch, that no sooner does
the regard of a philanthropist for the people of
his district come to be recognised, than their regard for him, and that, too, both from the con-
verted and unconverted, will attest of what kind
of material humanity is formed. The effect is so
beautiful that one cannot expatiate upon it, without meeting the imputation of romance from
those hackneyed, and secular, and incredulous
men, whose eyes have never once been directed to
this field of observation; but the effect is, at the
same time, so certain as to stamp on what we say
all the soundness of an experimental affirmation.
Christianity, indeed, is the alone agent by which
the elevating power of a sentiment so pure and so
celestial, as to have the effect of poetry upon the
imagination, will ever be realised on the familiar
and homebred scenes of ordinary life. But it is a
most inviting circumstance, in the great enterprise of spreading the light and influence of
Christianity around a population, where one sees

that the very humblest of its zealous votaries can thus work his secure and certain way to the universal acceptance of his fellows. Let suspicion be but once dissipated, and the enmity of nature be disarmed, by the true and touching demonstrations of a real principle of kindness, and ridicule have ceased from its uproar, and contempt have discharged all its vociferations, and the man's worth and benevolence become manifest as day; then, though the ministration of gold and silver be that which fortune hath altogether denied him, it is both very striking and very encouraging to behold, how, in spite of themselves, he steals the hearts of the people away from them; how, as if by the operation of some mystic spell, the most restless and profligate of them all feel the softening influence of his presence and of his doings; and how, in the cheap and humble services of tending their children, and visiting their sick, and ministering in sacred exercises at the couch of the dying, and filling up his opportunities of intercourse with the utterance of holy advice, and the exhibition of holy example, there is, in these simple and unaccompanied attentions, a charm felt and welcomed, even in the most polluted atmosphere that ever settled around the most corrupt and crowded of human habitations.

This is not credited by many of our citizens; and men who deliver themselves in a tone of grave, and respectable, and imposing experience, may be heard to affirm, that, unless an elder be vested with a power of administration over the public money, he will be an unwelcome visitor with the general run of our families—that he will meet with few to bid him God-speed, on the single and abstract errand of Christianity—and that, while the old system of payments without prayers was acceptable enough, the new system of prayers without payments will banish the whole host of eldership in our city from the acceptance and good will of its inhabitants. Surely this is a matter of proof and not of probability— a thing that may be committed to the decision of experience, instead of being left to the contentions of reason or of sophistry. Let an elder count it his duty to hold a habitual intercourse of kindness with the people of his district, and, for this purpose, devote but a few hours in the week to their highest interest; out of the fulness of a heart animated with good will to men, and, in particular, with that good will which points to the good of their eternity, let him make use of every practical expedient for spreading amongst them the light and influence of the gospel; let it be his constant aim to warn the unruly, to comfort the afflicted, to stimulate the education of children, to press the duty of attending ordinances, to make use of all his persuasion in private, and of all his influence to promote such public and parochial measures as may forward the simple design of making our people good, and pious, and holy;—then, though he should go forth among them stript of power, and patronage, and pecuniary administrations; though his honest and Christian good will be all he has to recommend him; though the various secularities, by which the offices of our Church have been polluted and degraded, shall be conclusively done away, and the whole armory of our influence among the people be reduced to the simple element of good will, and friendship, and personal labour, and unwearied earnestness in the prosecution of their spiritual welfare:—yet, with these, and these alone, will any of our elders, at length, find a welcome in every heart, and a home in every habitation. Others may then take up the ministration which he has put away. But it will be his presence which will awaken the finest glow of kindly and reverential feeling among our population. Though, out of any public treasury, he neither has gold nor silver to give, yet, let him just do with his means and his opportunities as every Christian should do, and feel as every Christian should feel, and he will rarely meet with a family so poor as to undervalue his attentions, or a family so profligate as to persist in despising them.

All the dispensations of Providence, and all the great events in the train of human history, are on the side of the Christian philanthropist. He has only to watch his opportunity, and there is not a family so hardened in the ways of impiety, where he may not, in time, establish himself. The stoutest hearted sinner he may have to deal with must, in a few little years, meet with something to soften and to bring him down. Death may make its inroads upon his household, and disease may come, with its symptoms of threatening import, upon his own person; and, in that bed of sickness which he dreads to be his last, may the terrors and reproaches of conscience be preparing a welcome for the elder of his district; and he who wont to laugh the ministrations of his Christian friend away from him will, at length, send an imploring message and supplicate his prayers. Such is the omnipotence of Christian charity. At the very outset of its enterprise, it will find a great and an effectual door opened to it: and, in the course of months, its own perseverance will work for it; and Providence will work for it; and the mournful changes which take place in every family will work for it; and all the frailties of misfortune and mortality to which our nature is liable will work for it: and thus may one single individual, acting in the capacity of a Christian friend, and ever on the alert with all the aid of Christian counsel, and all the offices of Christian sympathy, in behalf of his assigned population, be the honoured instrument of reviving another spirit, and setting up another style of practice and observation, in the midst of them. Thus may he obtain a secure hold of ascendency over the affections of hundreds; and, like unto a leaven for good, in the neighbourhood which has been entrusted to his care, may he, by the blessing of God, infuse into that mass of human immortality with which he is associated the fermentation of such holy desires, and penitential feelings, and earnest aspirations, and close inquiries after the truth, as may, at length, issue in the solid result of many being called out of darkness into light, of many being turned unto righteousness.

The Christian elder who has resigned the temporalities of his office should not think that, on that account, he has little in his power. His presence has a power. His advice has a power. His friendship has a power. The moral energy of his kind attentions and Christian arguments has a power. His prayers at the bed of sickness, and at the funeral of a departed parishioner, have a power. The books that he recommends to his people, and the minister whom he prevails on them to hear, and the habit of regular attendance upon the ordinances to which he introduces them, have a power. His supplications to God for them, in secret, have a power. Dependence upon him, and upon his blessing, for the success of his own feeble endeavours, has a power. And when all these are brought to bear on the rising generation; when the children have learned both to know and to love him; when they come to feel the force of his approbation, and, on every recurring visit, receive a fresh impulse from him to diligence at school, and dutiful behaviour out of it; when the capabilities of his simple Christian relationship with the people thus come to be estimated:—it is not saying too much, to say that, with such as him, there lies the precious interest of the growth and transmission of Christianity, in the age that is now passing over us; and that, in respect of his own selected neighbourhood, he is the depositary of the moral and spiritual destinies of the future age.

We shall conclude this department of the subject with three distinct observations relative to the office and duties of the eldership.

First. We are well aware how widely the practice of our generation has diverged from the practice of our ancestors: how the temporal, which form their superinduced duties, have taken place of the spiritual, which form the primitive and essential duties of the eldership; how, within the limits of our Establishment, the lay office-bearers of the Church are fast renouncing the whole work of ministering from house to house, in prayer, and in exhortation, and in the dispensation of spiritual comfort and advice, among the sick, or the disconsolate, or the dying. We are aware that a reformation, in this department, can only be brought about by an influence of a more gentle, and moral, and withal more effectual kind than that of authority. But we almost know nothing of greater importance than to have a connection of this kind established between the elders and the population of those districts which are respectively assigned to them. We know of nothing

which will tell more effectually, in the way of hu-
manizing our families, than if so pure an intercourse
was going on, as an intercourse of piety, between
our men of respectable station, on the one hand,
and our men of labour and of poverty, on the
other. We know of nothing which would serve
more powerfully to link and to harmonize into
one fine system of social order, the various classes
of our community. We know not a finer exhibition, on the one hand, than the man of wealth
acting the man of piety, and throwing the goodly
adornment of Christian benevolence over the splendour of those civil distinctions, which give a weight
and a lustre to his name in society. And we know
not a more wholesome influence, on the other
hand, than that which such a man must carry
around with him, when he enters the habitations
of our operatives, and dignifies, by his visits, the
people who occupy them; and talks with them,
as the heirs of one hope and of one immortality;
and cheers, by the united power of religion and
of sympathy, the very humblest of misfortune's
generation; and convinces them of a real and
a longing affection after their best interests; and
leaves them with the impression that here, at
least, is one man who is our friend; that here, at
least, is one proof that we are not altogether destitute of consideration amongst our fellows; that
here, at least, is one quarter on which our confidence may rest; aye, and amidst all the insignificance in which we lie buried from the observa-

tion of society, we are sure, at least, of one who, in the most exalted sense of the term, is now ready to befriend us, and to look after us, and to care for us.

Secondly. Those who have entered on the important and honourable office of the eldership, should have a full impression of its sacredness. We are fully aware that there is not a professing Christian who does not forfeit all title to the name and character of a Christian, if he do not honestly, and with all the energies of his soul, aspire at being not merely almost, but altogether a disciple of the Lord Jesus. It is the duty of the obscurest individual in a congregation, to be as heavenly in his desires, and as peculiar in the whole style of his behaviour, and as upright in his transactions, and as circumspect in his walk, and as devoted, in heart and in service, to the God of his redemption, as the minister who labours amongst them in word and in doctrine, or as the elders that assist him in the administration of ordinances, or as the most conspicuous among the office-bearers of the church with which he is connected. But they should remember that the very circumstance of being conspicuous forms a double call upon their attention to certain prescribed duties of the New Testament. It is this which gives so peculiar an importance to their example. It is this which, by making their light shine before men, renders it a more powerful instrument for glorifying God. And it is this, too, which stamps a tenfold malignity upon their misconduct. And under the impression of this, should they be careful lest their good be evil spoken of—to be, in all things, an example to the flock over which God hath appointed them the overseers—to remember that their conduct has a more decided bearing upon others than it had formerly—and that, as it is their duty to look, not to their own things, but to the things of others also, so it is their most solemn and imperious obligation, to take heed, and give no just offence, in any thing, that the religion of which they are the declared and the visible functionaries, be not blamed. We know not how a greater outrage can be practised on Christianity, we know not how a deadlier wound can be given to its interest and its reputation in the world, we know not how a sorer infliction can be devised on a part of greater tenderness, than for a man to usurp a place of authority and of lofty standing, in the church of our Redeemer, and then to exhibit such a life, and to maintain such a lukewarm indifference, and to hold out such a conformity to the world, as to all the levities, and all the secularities which abound in it; and above all, so to deform the path of his own personal history, by what is profane, and profligate, and unseemly, that the report of his misdoings shall spread itself over the neighbourhood, and, into whatever company it may enter, it shall scandalise the friends of Jesus, and become matter of triumph and of bitter derision to his enemies.

Thirdly. The gentlemen who have been invested with this office should make a conscience of their attendance upon the needs and the demands of their respective population; not to slur and superficialise the matter, but to give to it strength, and earnestness, and persevering attention; not to enter upon their offices, as if they were so many sinecures, but to feel that certain duties are annexed to them, and that, for the right and attentive performance of these duties, a weight of responsibility is lying upon them. In each parish there is an ample field for the exercise of such duties; a field so extensive that, if left to the solitary management of one individual, must be left in a great measure neglected; a field greatly beyond the time and the strength of the minister; a field which he is not able to cultivate to the full, by his own personal exertions, and to do justice to which he must avail himself of the assistance of his elders. And sure we are that, with a manageable extent of walk assigned to each of them, they would, at length, come to feel that to be an enjoyment which they may, perhaps, for some time, feel to be an oppression: and, though delicacy and inexperience should, at first, operate as restraints to their acting in the capacity of spiritual labourers, yet habitual and intimate intercourse with their people will soon reconcile them to their new employment, and render it a smooth, a pleasant, and an interesting concern.

It might be expected that, ere bringing this to-

pic to a close, we should deliver a few rules
for the right discharge and exercise of deaconship.   We do not plead for this as a permanent
institution of the church, believing as we do, that
it were vastly better for the people, if all public
charity, for the relief of indigence, were, as soon
as possible, done away.   Still, however, such an
order of men might be of important service, in
conducting society back again to its natural state,
as it respects pauperism.   And we are thoroughly persuaded that, by acting conformably to the
spirit of the few hints which follow, they will arrive at the conviction, that all public and ostensible charity might very safely be dispensed
with.

First.   The poor will feel themselves greatly
soothed and conciliated, by their ready attention,
by their friendly counsels, by their acts of advice
and assistance as to the conduct of their little affairs; by the mere civility and courteousness
which marks their transactions with them; and
that these will positively go farther to gladden
their hearts, and to endear their persons to them,
than all the money which they may find it necessary to award for the support of their indigent
families.

Secondly.   It will be said that, by this unre-
strained facility of manner, they will lay themselves
open to the inroads of the worthless and the undeserving.   In answer to this, we ask if there be
not room enough, in a man's character, for the

wisdom of the serpent along with the gentleness of the dove? That we may ward off the undeserving poor, is it necessary to put on a stern and repulsive front against all the poor who offer themselves to our observation? The way, we apprehend, is to put forth patience, and attention, and to be in the ready attitude of prepared and immediate service for all applications, in the first instance; to conduct every examination with temper and kindness: and surely it is possible to do this, and, at the same time, to conduct it with vigilance. Exercise will soon sharpen their discrimination in these matters, and when they have got a thoroughly ascertained state of the claim which has been advanced, and they find that it is not a valid one, then let them put forth their firmness, then let them make a display of calm and settled determination, then let them show their people that they have judgment as well as feeling, and that they know how to combine the habit of justice to the public, by not squandering their money on unsuitable objects, with the habit of sympathy for genuine distress, and of ready attention to the merits of every application.

On the strength of this principle, it will be in the power of a deacon to check, on the one hand, all unreasonable applications; and, on the other, still to preserve all that homage of attachment, which his kindness to real sufferers, and his candour and courteousness to all, are fitted to secure for him. His people will not like him the worse that they see him acting in a sound, judicious, and experimental way with them. They know how to appreciate good sense, as well as we; and they admire it, and they have an actual liking for it. They are scandalised when they see kindness lavished upon the unworthy. Though they like attention and sympathy, they have a greater esteem for them, when they see them combined with the exercise of judgment and a good understanding: and in proportion therefore as a deacon evinces himself to have the faculty of rejecting those claims which are groundless, in that very proportion will a real sufferer esteem that act of preference, by which he has had the discernment to single out his claim, and the benevolence most soothingly and most sympathisingly, and most amply, to provide for it.

But, lastly, we know not a more interesting case that can be submitted to a deacon, than when an applicant proposes, for the first time, to draw relief from a public charity. This he is often compelled to do, from some temporary distress, that hangs over his family: and if the emergency could be got over without a public and degrading exposure of him who labours under it, there would both be a most substantial saving of the public fund, and a most soothing act of kindness rendered to the person who is applying for it. If by the influence of the deacon, or that of his friends, work could be provided for a man in such circumstances, or some private and delicate mode of relief be devised for him, then we know not in what other way he could more effectually establish himself as the most valuahle servant of the public, and as the best and kindest friend of his own immediate population. All will depend upon the earnestness and the sense of duty which he brings to his offices along with him; and we should be much disappointed if it be not the result of his practice and observation, in this walk of philanthropy, that, after all, the cause of human indigence may be fully confided to the sympathy of individuals, and that even the demise of his own order is an essential step towards the conclusive establishment of that state of things where nature and Christianity will render their most effectual contributions, for alleviating the wants and the miseries of the species.

We may afterwards enlarge on the reasons why we regard a deaconship in the light of a temporary expedient, for the purpose of reducing that pauperism which has been accumulated upon us, under a former system of administration, rather than as an institution that is at all essential to the permanent well-being of a parish. So long as any method of public relief for indigence is perpetuated amongst us, whether by assessment or voluntary collection, we hold it greatly better that its whole conduct and management be devolved upon deacons than upon elders. But we are, at the same time, persuaded that it is not only a most practicable thing for an order of deacons so to manage,

as, in a few years, to transfer the whole expenses
of the parochial poor from a compulsory to a
gratuitous fund—we are further persuaded, that
as the result of their experience, these very men
will come to see with what perfect safety, and
even improvement, to the comfort of the lower
orders, the latter fund may also be dispensed
with; and thus their labours may come to be dispensed with, after having reached this most satisfactory of all consummations, that of having led
the people to repose on their own capabilities:
For, by giving them to understand that individual
sympathy, and their own foreseeing prudence,
are all they have to look for, against the day
of poverty, they will, at length, re-open those
mighty sources which an artificial charity had
sealed, and out of which nature, when not tortur-
ed and tampered with, as she has been, by the
intermeddling spirit of legislation, provides far
more abundantly for the wants of all her children.

CHAP. VIII.

ON SABBATH SCHOOLS.

It is well, that in the various religious establishments of Europe, provision should have been made for the learning as well as for the subsistence of a regular clergy. It is well, when a teacher of the gospel, in addition to the strict literature of his own profession, is further accomplished in the general literature of the times. We do not hold it indispensable that all should be so accomplished. But that is a good course of education for the church, which will not only secure the possibility that every minister may be learned in theology, but also a chance, bordering upon certainty, that some of them shall attain an eminence of authority and respect, in the other sciences. Christianity should be provided with friends and defenders, in every quarter of human society; and there should be among them such a distribution of weapons, as may be adapted to all the varieties of that extended combat, which is ever going on between the church and the world. And there is a special reason why the prejudices of philosophy against the gospel should, if possible, be met and mastered by men capable of standing on the very same arena, and plying the very same tactics, with the most powerful of its votaries;— and that, not so much because of the individual

R

benefit which may thereby be rendered to these
philosophers, as because of their ascendant influence over the general mind of society; and because of the mischief that would ensue to myriads
beside themselves, could an exhibition so degrading be held forth to the world, as that of Christianity which laid claim to the light of revelation,
retiring abashed from the light of cultivated nature, and not daring the encounter, when men,
rich in academic lore, or lofty in general authorship, came forth in hostility against her.

It is mainly to the learning of the priesthood
that Christianity has kept her ground on the
higher platform of cultured and well educated humanity, and that she enters so largely, as a bright
and much esteemed ingredient, into the body of
our national literature. It is true that, in this
way, she may compel an homage from many
whom she cannot subdue unto the obedience of
the faith; and save herself from contempt, in a
thousand instances, where she has utterly failed
in her attempts at conversion. But it is well,
whenever this degree of respect and acknowledgment can be obtained for her, among the upper
classes of life; and more especially in every free
and enlightened nation, like our own, where the
reigning authority is so much under the guidance
of the higher reason of the country, it is of un-
speakable benefit that Christianity has been so
nobly upheld by the talent and erudition of her
advocates. The fostering hand of the Legisla-

ture would soon have been withheld from all our Christian institutions, had the Christiam system not been palpably recommended by those numerous pleadings wherewith a schooled and accomplished clergy have so enriched the theological literature of our island. Nor do we believe that, in the face of public opinion, any political deference could have long been rendered to Christianity, had she been overborne, in her numerous conflicts with the pride and sophistry of able unbelievers. It is thus that we stand indebted to the learning of Christian ministers for the security of that great national apparatus of religious instruction, the utility of which we have already endeavoured to demonstrate: and hence, though learning does not, of itself, convert and Christianise a human soul, it may be instrumental in spreading and strengthening that canopy of protection, which is thrown, by our Establishment, over those humbler but more effective labourers, by whose Parish ministrations it is, that the general mass of our population becomes leavened with the doctrines of the gospel, and Christianity is carried, with light, and comfort, and power, into the bosom of cottages.

But, though learning must be enlisted on the side of Christianity, for the purpose of upholding her in credit and acceptance, among influential men; yet it is not indispensable for the purpose of conveying her moral and spiritual lessons into

the heart of a disciple. The truth is, that many
of the topics about which ecclesiastical learning
is conversant, are exterior to the direct substance
of that Bible which professes to be a written communication from God to man: such as the historic
testimonies that may be quoted in favour of religion, and those church antiquities, to acquire the
knowledge of which we must travel through many
a volume of ponderous erudition, and at least the
history, if not the matter, of the various contro-
versies by which the Christian world has been
agitated. We are aware that much of this controversy relates to the contents of the record, as
well as to the credentials of the record. Yet,
however its plainer passages may have been dark-
ened by heretical sophistry, on the one hand, and
its obscure passages may have divided the opinion
of critics and translators, on the other; this does
not hinder, that, from the Bible, and the English Bible, there may be made to emanate a flood
of light, on the general mass of an English peasantry—that, to evolve this light, a high and artificial scholarship is neither necessary nor available—that, on the understanding of a man, unlettered in all that proceeds from halls or colleges,
the Word of God may have made its sound, and
wholesome, and sufficient impression: and that
from him the impression may be reflected back
again, on the understandings of many others, as
unlettered as himself—that thus all, in the book
of God's testimony which mainly goes so to en-

lighten a man, as to turn him into a Christian, may be made to pass from one humble convert to his acquaintances and neighbours; and, without the learning which serves to acquire for Christianity the dignified though vague and general homage of the upper classes, he may, at least, be a fit agent for transmitting essential Christianity throughout the plebeianism that is around him.

To deny this, indeed, were to resist the affirmations of that very record in which all that may be known of Christianity is found. We are there told, and from the direct mouth of the Saviour, that things essential to salvation may be revealed unto babes, which lie hid from the wise and the prudent. The poor to whom the gospel is preached have a full share of this revelation. The Spirit of God, we are told, acts as a revealer; and yet it is not his office to make known any truths additional to those which are already engrossed in Scripture. The light that cometh from him is a light which shineth on the page of inspiration, and causes us to discern only what is graven thereupon. The doctrine of the Bible is made known to us by this process, and nothing else. Under the tuition of God's Spirit, we only learn what has already been fully expressed by the letter of the Bible, but which, without his influence, can never be fully apprehended in its meaning, or felt in its power. It is thus that he communicates nothing at variance with the written testimony, and nothing which has not been already.

declared by the written testimony; though his interference be necessary, in order that the testimony be received. The operation may be illustrated by the way in which an impression is given
to any substance, through the means of a stamping instrument. The substance may be so hard
and impracticable as to resist the impression,
when a weak arm is put forth to urge forward the
instrument; but it may be made to take in a full
and a fair impression, when a strong arm is employed. And thus may it be with the impression
of Bible doctrine, on moral, and thinking, and intelligent man. The Bible may be brought into
contact with the mind of the reader, and learning, and talent, and all the forces that mere humanity can muster, may be made to aid the impression of it, and be wholly ineffectual. The
Spirit of God may then undertake the office of
an enlightener; and, in so doing, he may keep
by the Bible as his alone instrument; and not one
truth may pass in conveyance from him to the spirit of that man, on whom he is operating, but simply and solely the truths which are taken off from
the written Word of God; and all the Christianity that he teaches, and that he leaves graven on
the hearts of his subjects, may just be a correct
transcript of the Christianity that exists in the
New Testament. And thus it is that a workman
of humble scholarship may be transformed, not
into an erratic and fanciful enthusiast, but into a
sound Scriptural Christian, without one other re-

ligious tenet in his understanding than what is strictly and accurately defined by the literalities of the written record, and without one other religious feeling in his heart than what is most pertinently called forth by the moral influence of the truths which have thus been made known to him.

If there be truth in this representation, it will appear that the Bible can be no more dispensed with, for the purpose of putting the impress of Christianity on a human soul, than the stamping instrument can be dispensed with, for the purpose of fixing the device which it bears on the piece of matter that is submitted to it. The disciple's mind must be brought into contact with Scripture, and it is so, when he is employed, either in hearing, or reading, or pondering, what is written thereon. And it will further appear that the Spirit, in his work of making good an impress of Christianity on man, no more varies in one feature, or one lineament, from the Christianity that is already engraven on the indelible Word of God, than that hand, which simply bears upon a seal, either alters or effaces the inscription which is fastened by it on the substance to which it is applied. It is thus that all the pretences of enthusiasm may be refuted and exposed; and that, while the teaching of the Spirit is held to be indispensable, the soundness and proficiency of the taught still remain to be tried, and may be taken cognizance of, at the bar of the law and of the testimony. There is no license given by

this statement to the vagaries of a credulous and
overheated imagination: being subject, as they
all are, to the touchstone of a word that is immu-
table, and cannot pass away. We know it to be
the fear of many, lest the doctrine of a special
and spiritual illumination, taking place in every
instance of conversion, should throw open the
Christian world to an influx of fancies and
fluctuations, that would be utterly interminable.
But the written record is the great barrier of defence against all such irregularities. There might
be room for this apprehension, were it still the
office of the Spirit to originate new and unheard
of truths, in the minds that he enlightens. But
this work has ceased long ago, and the Book in
which the truths thus originated were treasured
up has, for many centuries, had the seal of com-
pleteness set upon it; and the office of the Holy
Ghost now is not to inform any one mind of no-
velties that are yet unrevealed, bnt simply to
transcribe on the tablet of its understanding what
has already been inscribed on the tablet of the
written revelation. And thus it is both true that
it is through a distinct and personal work of the
Holy Spirit that each· believer is called out of
darkness unto marvellous light—and that, in respect of the essentials of Christianity, there has
been one stable and permanent belief among them
all. It is like the telescope pointed to a distant
landscape, which reveals the same objects to all
the numerous and successive spectators; and so

it is mainly one and the same doctrine that is held by the genuine disciples of all countries, and which has come unchangingly down, from generation to generation.

If it be thought that this statement serves very much to reduce the importance of human learning, let it be observed, on the other hand, that still to human learning there belongs an important function, in the matter of Christianity. One does not need to be the subject of a material impress upon his own person, in order to judge of the accordancy between the device that is submitted to his notice, and the seal that is said to have conveyed it. Both may be foreign to himself: and yet he, by looking to the one and to the other, can see whether they are accurate counterparts. And, in like manner, a man of sagacity and of natural acquirement may never have received, upon his own heart, that impression of the Bible which the Holy Spirit alone has strength to effectuate; but still, if such an impression be offered to his notice, in the person of another, he may be able both to detect the spurious, and, in some measure, to recognize the genuine marks of correspondence between the contents of Scripture, on the one hand, and the creed, or character, of its professing disciple, on the other. It is well, when such a man looks, in the first instance, to the written Word; and, by aid of the grammar and lexicon, and all the resources of philology, evinces the literal doctrine

s

that is graven thereupon. It is also well, when
he looks, in the second instance, to the human
subject, and by aid, either of natural shrewdness,
or of a keen metaphysical inspection into the *arcana* of character, drags forth to light that moral
and intellectual picture which the doctrine of the
Bible is said to have left upon the soul. If there
be a single alleged convert upon earth, who cannot stand such a trial, when fairly conducted, he
is a pretender, and wears only a counterfeit and
not the genuine stamp of Christianity. And thus
it is, that he who has no part whatever in the
teaching that cometh from God, who is still a
natural man, and has not received the things of
the Spirit, may, to a certain extent, judge the
pretensions of him who conceives that the Holy
Ghost has taken of the things of Christ, and
shown them to his soul. He can institute a sound
process of comparison between those testimonies
of Scripture which a natural criticism has made
palpable to him, and those traces upon the soul
which a natural sagacity of observation has made
palpable to him: and, without sharing himself in
an unction from the Holy One, or being sealed
by the Spirit of God into a personal meetness for
the inheritance of the saints, still may he both
be able to rectify and restrain the excesses of fanaticism, and also to recall the departures that her-
esy is making from the law and from the testimony.

The work of Bishop Horsley against Unitarianism is a work which erudition and natural talent are quite competent to the production of. It is the fruit of a learned and laborious research into ecclesiastical antiquities, and a vigorous argumentative application of the materials that he had gathered, to that controversy, on the field of which he obtained so proud and pre-eminent a conquest. We would not even so much as hazard a conjecture on the personal Christianity of this able and highly gifted individual. We simply affirm, that for the execution of the important service which he, at that time, rendered to the cause, his own personal religion was not indispensable; and, whether or not by the means of a spiritual discernment, he was enabled to take off, from the inscribed Christianity of the record, an effectual impression of it upon his own soul, it was well, that, by the natural expedients of profound sense and profound scholarship, he cleared away that cloud in which his antagonist, Dr. Priestley, might have shrouded the face of the record, both from the natural and spiritual discernment of other men. It is possible, both to know what the doctrine of the Bible is, and most skilfully and irresistibly to argument it, without having caught the impress of the doctrine upon one's own soul. It is possible for a man not to have come himself into effective personal contact with the seal of Holy Writ, and yet to demonstrate the characters of the seal, and to purge away its obscurity, and make it stand legibly out, which it must do, ere it can stand impressively out, to the view of others. There are many who look with an evil eye to the endowments of the English Church, and to the indolence of her dignitaries. But to that Church the theological literature of our nation stands indebted, for her best acquisitions; and we hold it a refreshing spectacle, at any time that meagre Socinianism pours forth a new supply of flippancies and errors, when we behold, as we have often done, an armed champion come forth, in full equipment, from some high and lettered retreat of that noble hierarchy; nor can we grudge her the wealth of all her endowments, when we think how well, under her venerable auspices, the battles of orthodoxy have been fought,—that, in this holy warfare, they are her sons and her scholars who are ever foremost in the field,—ready, at all times, to face the threatening mischief, and, by the might of their ponderous erudition, to overbear it.

But, if human talent be available to the purpose of demonstrating the characters of the seal, it is also, in so far, available to the purpose of judging on the accuracy of the impression. The work, perhaps, which best exemplifies this, is that of President Edwards, on the conversions of New England, and in which he proposes to estimate their genuineness, by comparing the marks that had been left on the person of the disciple, with the marks that are inscribed on the Book of the law and of the testimony. He was certainly much aided, in his processes of discrimination upon this subject, by the circumstance of being a genuine convert himself, and, so, of being fur-nished with materials for the judgment, in his own heart, and that stood immediately submitted to the eye of his own consciousness. But yet no one could, without the metaphysical faculty wherewith nature had endowed him, have con-ducted so subtle, and at the same time, so sound and just an analysis, as he has done; and no one, without his power of insight among the mysteries of our nature,—a power which belonged to his mind, according to its original conformation,—could have so separated the authentic operation of the Word upon the character, from the errors and the impulses of human fancy. It is true that none but a spiritual man could have taken so mi-nute a survey of that impression which the Holy Ghost was affirmed to have made, through the preaching of the Word, upon many, in a season of general awakening. But few, also, are the spi-ritual men, who could have taken so masterly a survey; and that, just because they wanted the faculties which could accomplish their possessor for a shrewd and metaphysical discernment among the *penetralia* of the human constitution. It is thus that, by the light of nature, one may trace the characters which stand out upon the seal; and, by the light of nature, one may be helped, at least, to trace the characters that are left upon the human subject, in consequence of this supernal application. Fanaticism is kept in check by human reason, and the soberness of the faith is vindicated. The extravagance of all pretenders to a spiritual revelation is detected, and made manifest; and the true disciple stands the test he is submitted to, even at the bar of the natural understanding.

We cannot take leave of Edwards, without testifying the whole extent of the reverence that we bear him. On the *arena* of metaphysics, he stood the highest of all his cotemporaries, and that, too, at a time, when Hume was aiming his deadliest thrusts at the foundations of morality, and had thrown over the infidel cause the whole *eclat* of his reputation. The American divine affords, perhaps, the most wondrous example, in modern times, of one who stood richly gifted both in natural and in spiritual discernment: and we know not what most to admire in him, whether the deep philosophy that issued from his pen, or the humble and child-like piety that issued from his pulpit; whether, when, as an author, he deals forth upon his readers the subtleties of profoundest argument, or when, as a Christian minister, he deals forth upon his hearers the simplicities of the gospel; whether it is, when we witness the impression that he made, by his writings, on the schools and high seats of literature, or the impression that he made, by his unlaboured addresses, on the plain consciences of a plain congregation. In the former capacity, he could estimate

the genuineness of the Christianity that had before been fashioned on the person of a disciple;
but it was in the latter capacity, and speaking of
him as an instrument, that he fashioned it, as it
were, with his own hands. In the former capacity, he sat in judgment, as a critic, on the resemblance that there was between the seal of God's
Word, and the impression that had been made on
the fleshly tablet of a human heart; in the latter
capacity, he himself took up the seal, and gave
the imprinting touch, by which the heart is con-
formed unto the obedience of the faith. The former
was a speculative capacity, under which he acted
as a connoisseur, who pronounced on the accordancy that obtained between the doctrine of the
Bible, and the character that had been submitted
to its influence; the latter was an executive capacity, under which he acted as a practitioner,
who brought about this accordancy, and so handled the doctrines of the Bible, as to mould and
subordinate thereunto the character of the people
with whom he had to deal. In the one, he was
an overseer, who inspected and gave his deliverance on the quality of another's work; in the
other, he was the workman himself: and while,
as the philosopher, he could discern, and discern
truly, between the sterling and the counterfeit, in
Christianity, still it was as the humble and devoted pastor that Christianity was made, or Christianity was multiplied, in his hands.

Now, conceive these two faculties, which were

exemplified in such rare and happy combination, on the person of Edwards, to be separated, the one from the other, and given respectively to two individuals. One of these would then be so gifted, as that he could apply the discriminating tests, by which to judge of Christianity; and the other of them would be so gifted as that, instrumentally speaking, he could make Christians. One of them could do what Edwards did, from the pulpit; another of them could do what Edwards did, from the press. Without such judges and overseers as the former, the faith of the Christian world might be occasionally disfigured by the excesses of fanaticism; but without such agents as the latter, faith might cease to be formed, and the abuses be got rid of only by getting rid of the whole stock upon which such abuses are occasionally grafted. It is here that churches, under the domination of a worldly and unsanctified priesthood, are apt to go astray. They confide the cause wherewith they are entrusted to the merely intellectual class of labourers, and they have overlooked, or rather have violently and impetuously resisted, the operative class of labourers. They conceive that all is to be done by regulation, and that nothing, but what is mischievous, is to be done by impulse. Their measures are generally all of a sedative, and few or none of them of a stimulating tendency. Their chief concern is to repress the pruriencies of religious zeal, and not to excite or foster the zeal itself. By this process they may deliver their Establishment of all extravagancies, so as that we shall no longer behold, within its limits, any laughable or offensive caricature of Christianity. But who does not see that, by this process, they may also deliver the Establishment of Christianity altogether; and that all our exhibitions of genuine godliness may be made to disappear, under the same withering influence which deadens the excrescencies that occasionally spring from it. It is quite a possible thing for the same church to have a proud complacency in the lore, and argument, and professional science, of certain of its ministers; and, along with this, to have a proud contempt for the pious earnestness, and pious activity, of certain other of its ministers. In other words, it may applaud the talent by which Christianity is estimated, but discourage the talent by which Christianity is made. And thus while it continues to be graced by the literature and accomplishment of its members, may it come to be reduced into a kind of barren and useless inefficiency as to the great practical purposes for which it was ordained.

To judge of an impression requires one species of talent, to make an impression requires another. They both may exist, in very high perfection, with the same individual, as in the case already quoted. But they may also exist apart; and often, in particular, may the latter of the two be found, in great efficiency and vigour, when the former of the two may be utterly awanting. The right way for a church is to encourage both these talents to the uttermost; and not to prevent the evils of a bad currency, by laying such an arrest on the exercise of the latter talent, as that we we shall have no currency at all. It must be produced, ere it can be assayed; and it is possible so to chill and to discourage the productive faculties in our Church, as that its assaying faculty shall have no samples on which to sit in judgment. This will universally be the result in every church where a high-toned contempt for what it holds to be fanaticism is the alone principle by which it is actuated; and where a freezing negative is sure to come forth on all those activities which serve to disturb the attitude of quiescence, into which it has sunk and settled. The leading measures of such a church are all founded on the imagination that the religious tendencies of our nature are so exuberant, as that they need to be kept in check, instead of being, in fact, so dormant as that they need work, and watchfulness, and all that is strenuous, and pains-taking, in the office of an evangelist, for the purpose of being kept alive. The true Christian policy of a church is to avail itself of all the zeal, and all the energy, which are to be found both among its ecclesiastics and its laymen, for the production of a positive effect among our population; and then, should folly or fanaticism come forward along with it, fearlessly to confide the chastening of all this exuberance to the sense, and the scholarship, and the sound intellectual Christianity, for the diffusion of which over the face of our Establishment, the Establishment itself has made such ample provision. Such is our impression of nature's lethargy, and deadness, and unconcern, that we are glad when any thing comes forward,—that we are pleased to behold any symptom of spiritual life or vegetation at all,—and so far from being alarmed by the rumour of a stir, and a sensation, and an enthusiasm, in any quarter of the land, we are ready to hail it as we would the promise of some coming regeneration. A policy the direct opposite of this is often the reigning policy of a church; and, under its blasting operation, spurious and genuine Christianity are alike obliterated; and the work of pulling up the tares is carried on so furiously, that the wheat is pulled up along with it,—the vineyard is rifled of its good-liest blossoms, as well as of its noxious and pestilential weeds; and thus the upshot of the process for extirpating fanaticism may be to turn the fruitful field into a wilderness, and to spread desolation and apathy over all its borders.

A church so actuated does nothing but check the excrescencies of spiritual growth, and may do it so effectually as to reduce to a naked trunk what else might have sent forth its clustering branches, and yielded, in goodly abundance, the fruits of piety and righteousness. There is no positive strength put forth by it, on the side of vegetation, but all on the side of repressing its hated overgrowth. It makes use of only one instrument, and that is the pruning-hook; as if, by its operation alone, all the purposes of husbandry could be served. Its treatment of humanity proceeds on such an excessive fertility of religion in the human heart, that all the toil and strenuousness of ecclesiastics must be given to the object of keeping it down, and so confining it within the limits of moderation; instead of such a natural barrenness that this toil and this strenuousness should rather be given to the various and everplying activities of an evangelist, who is instant in season and out of season. It is thus that the outfield of sectarianism may exhibit a totally different aspect from the inclosed and well kept garden of an Establishment. In the former, there may be a positive and desireable crop, along with the weeds and ranknesses which have been suffered to grow up unchastened; in the latter, there may be nothing that offendeth, save the one deadly offence of a vineyard so cleaned, and purified, and thwarted in all its vegetative tendencies, as to offer, from one end to the other of it, an unvaried expanse of earthliness.

We, therefore, do wrong, in laying such a weight of discouragement on the labourers who produce, and throwing the mantle of our protection and kindness only over the labourers who prune. And what, it may be asked, are the ingredients of mightiest effect, in the character and talent of a productive labourer? They are not his scholarship, and not his critical sagacity of discernment into the obscurities of Scripture, and not his searching or satirical insight among the mysteries of the human constitution. With these he may be helped to estimate the Christianity that has been formed, and to lop off its unseemly excrescencies; but with these alone we never shall positively rear, on the foundation of nature, the edifice itself. This requires another set of qualifications which may or may not exist along with that artificial learning to which, we trust, an adequate homage has been already rendered by us, and qualifications which, whether they are found among endowed or unendowed men, ought to be enlisted on the side of Christianity. They may exist apart from science, and they may most usefully and productively be exerted apart from science. The possessors of them are abundantly to be found in the private or humble walks of society, and may be the powerful instruments of propagating their own moral and spiritual likeness, among their respective vicinities. We are aware of the jealousy and disdain in which they are regarded by many a churchman,—that, held to be empirics, who invade the province of the regular faculty, there is, it is thought, the same mischief done by them, in theology, which is done by quacks in medicine,—that the diseases of the soul are liable to the same sort of injurious mismanagement, in the hands of the one, as the diseases of the body are, in the hands of the other; and this is very much the feeling of the great majority of our ecclesiastics, whether they look to the efforts of unlettered Methodism, in England, or to the Sabbath teaching, and the lay itinerancies, and the gratuitous zeal of the unofficial and the unordained of our own country.

Now, this parallel between physic and theology does not hold; nor is the power of working a given effect on the corporeal system arrived at by the same steps, with the power of working a given effect on the moral or spiritual system. To be a healing operator upon the body, one must be acquainted with the manifold variety of effects which the agents and applications innumerable of matter have upon the maladies equally innumerable, to which the body is exposed. To be a healing operator upon the soul, there is one great application revealed to us in Scripture, which, in every instance where it does take effect, acts as an unfailing specific for all its moral disorders. In the former profession, every addition of knowledge is an addition of power; and the best guarantees for an effectual exercise of the art medical are the science, and study, and experience, of a finished education. In the latter profession, these are useful too, for estimating the effect that has been made upon the character, but not indispensable for working that effect. That mighty truth, the belief of which is the power of God, and the wisdom of God, un-

to salvation, may be deposited, by one man, in
the heart of another, without the aid of any scholastic art, or scholastic preparation. It is too
simple to be illustrated by human talent, and the
mode of its conveyance from one bosom to another depends on certain influences which are as
much beyond the reach of a philosopher as of a
peasant, and as much within the reach of a peasant as of a philosopher. Grant that the one has
just as much of personal Christianity, and as much
of devotedness, in the cause of human souls, and
as much of the spirit of believing intercession
with God, in behalf of those among whom he is
labouring,—and then is he in possession of just
as powerful instruments as the other, for bringing
them under the dominion of the truth, as it is in
Jesus. So that it is not with bodily as it is with
spiritual innoculation. To work the one aright
there must be the contact of a right matter with
the material subject to which it is applied; and
one must study the properties of that which is
without them, ere they are qualified to make the
application. To work the other aright, there
must be the contact of a right mind with the moral subject to which it is applied; and the possessor of such a mind has simply to put its desires
and its tendencies into movement, that the wished for effect may follow; has to act on the impulse of its affections for others; and to pour
forth its Christian regards for their welfare; and
to gain them over by the exhibition of its worth,

and kindness, and piety; and to hold out that
Word of life, in which there is nothing dark, but
to those who love darkness; and to vent itself in
prayer for the saving illumination of those whom
it never ceases, so long as hope and prudence
warrant the exertion, to ply, with its most unwearied activities. To work a moral effect, such as
love, on the heart of another, one cannot fail to
perceive that mere science, even though it should
be the science of our own nature, were utterly
unavailing; and that the man who bears this affection in his own heart would do more to call
out a return of it, from the heart of his neighbour,
than he who, without love himself, has, at the
same time, a most intelligent discernment into
the law of its operation. And it is the same with
a Christian effect. He who can best work it on
another's mind is a Christian himself. It is the
sympathy of his kindred feelings—it is the observation of his actual faith, and of its bright and
beautiful influences upon his own character—it is
the winning representation of a doctrine that
may be read a thousand times over, without effect, in the written epistles of the New Testament, but which is armed with a new power to
engage and soften the heart of an inquirer, when
he sees it exemplified in the person of that believer who is a living epistle of Christ Jesus—it is
the melting tenderness by which he presses home
the overtures of the gospel on his fellow sinners,
and, above all, the efficacy of his prayers for grace

to turn and grace to enlighten them; these are
what may accomplish a man who is unlettered in
all but his Bible, to be a far more efficient Chris-
tianiser than the most profound or elaborate theo-
logian; these are what essentially constitute that
leaven by which, either with or without philosophy, a fermenting process for the growth and
the diffusion of Christianity is made to spread far
and wide among our population.

This is the reason why, though ecclesiastics
should be accomplished in the whole lore and
scholarship of their profession, they should not
discourage the effort and activity of lay operatives,
in the cause. They may inspect their work, but
they should not put a stop to it. When they discover a union of intelligence and piety in an individual, even of humble life, they should patronize
his attempts to spread around him the moral and
spiritual resemblance of himself. They else may
freeze into utter dormancy the best capabilities
that are within their reach of Christian usefulness: and thus it is possible for a clergyman, by
the weight of his authority, to lay an interdict on
a whole host of Christian agency, whom he should
have summoned into action, and of whom it is
possible that each may be far beneath him in the
literature of Christianity, and yet each far before him in the instrumental power of making
Christians.

Were the families of a city lane wholly overrun with the foul spirit of radicalism, it would not

be on the services of him who could best dissert
on the ethics of patriotism and good citizenship
that I should most build my hopes of reclaiming
them. I should look for a far more important
and practical reformation from the simple presence and contiguity among them, of one their
equal, perhaps, in station, and who himself was a
sound and a leal-hearted patriot. There would
be a weight of influence in the mere exhibition of
his wholesome and well-conditioned mind, which
no argument however skilful, and no penetration
however subtle into the casuistry of public and
political virtue, could have power to carry along
with them. The living exemplification of a sober,
and judicious, and regulated spirit, maintaining its
loyalty in the midst of surrounding fury and fermentation, would go farther to calm the tempest
than the most ingenious political sermon that
was ever framed: and more especially if the individual who so held forth among his neighbours
was one in whose friendship they had long trust-
ed, and to whose consistency and good conduct
they could all testify. There is no series of lectures delivered in any hall of public resort that
would have half the force which lay in the mere
personal communications of such a man with his
next-door associates; and what could not have
been done by the didactic efforts of any political
reasoner, will be far more readily done by the
present example and the untaught effusions of
him who simply realised, in his own character,

the worth and the practical wisdom of a good citizen.

Or, in some other cluster of families, did jealousy and dislike alienate the heart of each individual from all his fellows, it would not be to him who best understood the mysteries of our moral nature, that I would look, as the likeliest instrument for restoring peace and confidence among them. Through his insight into the *arcana* of the human constitution, he may be able both to perceive and to proclaim, that when there is good will to others in the bosom of one, this calls forth a reciprocal good will to him back again. It is not by sermonizing on the operation of this principle, that the wished for effect is carried : it is by actually having the principle, and operating therewith. Or, in other words, the simple presence of a man, humble it may be, in rank, but richly endowed either with Christian or with constitutional benevolence,—it is this, unaccompanied with all metaphysical discernment, or the power of metaphysical explanation, that will do more to expel the spirit of rancour from a neighbourhood, and to substitute the spirit of charity in its place, than any theoretical exposition of principles or processes can possibly accomplish. It is not the man who best lectures on the operation of the moving force, but the man who is possessed of the moving force, and actually wields it —it is he who works the practical consequence on the temper and mind of the neighbourhood

over which he expatiates. And thus it is that
the man of Christian love operates more powerfully as a leaven, in his vicinity, than the man of
Christian learning: and it is altogether a mistake,
that a long and laborious routine of scholarship
must be described, ere the exertions of a religious
teacher shall, with efficacy, tell on the moral
and spiritual habit of the disciples who repair to
him.

For, it is just in Christianity as in the cases we
have now quoted. All the essential truths of it
can be easily apprehended; insomuch, that on the
ground of mere intelligence with respect to its
most vital and important doctrines, the peasant
and the philosopher are upon a level. But to apprehend the truth with the natural understanding
is one thing, and it is another so to realise and so
to appropriate it, as that it shall bear, with power
and with personal influence, upon the character.
Now, we shall meet with instances of the latter
as readily in the humble as in the lofty walks of
society; and there we shall as soon find an individual who can hold forth a living picture of Christianity, and bring the whole moving force of its
affections and its virtues to bear on the vicinity
around him. It were bad philosophy, to confine the work of propagating a Christian influence
throughout a population to the adepts of a university; and just as strong a transgression against
the true philosophy of our nature, to confine it to
the regularly bred and ordained clergy, whether

of our city or our country parishes. And, however offensive it may be to the official pride and
the official intolerance of churchmen, it is not, on
that account, the less true, that, among the very
humblest of the flock, individuals may be found,
who, with no pretensions to the science of Christianity, yet, from the attractive sympathy that
there is in its virtues and in its graces, will
form into a more powerful as well as a purer leaven than is the minister himself: insomuch, that
the very best service which he is capable of rendering to the cause may be, to give freedom and
encouragement to the working of this leaven, in
every part of the mass, where it is known to exist.
Perhaps, the deadliest obstacle to the Christianity
of his parish is the rancour that he feels towards
the zeal and the activity of lay operatives,—the
contemptuous resistance, not less unphilosophical
than it is unscriptural, with which he is ever
bearing down the nascent piety of his neighbourhood, and stifling, in embryo, all those various
expedients of Sabbath schools, and fellowship
meetings, and assemblages for prayer and religious
conversation, wherewith the Christianity of the
few might diffuse and multiply its own image over
the whole of that parochial territory which is assigned to him.

In every church let securities be provided for
the highest attainments of Christian literature, so
as that many ecclesiastics shall be found in it,
rich in all the deep and varied erudition of theo-

logy. We know not a nobler intellectual eminence than that which may be gained on the
neglected walks of sound and scriptural philosophy, by one who, with a mind stored both in the
criticism and antiquities of his profession, further
knows how to impregnate his acquisitions with
the liberal and experimental spirit of our age;
and who, without commuting the orthodoxy of
God's imperishable record, could so far moder-
nize the science, of which he was, at the same
time, both the champion and the ornament, as to
envolve upon the world, not its new truths, but its
new applications. Christianity never changes,
but the complexion and habits of the species are
always changing: and thus may there be an ex-
haustless novelty both of remark and illustration,
in our intellectual treatment of a science which
touches at almost every point in the nature of
man, and bears, with decisive effect, on the
whole frame and economics of civil society. In
such a tract of literature as this, study, and speculation, and scholarship, may be carried to the
uttermost extent: and he who has done so may
well take his place with all that is dignified and
great, whether in moral or political philosophy.
But it were giving the last finish to the character
of his mind, if, amid the pride and the prowess
of its rare accomplishments, he could appretiate
aright the piety and the practical labours of an
unlettered Christian: and it would confer upon
him that very thing which is so touching, in the

simplicity of Newton, or in the missionary zeal and devotedness of Boyle, if, while surrounded by the trophies of his own successful authorship, he could be made to see, that, however profound in the didactics of Christianity, yet, in the actual work of giving a personal spread to Christianity, there is many a humble man of privacy and of prayer who is far before him.

According to our *beau ideal* of a well going and a well constituted church, there should be among its ecclesiastics the very highest literature of their profession, and among its laymen the most zealous and active concurrence of their personal labours in the cause. The only check upon the occasional eccentricities of the latter should be the enlightened judgment of the former: and this, in every land of freedom and perfect toleration, will be found enough for the protection of a community against the inroads of a degrading fanaticism. It is utterly wrong, that because zeal breaks forth, at times, into excesses and deviations, there should, therefore, be no zeal; or, because spiritual vegetation has its weeds as well as its blossoms, all vegetation should, therefore, be repressed. The wisest thing, we apprehend, for adding to the produce of the Christian vineyard is to put into action all the productive tendencies that may be found in it. The excrescencies which may come forth will wither and disappear, under the eye of an enlightened clergy: so that while, in the first instance, the utmost space and enlargement should be permitted, for the manifold activities of Christian love, upon the one hand, there should be no other defence ever thought of, against the occasional pruriencies that may arise out of this operation, than the mild and pacific, but altogether efficacious corrective of Christian learning, upon the other.

There are two sets of clergy, in every establishment; and it were curious to observe how each of them stands affected to the two questions, whether the ministers of the gospel shall be more richly furnished with Christian literature, and, whether the laymen who are under them shall be permitted to supplement the duties of the clerical office, with Christian labour. There is one class of our ecclesiastics, both in England and Scotland, who have a taste for popular agency, and lay enterprises, and the whole apparatus of religious schools and religious societies, which are so multiplying around us, in this busy age of philanthropic activity and adventure. Now, what we would ask of such ecclesiastics is, whether they would feel a relish or repugnance towards those measures, the effect of which is to exalt the clergy of the church to a higher pre-eminence than they even now occupy, for all the accomplishments of sacred literature? Will they come forward and say that they are afraid of literature?—that a clergy too enlightened would not suit them?—that, loving to breathe in the muddy atmosphere of popular ignorance and popular folly, they want no science and no scholarship, whose hateful beams might disperse the congenial vapours wherewith the effervescence of plebeianism has filled and overspread the whole scene of their ignoble labours? Do they tremble, lest the light of philosophy should penetrate into the dark unknown of their own inglorious sculking places? And are they really conscious, after all, that what they have headed and patronised is a low paltry drivelling fanaticism, which would shrink before the full gaze of a lettered and intellectual church, where every minister were a luminary of science as well as a luminary of the gospel? These are the degrading imputations they will bring upon themselves, by any resistance they shall make to the learning of the clergy: and such a resistance, if offered, is the very thing that will propagate the timely alarm to another quarter, and will cause, we trust, the friends of learning to rally, and to form into strength elsewhere. Those ministers who, whether under the name of the high church, or of the moderate, or of the rational party, feel a strong disrelish towards the active interference of laymen in the work of religious instruction, will know how to act should they perceive, in the party of their antagonists, an equally strong disrelish towards any measure that goes to augment the professional literature of all our future ecclesiastics. They cannot be blind to the fact, that, at this moment, there is a fermentation, and a brooding activity,

x

and an unexampled restlessness, and a busy movement of schemes and of operations, before unknown in the walks of popular Christianity; and if, additional to all this, they should further see a dread, on the part of zealous champions and overseers, lest the lamp of Christian literature should be lighted up into greater brilliancy than before, we trust that this will be felt and understood by those who nauseate what they term the missionary and methodistical spirit of our age, as the intimation of what they ought to do. It is not by putting forth the arm of intolerance, that they will reach it its exterminating blow. It is not by fulminating edicts that they will smother it. It is not by raising and strengthening all the mounds of exclusion, that they will be able to guard our Establishment against what they deem, and honestly deem, to be the inroads of a pestilence. These are not the legitimate defences of our Church against hateful fanaticism: and they who have set themselves in array against this hydra, whether she be indeed a reality or only a bugbear of their own imagination, can do nothing better than to rear a literary and enlightened priesthood, under the eye of whose vigilance all that is truly noxious - and evil will be most effectually disarmed also.

But should the friends of this so called fanaticism among the clergy be also the friends, and not the enemies, of scientific and theological accomplishment in their own order; should they dare their antagonists to the open arena of light and of liberty; should their demand be that the torch of learning shall be blown into a clearer and intenser flame, and be brought to shine upon all their opinions and all their ways; should the cry which they send forth be for more of erudition, and more of philosophy, and that not one single labourer shall be admitted to the ministerial field, till our universities, those established luminaries of our land, have shed upon his understanding a larger supply of that pure, and chaste, and academic light, the property of which is to guide, and not to bewilder, to clarify the eye of the mind, and not to dazzle it to the overpowering of all its faculties;— if this be the beseeching voice of fanaticism, and it be left to pass unregarded away, then shall the enemies of fanaticism have become the enemies of knowledge; and our Church, instead of exhibiting the aspect of zeal tempered by wisdom, and of a warm, active, busy spirit of Christian philanthropy, under the control and guardianship of accomplished and well educated clergymen, may, at length, desolated of all its pieties, be turned into a heartless scene of secularity, and coarseness, and contempt for vital religion, where the sacredness of Christianity has fled, and left not behind it one redeeming quality in the science of Christianity among its officiating ministers; and, alike abandoned by the light of the Divine Spirit, and the light of human philosophy, it will offer the spectacle of a dreary and extended waste, without one spot of loveliness or verdure which the eye can delight to rest upon.*

But, it is now time to enter on the more familiar objections which have been alleged against Sabbath schools: and there is none which floats so currently, or is received with greater welcome and indulgence, than that they bear with adverse and malignant influence, on family religion,—that they detach our young from the natural guardianship of their own family; and come in place of that far better and more beautiful system which, at one time, obtained over the whole Lowlands of Scotland,—when almost every father was, at the same time, the Sabbath teacher of his own

---

* We have been insensibly led to some of the above remarks, by the circumstance of a measure being now in progress, for augmenting the academic preparations of our students, ere they shall be admissible to the ministerial office in Scotland. There can be no doubt as to the fact of a very wide diversity of sentiment between two bodies of clergy, about the expediency of enlisting, as subsidiary teachers, laymen who have not had the advantage of a university education. We think, on the one hand, that, without such education, there is many a private Christian, who might thus be most usefully and most effectively employed; but, on the other hand, we would have this education rendered far more complete, and perfect among the regular teachers of the Establishment. And we therefore conceive that the measure in question should have friends and zealous supporters from both sides of the Church. They who see ground for fear, lest, in the novel institutions of Sabbath teaching, and lay agency, the Church shall be trodden under foot by a sort of fanatical usurpation, should wish for a more accomplished clergy, as the most effectual barrier against this mischief. And it is for the credit of those again who patronise such institutions, to manifest their utter fearlessness of light and learning; but rather to court its approaches, and prove, by their doing so, that they regarded their own practice as accordant with the doctrines of revelation, and the sound philosophy of our nature.

offspring; when the simple voice of psalms was heard to ascend from our streets and our cotages, and the evening of God's hallowed day was consecrated, in many a mansion of domestic piety, to those holy exercises which assembled the children of each household around their venerable sires, and transmitted the Christian worth and wisdom of the former to its succeeding generation. It is some such picture as this which kindles the indignation of many a sentimentalist against the institutions that we are pleading for; and they have to combat not merely the unconcern and enmity which obtain with the many, towards all schemes of Christian philanthropy whatever, but also the generous emotions, and even the pious recollections, of a few men, who are disposed, at least, to give the question a respectful entertainment.

Now, it ought to be remembered, that to come in place of a better system is one thing, and to displace that system is another. Is it possible for any man, at all acquainted with the chronology of Sabbath schools, to affirm that they are the instruments of having overthrown the family religion of Scotland? Have they operated as so many ruthless invaders, on what, at the time of their entrance, was a beauteous moral domain, and swept away from it all that was affecting or graceful in the observations of our forefathers? Whether did they desolate the territory, or have they only made their lodgement on what was already a scene of desola-

tion? The truth is, that for many years previous
to the extension of this system, a woful degeneracy was going on in the religious habit and character of our country;—that, from the wanton out-
rages inflicted by unrelenting patronage on the
taste and demand of parishes, the religious spirit, once so characteristic of our nation, has
long been rapidly subsiding—that, more particularly in our great towns, the population have so
outgrown the old ecclesiastical system, as to have
accumulated there into so many masses of practical heathenism:—and now the state of the alternative is not, whether the rising generation shall
be trained to Christianity in schools, or trained to
it under the roof of their fathers; but whether
they shall be trained to it in schools, or not trained
to it at all. It is whether a process of deterioration,
which originated more than half a century ago, and
has been rapid and resistless in its various tendencies
ever since—whether it shall be suffered to carry our
people still more downward in the scale of moral
blindness and depravity; or whether the only remaining expedient for arresting it shall be put into
operation. Were it as easy a task to prevail on
an irreligious parent to set up the worship and
the instruction of religion, in his family, as to get
his consent, and prevail upon his children, to attend the ministrations of a Sabbath school, there
might then be some appearance of room for all
the obloquy that has been cast upon these institutions. But as the matter stands, in many a city

and in many a parish, the Christian philanthropist
is shut up to an effort upon the young, as his last
chance for the moral regeneration of our country.
In despair (and it is a despair warranted by all
experience) of operating, with extensive effect, on
the confirmed habit and obstinacy of manhood, he
arrests the human plant, at an earlier and more
susceptible stage, and puts forth the only hand
that ever would have offered for the culture and
the training of this young immortal. In the great
majority of instances, he does not withdraw his pupils, for a single moment, from any Christian influence that would have descended upon them
in another quarter, but showers upon their heads
and their hearts the only Christian influence they
ever are exposed to. He is, in fact, building up
again that very system, with the destruction of
which he has been charged, and rearing many
young, who, but for him, would have been the
still more corrupt descendants of a corrupt parentage, to be the religious guides and examples of a
future generation.

It is not true that family religion is superseded by
these schools, so as to make Christianity less the
topic of mutual exercise and conversation between
parents and children, than before the period of
their institution. Instead of banishing this topic
from families, they have been known, in very many instances, to have first introduced it into dwelling-places where before it was utterly unknown.
The most careless of parents are found to give

their ready and delighted consent to the proposal which comes to them from the Sabbath teacher, for the attendance of their children. And the children, instead of carrying off from their own houses an ingredient of worth which truly had no place in them, do, in fact, impart that very ingredient from the seminaries which have been branded as the great absorbents of all the family religion in the land. Parents, in spite of themselves, feel an interest in that which interests and occupies their children; and through the medium of natural affection have their thoughts been caught to the subject of Christianity; and the very tasks and exercises of their children have brought a theme to their evening circle, upon which, aforetimes, not a syllable of utterance was ever heard; and still more, when a small and select library is attached to the institution, has it been the mean of circulating, through many a household privacy, such wisdom and such piety as were indeed new visitants upon a scene, till now untouched by any print or footstep of sacredness.

We have one prophecy in the Bible, that many shall run to and fro, and knowledge shall be increased. It was thus at the outset of Christianity, when apostles itinerated from one country to another; it is thus still with missionaries who go abroad; and it is also thus, though in a greatly more limited degree, with Sabbath teachers, who go forth on the errand of Christianising, each stepping beyond his own threshold, and travelling his benevolent round among other families. In the natural progress of things, the loco-motive operation will gradually contract itself within narrower boundaries. Christianity, by a more extended set of movements, will first be established, in a general way, throughout all lands. Then, by a busy internal process among towns and parishes, will there be a filling up of each larger territory. The local system of Sabbath schools may be regarded as a step, in this transition, from a wore widely diffusive to a more intense and contracted style of operation. So far from superseding the household system of education, its direct consequence is to establish that system in places where it was before unknown, or to restore it in places, where, through the decay of Christianity, for one or more generations, it had, for some time, been suspended. We shall not affirm, at present, whether it is destined to continue a wholesome institution, to the end of time; or, whether, like the general enterprise of missionaries, it too may come to be dispensed with, having served its own important but temporary purpose of conducting the world onward to that state, for the arrival of which we have another prophecy of the Bible, when " they shall not teach every man his neighbour, and every man his brother, saying, ' know the Lord;' for all shall know him, from the least to the greatest."

Meanwhile, we not only see that the Sabbath school system tends directly to the establishment

of the househould system of education, but that,
even in those families where the latter is in full
operation, the former does not interfere with it.
There are many who concede the advantage of
Sabbath schools, in those cases where the parents
are neither able nor willing to teach their children, but who regard them as a bane and a nui-
sance, when they come into contact with our religious and well ordered families. In this state
of opinion, it is impossible to conduct a Sabbath
school, without a feeling of very awkward embarrassment, on the part both of the teacher and of
the people among whom he expatiates. No children can be admitted, without a severe reflection
against their parents being implied by it; and if
such be the prevalent style of sentiment respecting these institutions, no parent will consent to
send his children, without feeling, that by this
step, he brings down upon his own character and
respectability the heaviest of all imputations. For
our own parts, we feel ourselves to be clear of
this embarrassment altogether. We would make
no distinction in the invitation that we offered to
families for their attendance on our schools, between religious and irreligious parents. In large
towns, where the church accommodation is still
in such wretched scantiness, we know that, with
respect to the great majority of children, such a
school affords the only opportunity they have,
through the day, for meeting in a place of public
worship or instruction,—and that attendance upon

it would no more interfere with household exercises, than does attendance upon the ministrations of a regular clergyman, in a well provided country parish. This argument for the sufficiency and the superiority of family instruction would apply, with as great force, against the attendance of children on a church, as against their attendance on a Sabbath school, in all those cases where there is no church open to receive them. The truth is, that these schools afford the only supplement we can at present command, in a large town, for the defects of its ecclesiastical system. They come in place of the churches yet to be provided, and the existing number of which we have already demonstrated to be so fearfully short of the needs of the population. Nor does the time in which a Sabbath school keeps its children detached and at a distance from their natural guides and protectors, exceed the time at which, under a better economy, these same children would be sitting, from under the parental roof, in a chapel, or meeting-house.

But, even granting the case of parents altogether religious, and granting them to be fully observant of all the ordinances, and that, in particular, their well-filled family pew holds out, Sabbath after Sabbath, the pleasing aspect of a well-conditioned and a well disciplined household; still we do not hold a Sabbath school for the children of such parents to be at all hurtful, or even superfluous. There is time both for the household and the school exercises, during the currency of a Sabbath evening, consisting, at the very least, of four hours; and it is, on many accounts, better that this time should be so partitioned, than that it should all be spent by the children, in what they are apt to feel the weary imprisonment of their own dwelling places. It is well that there should be such a variety to keep up and enliven their attention, among religious topics. It is well that the parent should guide their preparations for the teacher; and that a judicious teacher should lead on the parent to a right track of exercise and examination, for the children. There is time, under such a system, both for the lessons and the prayers of the family; and it is further right that there should be time for the heads of the family to have their own hours of deeper sacredness, not to be interrupted even by the religious care of those who have sprung from them. The seminaries we plead for, instead of having any effect to mar, do, in fact, harmonise, at all points, with the spiritual complexion of our most decent and devoted families. Nor can we conceive any degree of piety, or Christian wisdom, on the part of parents, that should lead them to regard a well conducted Sabbath school in any other light than as a blessing and an acquisition to their children.

And here it may be remarked of a local school, that it possesses a peculiar advantage over a general school, in the attraction which it holds out

to all sorts of families. It lies either within its
own little district, or in its own immediate vicinity; and, separated only by a few houses from
each dwelling-place, the whole line of distance
which is described by each of the scholars from
his home, can, both in going and returning, be
easily followed or overseen by his parents. Thus
will there be no corruption to meet him on his
path, and no possibility, between the parent and
the teacher, to evade the attendance of a single
evening, on any excursion of vice or idleness.
The shield and the security of domestic guardianship are thus thrown over the system; and even
the children of the religious and irreligious
mingle together only under the eye of their
teacher, and may be separated instantaneously at
the breaking up of the juvenile congregation.
They mix only at the season when the example
and proficiency of the good have a predominating
influence over the depraved and the careless;
and passing, in a single moment, from the eye of
the teacher to the eye of the parent, there is no
time for the influence of the depraved to assume
its natural ascendency. Through a Sabbath
school, as through a conduit, the spirit and character of the better families may send a moralising
influence upon the others; while, in their passage
to and from the schools, all the guards of parental jealousy might be put forth, to intercept the
stream that else might flow in an opposite direction. It is thus that the presence and the exer-

tions of a Sabbath teacher may bring about just such a composition of the families as to give scope for the assimilating power of every good ingredient, and, at the same time, to check the assimilating power of every bad one. He may hasten inconceivably the fermentation of that leaven, by the working of which it is that we are taught to expect, at length, the spread of Christianity throughout the whole population. Nor are we aware of a single office, within the regular limits of any ecclesiastical constitution, from the pious and faithful discharge of whose duties so signal a blessing may be anticipated, both for the present and for future generations.

We are glad, however, that so much has been said, in Scotland, about the invasion of the Sabbath school system on family religion. It will have a salutary re-action both on teacher and parents, and make all who are religiously disposed be careful, lest so interesting a vestige of the Christianity of other days should be any further defaced or trampled upon, by an institution the design of which is to restore our population to all that was pious, and venerable, and affecting, in the style and habit of the olden time. And there is one thing that may be said to those who urge this objection most vehemently. In so doing they give up the principle of the former objection. By admitting the competency of parents to teach Christianity to their children, they admit, that part of this work, at least, may be confided to other hands than those of regular and ordained clergy. They admit that a father, in humble life, may be the instrument of transmitting Christian wisdom and Christian worth to his own children, —and that though it·were quackery for each parent to undertake the cure of family diseases, it is not quackery for each to undertake the work of family instruction. Thus the comparison between the efforts of the unlicenced in theology and medicine is, by them at least, practically given up. We hold this to be a signal testimony, and from the mouths of adversaries too, to the power of unlettered Christianity, in propagating its own likeness, throughout the young of our rising generation,—a power which most assuredly would not all go into dissipation, though, for a short time every Sabbath evening, it were transported from its place in the family to a new place in such a seminary of religious instruction as we have attempted to advocate.

And there is one point of superiority which a Sabbath teacher, humble in circumstances, has over one who is much and visibly raised above the level of the families among whom he labours. It is true that the latter has an advantage, in the mere ascendency of rank, and in that peculiar homage which the very exhibition of piety, when conjoined with affluence, is ever sure to draw from the multitude. But the former has his compensation in the more unmixed influence of his ministrations. His presence awakens no sordid or mercenary expectation among the poor. The welcome he gets from them is altogether disinterested: and, as we have already attempted to evince, in the proportion that the acceptance of a religious visit is untainted, in respect of its character, is the visit itself unimpaired in respect of its practical efficacy. To us the purity of the ministration appears indispensable to the power of it: and it is to him who is the bearer of Christianity and nothing else, among the habitations of the common people, that we would look for the most ready and rapid diffusion of its principles. This is a circumstance which goes far to counteract any loss that may be conceived to arise from the defect of a more regular or refined scholarship. Let there be sincere piety united with plain but good intelligence, and we would have no scruple, but the contrary, in employing, as Sabbath teachers, men from the very humblest classes of life. The weight of an exalted character will ever carry it over the want of an exalted condition: and it is, indeed, a striking testimony to the worth and importance of the poor, that among them the best capabilities are to be found for transforming a corrupt into a pure and virtuous community.

This holds out a very brilliant moral perspective to the eye of a philanthropist. In a few years, many of the scholars at our present seminaries will be convertible into the teachers of a future generation. There will be indefinite additions made to our religious agency. Instead of having to assail, as now, the general bulk of the population, by a Christian influence from without, the mass itself will be penetrated, and, through the means of residing and most effective teachers, there will be kept up a busy process of internal circulation. It is thus that he who can patiently work at small things, and be content to wait for great things, lends by far the best contribution to the mighty achievement of regenerating our land. Extremes meet; and the sanguine philanthropist, who is goaded on by his impatience to try all things, and look for some great and immediate result, will soon be plunged into the despair of ever being able to do any thing at all. The man who can calmly set himself down to the work of a district school, and there be satisfied to live and to labour without a name, may germinate a moral influence that will, at length, overspread the whole city of his habitation. It is rash to affirm of the local system that it is totally impracticable in London; while most natural, at the same time, that it should appear so to those who think nothing worthy of an attempt, unless it can be done *per saltum*,—unless it at once fills the eye with the glare of magnificence, and it can be invested, at the very outset, with all the pomp and patronage of extensive committeeship. A single lane, or court, in London, is surely not more impracticable than in other towns of this empire. There is one man to be found there, who can assume it as his locality, and acquit himself thoroughly and well of the duties which it lays upon him. There is another who can pitch beside him, on a contiguous settlement, and, without feeling bound to speculate for the whole metropolis, can pervade, and do much to purify his assumed portion of it. There is a third who will find that a walk so unnoticed and obscure is the best suited to his modesty; and a fourth, who will be eager to reap, on the same field, that reward of kind and simple gratitude, in which his heart is most fitted to rejoice. We are sure that this piece-meal operation will not stop for want of labourers,—though it may be arrested, for a while, through the eye of labourers being seduced by the meteoric glare of other enterprises, alike impotent and imposing. So long as each man of mediocrity conceives himself to be a man of might, and sighs after some scene of enlargement, that may be adequate to his fancied powers, little or nothing will be done; but so soon as the sweeping and sublime imagination is dissipated, and he can stoop to the drudgery of his small allotment in the field of usefulness, then will it be found, how it is by the summation of many humble mediocrities, that a mighty result is at length arrived at. It was by successive strokes of the pickaxe and the chisel that the pyramids of Egypt were reared: and great must be the company of workmen, and limited the task which each must occupy, ere there will be made to ascend the edifice of a nation's worth, or of a nation's true greatness.

In this laborious process of nursing an empire to Christianity, we know not, at present, a readier or more available apparatus of means than that which has been raised by Methodism. In every large town of England, it owns a number of disciples, and, through a skilful mechanism that has been long in operation, there is a minute acquaintance, on the part of their leaders, with the talents and character of each of them. Why should not they avail themselves of their existing facilities for the adoption of this system, and so, thoroughly pervade that population by their Sabbath schools, which they only, as yet, have partially drawn to their pulpits? It would be doing more, in the long run, to renovate and multiply the chapels of Methodism, than all that has yet been devised by them : and thus might they both extend religious education among the young, and a church-going habit throughout the general population. We doubt not that, with this new style of tactics, they would mightily alarm the Establishment. But so much the better. This is just the salutary application which the Establishment stands in need of. And, from all that we have learned of the catholic and liberal spirit of this class of dissenters, we guess that, though they did no more than simply stimulate the Church of England to do the whole work, and to do it aright, they would bless God and rejoice.

Such is the good will we bear to sectarians, that we should rejoice in nothing more than to behold their instantaneous adoption of an expedient which, we honestly believe, would add tenfold to their resources and their influence. Let them operate in large towns, on the principle of locality. Let them enter on the territorial possession of this peopled wilderness. Let them erect as many district schools and district chapels as they find that they have room for; and if the Establishment will not be roused by this manifold activity, out of its lethargies, then sectarianism will, at length, earn, and most rightfully earn, all the honours and all the ascendency of an Establishment. It is, indeed, a most likely thing that the Church would be put into motion; and this, of itself, were an important good rendered to the country, by the industry and zeal of dissenters. But when we look to the fearful deficiency of our ecclesiastical system, there is no fear lest all the galley-boats of sectarianism, with the slow and ponderous Establishment in tow, will too soon overtake the mighty extent of our yet unprovided population. Nor do we know of any common enterprise that would promise fairer, at length, for embodying the Church and the dissenters together, by some such act of comprehensive union, as has lately reflected so much honour on the two most numerous classes of dissenters in our country.

NOTE.

SINCE the publication of the chapters on Church Patronage, the Author has been kindly honoured by a specific communication from Mr. Gladstone, respecting the returns of the churches that were endowed by him.

One of them is in the town of Liverpool, and there is attached to it a school for the education, at present gratuitous, of 280 children. The cost and annual expense of this establishment form a heavy deduction from the surplus of seat rents that would otherwise have accrued out of the capabilities of the church alone; and, accordingly, the return is only between three and four per cent. per annum, on the whole cost.

The other church is at Seaforth, a small distance from Liverpool, where there is likewise a school attached to the church. In both cases there are also school-houses. It is obvious that the circumstance of the church at Seaforth being smaller than the other, is unfavourable to the amount of surplus return upon the capital; and, accordingly, though the schools there be only endowed partially, whereas it is still a wholly endowed school in Liverpool, the return upon the whole cost is about two and a half per cent.

358

The Author thinks it necessary to supplement, by these details, the information of the text; and he does so, not at the desire of Mr. Gladstone, who kindly left him to his own discretion, in this respect, but to prove how small the hazard of such a speculation is, in populous cities, and with large churches, provided only, however, that the subscribers restrict themselves to the single object of a church, and not, as has been most benevolently done in the instances at Liverpool, extend the charity of their enterprise to additional objects.

END OF VOL. I.